MUD, BLOOD & DETERMINATION

Wolverhampton Military Studies

www.helion.co.uk/wolverhamptonmilitarystudies

Submissions

The publishers would be pleased to receive submissions for this series. Please contact us via email (info@helion.co.uk), or in writing to Helion & Company Limited, 26 Willow Road, Solihull, West Midlands, B91 1UE.

Titles

Mud, Blood & Determination

The History of the 46th (North Midland) Division in the Great War

Wolverhampton Military Studies No.8

Simon Peaple

 Helion & Company Limited

Helion & Company Limited
26 Willow Road
Solihull
West Midlands
B91 1UE
England
Tel. 0121 705 3393
Fax 0121 711 4075
Email: info@helion.co.uk
Website: www.helion.co.uk
Twitter: @helionbooks
Visit our blog http://blog.helion.co.uk/

Published by Helion & Company 2015

Designed and typeset by Bookcraft Ltd, Stroud, Gloucestershire
Cover designed by Euan Carter, Leicester (www.euancarter.com)
Printed by Gutenberg Press Limited, Tarxien, Malta

Text © Simon Peaple 2015
Photographs © as individually credited
Maps © Barbara Taylor 2015

Front cover: Territorials in action on the Western Front, autumn 1915 (Author's collection). Rear cover: Major General Montagu-Stuart-Wortley, GOC 46th Division 1914-16 and staff (Author's collection).

ISBN 978 1 910294 66 6

British Library Cataloguing-in-Publication Data.
A catalogue record for this book is available from the British Library.

For details of other military history titles published by Helion & Company Limited contact the above address, or visit our website: http://www.helion.co.uk.

We always welcome receiving book proposals from prospective authors.

To Sheree

For your love and support over the past 30 years, without you this would never have seen the light of day

Contents

List of Illustrations

List of Maps

General Key for all maps.

Red	German
Blue	Allied

XXXX ▢	Army
XXX ▢	Corps
XX ▢	Division
X ▢	Brigade
I I I ▢	Regiment (German only)
I I ▢	Battalion
I ▢	Company
• ▢	Section
⊠	Infantry

List of Abbreviations

1/8 Blankshires	A first line territorial battalion which has volunteered / is serving overseas
2 Blankshires	A regular battalion in existence prior to the outbreak of war
5 (Service) Blankshires	A service battalion raised after 4 August 1914
AA & QMG	Adjutant and Quarter master Branch of Staff
AIF	Australia Imperial Force
BEF	British Expeditionary Force
BGGS	Brigadier General General Staff
BGRA	Brigadier General Royal Artillery
CCC	Churchill College Cambridge
CO	Commanding Officer, the officer appointed to command the battalion / company
CRA	Commander Royal Artillery, the senior artillery officer of a division.
CRE	Commander Royal Engineers, senior engineer officer of a division
DAC	Divisional Ammunition Column
DSO	Distinguished Service Order
GHQ	General Headquarters, the Headquarters of the BEF at Montreuil
GOC	General Officer Commanding, the senior officer commanding a division of higher formation
GSO1	The chief staff officer of a division
GSO2	The second most senior staff officer of a division
HE	High explosive
IWM	Imperial War Museum
KCB	Knight of the Order of the Bath
KCMG	Knight of the Order of Michael and George
LRO	Record Office for Leicestershire, Leicester and Rutland
MC	Military Cross
MGC	Machine Gun Corps

MGO	Machine Gun Officer (belonging to a higher formation) e.g. Corps MGO
MLL	Museum of Lincolnshire Life
MM	Military Medal
MO	Medical Officer
NCO	Non Commissioned Officer
OC	Officer Commanding, the officer in command at the time
OH	Edmonds J.E., *Military Operations in France and Belgium*, known as the Official History
ORs	Other Ranks
QM	Quarter Master
RE	Royal Engineers
RFA	Royal Field Artillery
RFC	Royal Flying Corps
RGA	Royal Garrison Artillery
RSM	Regimental sergeant Major, the senior NCO of a battalion
SAA	Small Arms Ammunition – usually bullets for rifles / machine guns
TNA	The National Archives
VC	Victoria Cross
WSF	Regimental Headquarters of the Worcestershire and Sherwood Forresters Regiment

The Wolverhampton Military Studies Series
Series Editor's Preface

As series editor, it is my great pleasure to introduce the *Wolverhampton Military Studies Series* to you. Our intention is that in this series of books you will find military history that is new and innovative, and academically rigorous with a strong basis in fact and in analytical research, but also is the kind of military history that is for all readers, whatever their particular interests, or their level of interest in the subject. To paraphrase an old aphorism: a military history book is not less important just because it is popular, and it is not more scholarly just because it is dull. With every one of our publications we want to bring you the kind of military history that you will want to read simply because it is a good and well-written book, as well as bringing new light, new perspectives, and new factual evidence to its subject.

In devising the *Wolverhampton Military Studies Series*, we gave much thought to the series title: this is a *military* series. We take the view that history is everything except the things that have not happened yet, and even then a good book about the military aspects of the future would find its way into this series. We are not bound to any particular time period or cut-off date. Writing military history often divides quite sharply into eras, from the modern through the early modern to the mediaeval and ancient; and into regions or continents, with a division between western military history and the military history of other countries and cultures being particularly marked. Inevitably, we have had to start somewhere, and the first books of the series deal with British military topics and events of the twentieth century and later nineteenth century. But this series is open to any book that challenges received and accepted ideas about any aspect of military history, and does so in a way that encourages its readers to enjoy the discovery.

In the same way, this series is not limited to being about wars, or about grand strategy, or wider defence matters, or the sociology of armed forces as institutions, or civilian society and culture at war. None of these are specifically excluded, and in some cases they play an important part in the books that comprise our series. But there are already many books in existence, some of them of the highest scholarly standards, which cater to these particular approaches. The main theme of the *Wolverhampton Military Studies Series* is the military aspects of wars, the preparation for wars or their prevention, and their aftermath. This includes some books whose main theme is the technical details of how armed forces have worked, some books on wars and battles, and some books that re-examine the evidence about the existing stories, to show in a different light what everyone thought they already knew and understood.

As series editor, together with my fellow editorial board members, and our publisher Duncan Rogers of Helion, I have found that we have known immediately and almost by instinct the kind of books that fit within this series. They are very much the kind of well-written and challenging books that my students at the University of Wolverhampton would want to read. They are books which enhance knowledge, and offer new perspectives. Also, they are books for anyone with an interest in military history and events, from expert scholars to occasional readers. One of the great benefits of the study of military history is that it includes a large and often committed section of the wider population, who want to read the best military history that they can find; our aim for this series is to provide it.

Stephen Badsey
University of Wolverhampton

Acknowledgements

In researching the thesis from which this book is derived I received great benefit from the vast knowledge of Dr John Bourne in addition to the original suggestion that I study the 46th Division. To John too, I owe being introduced to the Staffordshire Police Military History Society and all the subsequent enthusiasts encountered in speaking at WFA events.

In conducting the research I was assisted by a variety of staff and volunteers at the archives where I went, sometimes at irregular intervals, to pursue particular aspects or records. In particular, I would like to thank the staff and volunteers at the Staffordshire Regimental Museum, the Museum of Lincolnshire Life, the Sherwood Foresters HQ, the Record Office for Leicestershire, Leicester and Rutland and the staff of Churchill College, Cambridge, the Liddell Hart Centre (then in Leeds), the Imperial War Museum in London and The National Archives, Kew.

I am also very grateful to the late Mabel Jarman for awarding me a Tom Jarman Scholarship to enable me to stay at the Gladstone Library in Hawarden to assist me in writing up my research. The scholarship was awarded at the proposal of Dr Malcolm Lambert whose support for my academic endeavours now spans over 30 years; he is a gentleman and international scholar of distinction and I can only hope some of that depth is evident in my work. Joyce Lambert has always encouraged me to persevere as well as being incredibly supportive to Sheree and I ever since we first met.

The dedication to Sheree, being compiled from words, cannot do justice to her role in helping an introverted scholarly person like me survive the challenges of life – I can still remember the moment our eyes first met and will treasure it in my heart until I die. Her love for me and the care she has taken of our sons Thomas and Edward is the root cause of all our achievements.

I first visited the Western Front, on which my grandfather and great uncle served and where the latter still lies, under the guidance of the late great John Giles. He inspired me and subsequent visits have included a number where I have enjoyed the privilege of taking students from Solihull FE College and since 2001 the pupils of Princethorpe College, especially my A level students, whose interest and enthusiasm is inspirational.

I would also like to thank Duncan Rogers for agreeing to publish an author without the stellar profile of Bourne and Sheffield. I did not want to break the story into articles and I am very grateful for his willingness to take a risk in publishing a divisional history. My editor, Michael LoCicero has been a source of unfailing enthusiasm as well as expert guidance.

Simon Peaple
Tamworth, 2014

Introduction

With the outbreak of war the Germans had set in train the Schlieffen Plan and the French their Plan XVII each mobilising over a million men. The British despatched the BEF to the left of the French – the French had requested this in case the BEF never came! Ironically, the British were in just the right place to block the outer wheel of the German armies endeavouring to encircle the French. Heavily outnumbered, the expertly trained BEF fell back in the "Retreat from Mons" with Haig playing a less distinguished role than his fellow Corps Commander Smith-Dorrien whose accurate appreciation of what a European war would mean had shocked cadets at the annual Public Schools Camp in 1914.

Thanks to the BEF slowing down the German advance, Joffre, the French Commander in Chief, had time to recognise the need to transfer troops to his left wing and eventually to halt the Germans at the Marne. Schlieffen had explained this manoeuvre to his staff officers during an exercise and the failure of Moltke the Younger to adapt the plan or to ensure that the German right was sufficiently strong enabled the French to survive with British assistance. As both sides failed to land a knock out blow, they attempted to outflank each other which created "The Race to the Sea" that would create a line of trenches running from the sand dunes on the Belgian Coast to the Alps. Known to history by its German designation as the "Western Front", it was here that the bulk of the British effort would be committed and where the vast majority of its dead would subsequently lie.

It was to this blood soaked stalemate that the British 46th North Midland Division would be sent in February 1915. By the time they arrived, the naive "over by Christmas" statements of August 1914 had proven themselves to be hollow. The 46th Division would therefore enter the stage when it was clear that the war would last a long time; the men of Staffordshire, Nottinghamshire, Derbyshire, Leicestershire and Lincolnshire were about to embark upon a learning curve which they would complete through blood, toil and determination.

According to the pre-war military doctrine, the two sides were now engaged in a "wearing out" phase of an enormous battle. In truth, the era of "Total War" had begun and the means to achieve the final victory were not yet available, nor the ideas needed to maximise their impact or the skills needed to execute them sufficiently appreciated. The British Army's search for victory and in particular the 46th Division's progress along that learning curve inspired my research but this is their story.

1

The Reality of War

The purpose of this chapter is to assess the level at which the 46th Division began upon the learning curve of the British Army. Unlike troops arriving on the Western Front after Gallipoli, such as the Australians, it had no previous combat experience. The Division now had to undergo a period of training and assessment. It is the modern practice to evaluate children's performance when they enter school in order to arrive at a baseline against which their subsequent progress can be measured. Bidwell and Graham, and Neillands, assert that all the territorial divisions began lower down the curve because they were initially equipped with obsolete artillery and had retained the eight-company battalion structure until after war mobilisation in 1914.[1] The judgements formed of 46th Division in this early phase seem to have been negative and to have affected the expectations of higher command.

Following an inspection by King George V on 19 February 1915, 46th Division made its way to the channel and crossed to France. On 2 March 1915, Major General Hon. E.J. Montagu-Stuart-Wortley was able to open his Divisional Headquarters at the Chateau du Jardin near Le Havre.[2] On the following day, as his division concentrated after a difficult crossing, Montagu-Stuart-Wortley and Lieutenant Colonel W.H.F. Weber, the GSO1, went to meet Field Marshal Sir John French, Commander in Chief of the British Expeditionary Force, at Bailleul. It seems that this was a friendly meeting.[3]

4/1 Midland Brigade RFA left on 3 March to begin training with 4th Division whilst the infantry were allocated in the ratio of one brigade to a division in the

---

1 S. Bidwell & D. Graham, *Firepower* (1982) pp.13 and 36 et passim. See also R. Neillands, *The Great War Generals* (1999), p.36.

2 All references in this chapter are to the Divisional War Diary for March 1915 (WO95/2662) unless otherwise stated. Major-General Hon. Edward James Montagu-Stuart-Wortley CMG DSO MVO (1857-1934), commanded 46th Division from 1 June 1914 until 6 July 1916 when he was effectively sacked and returned to England. He never subsequently held a command on the Western Front.

3 See Chapter 8 and TNA: WO 138/29 for details.

Major General Montagu-Stuart-Wortley, GOC 46th Division 1914-16 and staff.
(Author's collection)

A lively send off for C Company 1/6th Sherwoods, August 1914. (Author's collection)

line and one battalion to each brigade in the line. For example, 137 (Staffordshire) Brigade was attached to 6th Division and 1/5 North Staffords received instruction from 18 Brigade. 46th Division's concentration did not go smoothly and so a mixed brigade was attached to 4th Division. This mixed brigade comprised 1/5, 1/6 and 1/7 Battalions Nottinghamshire and Derbyshire Regiment (Sherwood Foresters) and 1/5 Leicesters as 1/8 Sherwoods were temporarily attached to 2nd Cavalry Division on 10 March 1915.

1/5 Leicesters were inspected by the GOC Second Army, General Sir Horace Smith-Dorrien,[4] who later "interviewed all the officers".[5] The battalion then underwent instruction at the hands of the 12 Infantry Brigade. On 5 March, 'A' and 'C' companies were the first to enter the trenches. The battalion diary noted:

> For the first 24 hours in the trenches each man was placed between two regular soldiers to learn the routine and become accustomed to conditions of trench warfare.

Meanwhile, the platoon commanders and sergeants were placed with their corresponding Regular opposite numbers. A similar experience is described in the history of 7 Somerset Light Infantry.[6]

2/Essex's Headquarters was host to the CO, Adjutant and Second in Command of 1/5 Leicesters since they too needed field guidance. The reality of trench warfare was soon apparent to 'C' company, when Second Lieutenant G. Aked was killed in the trenches that night, 5 March 1915. The battalion history records that a stray bullet killed him.[7] The battalion diary baldly notes the death of an officer and an Other Rank but names neither. The Divisional diary records its 'first casualty report' on 9 March 1915 as being from 139 Brigade not 138 Brigade. The report does not mention to whom the report related. Three men's deaths are recorded in their battalion's diaries by this date. Sergeant John Ware, 1/5 Sherwood Foresters, was fatally wounded on 5 March 1915 whilst 'C' Company and 1 Platoon of 'B' were moving up to the trenches for instruction. He died on 6 March and he too was noted as a victim of a stray bullet.[8] On 8 March, Lance-Corporal Allen Redfern, 'C' Company, 1/6 Sherwoods was killed during a working party.[9] These deaths initiated the battalions into the myriad of dangers facing them especially from snipers.

---

4   General Sir Horace Lockwood Smith-Dorrien (1858-1930) was GOC II Corps (August 1914-April 1915), when he was sacked by Field Marshal French. The two men loathed one another.
5   LRO: 22D63/137, War Diary 1/5 Leicesters, 4 March 1915.
6   B. Moorhouse, *Forged by Fire*, (2003).
7   Op.cit, 6 March 1915. The other references relate to entries in the relevant battalion war diaries on the dates given.
8   WSF: War Diary 1/6 Sherwood Foresters, 8 March 1915.
9   Ibid.

Officers of the 1/4th Leicesters at Luton, October 1914. (Milne)

The death of Private C.W. Sheppard, 1/7 Sherwoods, on 6 March called for detailed note in his battalion's diary as he was "accidentally shot" whilst in the trenches by a Lance-Corporal of the Hampshire Regiment. One can imagine the strain this would put on inter-unit relationships. The battalion historian of 1/8 Sherwoods provides an interesting account of their initiation and stresses they were commended on their silence entering the trenches.[10]

The War Diary of 1/5 Leicesters records that after all the companies had spent 24 hours in the trenches as individuals the men were given group training. This involved sections being allocated section frontages within platoon frontages of the instructing battalions. All this meant that overall the men would have some idea what to expect when they were allocated trenches in the line and of their particular roles within their sub-unit. Meanwhile, the future of the Division was being decided as reports were compiled by the instructing formations. The request for information on the overall preparedness of 46th Division was sent by Lieutenant Colonel Hon. J.F. Gathorne-Hardy of Second Army Staff.

The man formally responsible for commenting on 46th Division was Lieutenant General Sir W.P. Pulteney, GOC III Corps.[11] He adopted a minimalist approach and simply topped and tailed the incoming reports and forwarded them to Gathorne-Hardy.[12] It was the subordinate commanders whose opinions counted. The key report

---

10   W.C.C. Weetman, *History of the 1/8 Battalion Sherwood Foresters* (1920).
11   Lieutenant General Sir William Pulteney Pulteney (1861-1941) was GOC III Corps from September 1914 until February 1918.
12   All the material quoted on the reports on the training and proficiency of 46th Division is drawn from TNA: WO95/2662, General Staff Records, 46th Division.

on the 1/5, 1/6 and 1/7 Sherwoods and the 1/5 Leicesters came therefore from Major General Henry Wilson, GOC 4th Division.[13] Wilson seems to have added, in his own handwriting, some negative comments to the reports drawn up by his brigadiers, in a report he forwarded to Pulteney on 12 March 1915. Thus on "Military Bearing" the report read: "Good – the behaviour of working parties in exposed conditions was excellent." To which Wilson added: "Some lack of keenness was noticed." It is difficult to reconcile the two halves of this judgement but perhaps the comments on training help to explain the situation. For Wilson wrote on Training: "The state of training is reported as good on the whole, but in some cases only fair." Thus the unevenness of the battalions may be an explanation of the judgement on military bearing.

It is not known when these reports were copied to 46th Division but on 18 March 1915 the War Diary records a visit from Lieutenant Colonel C.H. Harington of III Corps to "settle questions" relating to divisional instruction. Given the time that elapsed between Wilson's report and Harington's visit it is conceivable that Montagu-Stuart-Wortley had objected to some of the negative comments.

Montagu-Stuart-Wortley's disagreements with his superiors will be discussed at length in the chapters on Loos and the Somme but it would seem that he was already creating 'negative waves'. If Montagu-Stuart-Wortley did cavil, it reflects poor judgement because many of the reports were positive. Thus, the CRA 6th Division reported: "The officers appear to know their work and the detachments are very well drilled and perform their duties quickly and efficiently." Although he added that ranging officers had at first taken gambles and therefore wasted ammunition he also noted that they had since improved. 6th Division had also hosted the Divisional Cavalry and the officers of the Yorkshire Hussars were described as "quite up to standard". The GOC 6th Division, Major General J.L. Keir, said of 137 Brigade that, "I am glad to receive such good accounts of their training, especially of their officers". His Brigadiers provided the substance for this view. Brigadier General E.C. Ingouville-Williams, GOC 16 Brigade's view of the 1/5 South Staffords was that they would be a "very good battalion in all respects" whilst the 1/6 South Staffords were described as "generally intelligent and zealous" by his opposite number in 17 Brigade, Brigadier General G.M. Harper.[14]

In the light of future events, Brigadier General W.N. Congreve VC,[15] GOC 18 Brigade's judgement on 1/5 North Staffords was notable for the comparison it makes.

---

13 Field Marshal Sir Henry Hughes Wilson (1864-1922) was a key actor in pre-war military discussions with the French and mastermind of British mobilisation in 1914. He lost the chance to become Field Marshal French's chief of staff owing to his involvement in the 'Curragh Incident' of March 1914. He was appointed Chief of the Imperial General Staff in February 1918 and worked well with Foch. He was assassinated by the IRA in 1922.

14 Lieutenant General Sir (George) Montague Harper (1865-1922) later commanded 51st (Highland) Division (1915-18) and IV Corps (1918).

15 Lieutenant General Sir Walter Norris Congreve VC (1862-1927) was later GOC XIII Corps (1915-17) and GOC VII Corps (1918). He was the only corps commander to be wounded during the war, losing a hand at Arras.

1/6th South Staffs at Bishop's Stortford, November 1914. (6th South Staffs)

Having stated that the battalion had been given identical training to recent Canadians "attached for instruction" he went on: "The men seem of a good type, keen to learn, and their officers are better soldiers than the Canadians." In early 1915 it was still possible for Territorials to rank above 'colonials'. 1/6 North Staffords received a similarly positive report from 19 Brigade. Second Echelon formations, such as 2 Company of the Divisional Train and No. 2 Field Ambulance, also received good reports.

Harington's visit to 46th Division on 18 March is interesting in that it comes six days after Wilson's critical reports and six to eight days before the more positive reports were despatched by Pulteney. Wilson was to prove to be a very political general and it is interesting that he is the most critical officer. Three of the battalions criticised by Wilson were 1/5, 1/6 and 1/7 battalions of the Sherwoods. The contrast can therefore be made with 1/8 Sherwoods, who "very favourably impressed" the GOC 10 Brigade (Brigadier General C.P.A. Hull). Since all four battalions had undergone the same training until two weeks previously such a favourable review casts further doubt on Wilson's additions to his Brigadiers' reports.

The four battalions shared another common experience. All the battalions were inspected by General Smith-Dorrien, GOC Second Army, whose regiment was the Nottinghamshire and Derbyshire. The diary of 1/7 Sherwoods records Smith-Dorrien as saying that it was a "great pleasure" to have them. Of course such a statement to an incoming battalion is simply 'good form' but equally office politics would also normally preclude pot shots at your own army commander's regiment. Wilson would appear to feel few inhibitions perhaps being already aware of the rift between Smith-Dorrien and Field Marshal French.

Officers' mess, 1/6th South Staffs, Rue de la Lys, 1915. (6th South Staffs)

It would seem that on the whole the Division passed muster with its trainers. The vast majority of the troops were seen as keen but inevitably inexperienced. The verdict of the GOC 12 Brigade, Brigadier General F.G. Anley, on 1/4 Leicesters seems to sum up contemporary views: "The officers were also good and their training reached on the whole as high a standard as the other territorial regiments seen out here."

The main concern expressed was regarding the quality of NCOs. For example, the otherwise very positive report on 1/8 Sherwoods, noted on Discipline: "Good. NCOs the weakness as usual." As will be seen in later chapters, all regulars had doubts about the ability of Territorial NCOs to exert authority given that they had had separate civilian relationships with the men.

The main concern appeared therefore to be the Divisional Commander. These concerns are reflected in the correspondence of Lieutenant Colonel P.W. Game, who was GSO1 46th Division from 18 July 1915 to 19 March 1916. Fortunately, for the historian, Game wrote a steady stream of letters to his wife.[16] Game, educated at Charterhouse and subsequently commissioned into the Royal Field Artillery in 1895, was an experienced regular officer. Having served in the Boer War he graduated from Staff College in 1909 winning the Royal United Services Institute Gold Medal. His first staff posting was as GSO3 at the War Office in the Directorate of Military

16   IWM: Papers of Air Vice Marshal P.W. Game.

Training. Arriving in 1910 he inherited Douglas Haig's work and although he did not work with Haig he would have been involved in implementing the work Haig had begun. One may therefore conclude he would have numbered amongst the "new school of young officers" referred to by Haldane. Having been promoted Major in 1912, Game left the War Office in November 1914 to become GSO2 IV Corps, then under the command of Sir Henry Rawlinson.[17]

On 19 July 1915, Game compared his new boss with his old one, describing Montagu-Stuart-Wortley as 'cynical' – unlike Rawlinson. Game also observed to his wife that he was "further back from the trenches that even with the Corps". Even if there is some hyperbole one may reasonably conclude that 46th Division HQ was indeed well back. In this letter, Game also asserts that he does not think he will like Montagu-Stuart-Wortley, though he had not seen him much yet. Given the key role of the GSO1 and the absence of any significant entry in the Divisional diary such a statement may imply Montagu-Stuart-Wortley's distance from detail. This interpretation is borne out by Game's statement in a letter on the following day that Montagu-Stuart-Wortley "prides himself on letting his staff do their own work". Since Game also describes Montagu-Stuart-Wortley as "childishly peevish and inclined to whine" we can reasonably deduce that Game's first impressions were negative.

That Stuart-Wortley's new GSO1 found him difficult to work with might explain why Game was happy to be posted to GHQ RFC in 1916 but it does not explain why he became disliked by his fellow senior officers. However, Game's letter to his wife, dated 15 July 1915, shows that he did not arrive with an entirely open mind. In this letter Game tells his wife he is glad to go despite three reservations: Flanders; Montagu-Stuart-Wortley being 'somewhat difficult and requiring careful handling'; and superseding Price-Davies. The last point reflects the fact the Captain Price-Davies, the acting GSO1, was a holder of the Victoria Cross and perhaps Game as a Regular staff officer felt that there might be some hostility to an outsider even though Captain Price-Davies was too junior to be considered for the permanent posting.

The key point is the second reservation since Game writes that 'he is told' this about Montagu-Stuart-Wortley. In an A.J.P. Tayloresque way one can picture the scene in IV Corps HQ when Rawlinson congratulates Game on promotion to Lieutenant Colonel but then gives him a 'few words to the wise' regarding his new appointment. Both Rawlinson and Montagu-Stuart-Wortley had been to Eton but as Rawlinson was seven years younger their paths would probably not have crossed. However, Rawlinson would almost certainly have met Montagu-Stuart-Wortley when he visited Malta in 1894 since the latter was Brigade-Major at Malta from August 1893 to August 1896. In fact, when Rawlinson graduated from Staff College in 1895, and with his posting as Brigade-Major, he effectively caught up with the older Montagu-Stuart-Wortley.

Rawlinson's subsequent rise in seniority might help to account for the tension between the two men. Thus Rawlinson was commanding an infantry brigade in 1905

17   General Sir Henry Rawlinson Bt. (1864-1925) later commanded Fourth Army (1916-18).

whilst Montagu-Stuart-Wortley was not given 10 Brigade until April 1908 despite having returned from being the Military Attaché in Berne in 1904. By 1910 Rawlinson was a Major General, a rank attained by Montagu-Stuart-Wortley only on 5 March 1913. Rawlinson and Haig[18] were associated with the Haldane group. If this group were the 'insiders' then it seems probable that Montagu-Stuart-Wortley was one of the 'outsiders' – older officers not imbued with the new spirit. Ironically, like Pétain, by 1913 retirement was beckoning for Montagu-Stuart-Wortley and so the Great War presented a final opportunity. The difficulty for Montagu-Stuart-Wortley was that he found himself in France with superiors whose opinion of him was essentially negative. Montagu-Stuart-Wortley's reputation as a 'whiner' and this hostile audience were to combine to end his career in 1916.

Therefore when the 46th Division emerged from its initial introduction to trench warfare it was seen as about average and therefore it was entering upon the learning curve of the British Army roughly on a par with other newly arriving units. As a territorial division it faced the material hurdles described by Bidwell but at this early stage this disadvantage would not have been very apparent since it was not involved in offensive operations.[19] Since the learning curve was to involve the British Army in learning to devolve operational authority to platoons by 1918 the perceived weakness in the quality of NCOs might prove to be a significant handicap in the future but it would have an impact on the pace of development not its starting point. The relationship between Montagu-Stuart-Wortley and his fellow senior officers was to have a more immediate impact in that the assignment of 46th Division to a trench holding role was to physically separate it from the learning curve experienced by those conducting offensive operations.

18   Richard Burdon Haldane (1856-1928), reformist Secretary of State for War (1905-12).
19   See above, note 1.

2

Surviving Trench Warfare: 1915

Between April and October 1915, 46th Division entered upon its learning curve. In common with most divisions arriving on the Western Front in 1915, its initial role was to defend an area of the line, as part of II Corps, Second Army, at Wulverghem in Flanders. Although it had undergone a period of "trench instruction", 46th Division now had to learn to be self-reliant. As was seen in the last chapter, the 46th Division did not receive uniformly positive reports during its initial field familiarisation programme and so this period is important in identifying any early signs that 46th Division lacked the ability to absorb lessons from the experience it was gaining. This was a difficult time for British divisions as the Germans were in the ascendant technically, for example in sniping, as well as physically, since the Germans usually occupied the higher ground.[1] Historians of the Learning curve such as Prior and Wilson focus on offensive operations so the 46th Division is at this point only able to progress within the more limited sphere of general battle worthiness and competence.

On 12 May 1915, Brigadier General W.R. Clifford (GOC 138 Brigade) issued Standing Orders "for Trench Duties and Reliefs and Battalions in Billets".[2] These Standing Orders certainly sought to be comprehensive, covering such subjects as Sentries, Sandbags and Signposts as well as containing several appendices for example, "B" on "Handing Over Certificate".[3]

The Standing Orders begin with very detailed instructions about the deployment of the men in the line. At that time the Brigade had two battalions in line and the instructions not only set out the site for battalion HQs but also specify the number of men to be deployed in the different trenches:

---

1   H. Hesketh-Pritchard, *Sniping in France*, (1994).
2   LRO: 22D 63/177/1.
3   Ibid.

Saps between E1R & E1L are to be garrisoned by 20 men from the same company which is deploying 30 men in E1R and 20 men in E1L.[4]

Given that we know there was a general shortage of artillery ammunition it is not surprising to find that paragraph 2 is devoted to machine guns. The fact that the machine gun was seen as vital for defence is evidenced by the instruction that:

At all times each gun must have two reliefs (6 men) actually in the trench or work occupied by it.

and that

A complete belt equipment should be left with each gun.[5]

The typed orders leave blank the number of machine guns but the number "10" has been written in. Therefore on a two battalion front we can say that each battalion has five machine guns, which shows that by 1915 even Territorial battalions were better equipped than their regular confreres of 1914. On 30 April 1915 1/4 Leicesters recorded eight machine guns in their positions.[6] However, this apparent abundance is tempered by the fact that the guns were permanently deployed and each battalion in turn took over responsibility for them with the trenches themselves.

The Brigade Major, Major R.L. Aldercron, was also very specific about the number and role of sentries. He laid down that one man in six should act as sentry during the day whilst this should rise to one in three at night.[7] Since the Brigade Major also said that sentries should be relieved every hour this scheme, where fully implemented, would have created a night shift pattern of two hours off/one hour on. Such a pattern would have contributed to fatigue but since the orders also specified that:

On no account are men to be allowed to cover up their ears with mufflers or cap comforters, etc.

it also reduced the risk of men suffering unduly in inclement weather.

The problem of maintaining vigilance is also evident in the instruction that men "required for Listening Patrols or specially arduous and responsible duty" should be given at least six hours warning so that they can get a proper rest.[8] One suspects that

---

4   Ibid., para 1.
5   Ibid., para 2.
6   LRO: War Diary 1/4 Leicesters April 1915, Appendix A.
7   Ibid., para 5.
8   Ibid., para 6.

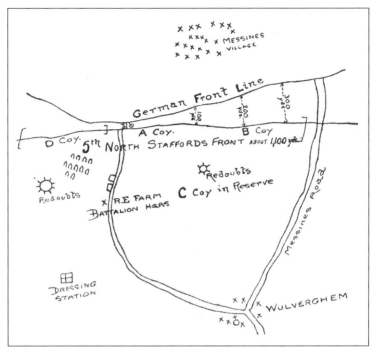

A contemporary sketch of the trenches, 1915. (Meakin)

Trenches of the 1/6th South Staffs at Wulverghem, 1915. (6th South Staffs)

this may have frequently proved to be a counsel of perfection. The orders also stated the three main objectives of listening posts and patrols, viz.:

- to secure the safety of the line
- to obtain information about the enemy
- initiate active enterprises against German snipers, patrols etc.

All these statements suggest that the idea of "No Man's Land beginning at the German wire" was a doctrine that had become widely disseminated by the middle of 1915 to Brigade level so the 46th Division was in touch with the learning curve.

Execution

However, the diary of 1/4 Leicesters records criticism of Captain R.A. Faire for not opening fire or capturing a German working party found whilst on patrol.[9] The diary of 1/5 Leicesters does not record a single patrol in May 1915 but the frequent use of the battalion for working/wiring parties may help to explain this. The difficulty of gaining accurate information is wryly recorded by the Adjutant of 1/5 Lincolns, when he says that a Listening Patrol reported sounds of German mining: "(This turned out to be rats!!!)."[10]

The general state of the British Army in 1915, and the commitment of many Regular units to battles such as Ypres and Aubers Ridge, can be deduced from the fact that even these apparently inactive battalions with three months trench experience were now expected to act as tutors. For example, 'B' and 'D' companies of the 10th (Service) Battalion of the Durham Light Infantry joined 1/5 Lincolns in the trenches on 19 June. 1/4 Lincolns had received 'B' and 'D' companies of the 7th (Service) Battalion Rifle Brigade on 29 May and 31 May respectively before being visited by that Battalion's officers on 1 June.[11] Nonetheless, this responsibility suggests that 46th Division was seen as competent.

One of the officers serving in the Brigade at this time was Second Lieutenant A.P. Marsh, 1/5 Leicesters. Fortunately for the historian, he had fallen in love with Miss Adine Walker whilst the Division was based in Sawbridgeworth, Hertfordshire, and his almost daily letters to her reveal something of the spirit of the young officers in the Brigade.[12] Obviously, there is an element of self-censorship with regard to the dangers faced, but so much of the early correspondence deals frankly with his yearning to

---

9   LRO: War Diary 1/4 Leicesters, 1 May 1915.
10   MLL: War Diary 1/5 Lincolns, 14 June 1915. Ibid., 19 June 1915 and War Diary 1/4 Lincolns, 18 June 1915.
11   Op. cit., 1 June 1915.
12   Letters of Lieutenant Marsh, passim.

receive his mother's consent to his engagement that one senses the military comments can generally be relied upon not to be an overstatement of his feelings.

Thus he records that, on 8 March 1915, he was in charge of 60 yards of trench for the first time. His transparent honesty might not have pleased his Brigade Major:

> I'm writing this sitting in an old cart and nominally superintending a bayonet fighting parade.[13]

However, life became more serious. For example, he and two men had to go out into No Man's Land on 4 April 1915 to clear a blocked drain, which threatened to cause the trench to collapse, coming under heavy German fire. [14] This dose of realism did not prevent him from leading patrols, for example, one on 23 April, but does lead to this passage in a letter to Adine; "I have just written to Kenneth and told him not to get too excited to get out here as when he does he will not like it."[15] Only a day earlier he had stressed to her that there had been no officer casualties in the Battalion since Armentières,[16] but on that day Second Lieutenant Christopher Selwyn died of his wounds whilst Captain J. Chapman was wounded.[17] Marsh, who had been commissioned into 1/5 Leicesters in 1908, was subsequently wounded in the shoulder on 1 July 1915 and was eventually evacuated to England via Le Touquet where he served out the war as an Adjutant to the Volunteer Force, having married Adine in 1915.[18]

That the demands of war were putting pressure on these territorial soldiers now serving full time is evident in the records of 1/4 Leicesters. Their Adjutant, Captain R.S. Dyer-Bennet, himself a Leicestershire Regiment officer, makes some very direct observations in the War Diary. On 19 April 1915 he records that Lieutenant Colonel Harrison inspected the companies in Field Service Marching Order and that whilst 'A' were good and 'B' and 'D' were 'fair', 'C' was judged to be 'bad'. Ten days earlier he had recorded that 'C's march discipline had 'gone to the wind' whilst returning to Dranoutre from the trenches.[19] Self-criticism suggests the source here is reliable and since discipline on the march was primarily down to NCOs this may reflect the weakness identified during induction.

This view is borne out by the NCOs of 'B' and 'D' who were seen as being very keen and interested at the CO's lecture on 27 April but it was still felt that not many NCOs were ready for promotion when the Colonel reviewed the situation with the company commanders on 28 April. The Adjutant recorded that many of the senior NCOs were "older hands, but not very bright & so considered less fit than younger soldiers". In

---

13   LRO: Letters of Second Lieutenant A.P. Marsh, letter dated 14 March 1915.
14   Ibid., Letter dated 4 April 1915.
15   Ibid., Letter dated 21 April 1915.
16   Ibid., Letter dated 20 April 1915.
17   LRO: War Diary 1/5 Leicesters 20 April 1915.
18   Ibid., 1 July 1915 & Letter 2 July 1915 and *Tally Ho*, 1.4 (3) (1959).
19   LRO: War Diary 1/4 Leicesters, 19 April 1915.

coming to this view, Captain Dyer-Bennet presumably had in mind such incidents as that when 40 men sent to work under the Royal Engineers went off to the wrong job: "A case of incompetent NCO – not looking after his men whilst his officer was away getting orders."[20]

Since the Adjutants of the North and South Staffords are more reticent in this period it is hard to know if they were finding similar difficulties. If Brigadier General H.B. Williams is to be believed, see below in Chapter 4, then it is likely that they were.

The standard of NCOs had been raised in December 1914 in 139 Brigade when it was noted that

> [Discipline] continues to improve – the Officers 'take charge' more and NCOs also are asserting their authority more than they used to.[21]

Perhaps as a result of this earlier attention Company Quarter-Master Sergeant Dickenson, 1/6 Sherwoods, was gazetted Second Lieutenant from 13 March 1915.[22] Subsequently, Acting Sergeant-Major W. Seaton was gazetted Second Lieutenant and Temporary Captain from 1 April 1915.[23]

The NCOs of 1/8 Sherwoods were lectured on discipline by their Commanding Officer on 7 March 1915, having only recently landed in France. Their Adjutant makes no subsequent remarks about their effectiveness. Interestingly, the battalion subsequently had joint bomb-throwing and advance guard practices in which the Officers and NCOs were instructed together.[24]

Having urged all battalions to actively seek out information the Standing Orders also gave detailed instructions about observing artillery fire. Officers were required not only to note the time between flash and burst but also to take a compass map reading from the flash. This suggests the 46th division were at least in line with best practice at the time if these orders were carried out. They were also to note the exact time of firing and to obtain a fuse as this would often give the CRA information about range.[25] There is no extant record of such activity. Nonetheless, further requests for detailed information to be gathered were received. For example, on 13 April 1915 Brigadier General G.M.W. MacDonagh, BGGS (Intelligence) at GHQ staff,[26] had his request for information passed on to 1/4 Leicesters via Second Army, II Corps, 46th Division and 138 Brigade. MacDonagh not only wanted information on the

---

20   Ibid., 14 April 1915.
21   LRO: 139 Brigade War Diary, 12 December 1914.
22   WSF: War Diary 1/6 Sherwood Foresters, 30 March 1915.
23   Ibid., 16 April 1915.
24   WSF: War Diary 1/8 Sherwood Foresters, 15 March 1915 and 23 March 1915.
25   Standing Orders – Ibid., para 13.
26   Lieutenant General Sir George Mark Watson MacDonagh (1865-1942), later Director of Military Intelligence at the War Office.

changing composition of German fuses but also the average proportion of blind shells and their causes as well as the composition of bursting charges. In forwarding this request to the battalion via Brigade the GSO2, Captain Price-Davies VC, had felt it necessary to stress that the artillery would provide information on fuses and bursts but that the proportion of 'blinds' should be included in shelling reports by battalions. Price-Davies had also stated, and underlined, that only Artillery personnel should handle/investigate unexploded shells.[27] For the further guidance of the infantry they were to note the condition of the ground if it was likely to have caused the failure to explode. Even with this hint one suspects that a conscientious officer could have felt like the Sales Director who receives a call from the International Vice President asking why the company's fish fingers were not on sale at Arkwright's corner shop in Darlington last Friday! One is also left to wonder at the quality of the information collected by men who, in daylight, could hardly afford to look over the parapet to check whether an unexploded shell was lying in mud or on rock. The ever-present danger is brought out in the diary of 1/5 South Staffords for April 1915, which records that Private William Durrant, a member of the machine gun section, and Private H.J. Rock of 'C' Company were shot through the head.[28] Subsequent entries ascribe four further casualties in April to sniper fire.

That the Division felt at a disadvantage to the Germans is evident from the minutes of the Leicestershire Territorial Force Association. At its meeting on 1 July 1915, the Leicestershire TFA noted that the Emergency Committee had responded to a request from Major General Montagu-Stuart-Wortley for rifles with telescopic sights. The committee had approached the Mayor of Leicester who had agreed to provide £80 to purchase four rifles per battalion, "thus enabling our men to compete on equal terms with the enemy's snipers". At a subsequent meeting on 23 September 1915 it was noted that four rifles with telescopic sights had been sent to the 1/4 and 1/5 Leicesters within the past fortnight. This ad-hoc approach to provision demonstrates the difficulties the official channels were experiencing in meeting the army's needs.[29] That the importance of sniping had not been anticipated even at the lower level is clear from its omission from Brigade Standing Orders.

The Sniping Officer for 1/5 Leicesters was Second Lieutenant A.P. Marsh, who records that he tried to resign at the end of April 1915 but was told to carry on.[30] He went on to note:

> They have provided me with two telescopic sight rifles so now I have not got to get anywhere near so close to do good shooting.

27 LRO 22D 63/162: Brigade Orders, ibid.
28 SRO: War Diary 1/5 South Staffords 11 April 1915.
29 LRO DE819/1: Minutes of Leicestershire TFA.
30 Letter 67, dated 'Sunday'; letter 66 was dated 29 April 1915 and letter 68 dated 2 May 1915.

As part of his duties, Marsh had to visit the sniper posts but it seems that the rifles were not always deployed effectively. Marsh recounts that he had 'lent' a telescopic rifle to Second Lieutenant Wollaston one of the Platoon commanders. Wollaston had only joined the battalion a week earlier having previously completed a machine gun course at Bailleul.[31] Marsh continues that he found Wollaston firing at some German smoke about 1,000 yards distant and that when Marsh asked him how much ammunition he intended to waste it transpired that

> this morning his [Wollaston's] breakfast had, as not infrequently happens, been spoilt by a German bullet filling it with earth from the parapet. Now he was doing a little 'frightfulness' trying to hurt someone else's meal[32]

Whilst such accounts can be disparaged as contemporary anecdotes but Ashworth suggests meals were the first area in which "Live and let Live" developed and this would appear to support the view that meals were psychologically very important.[33]

The serious efforts to compete with the Germans began to bear fruit. This is indicated when Marsh writes on 3 June 1915 that he was now hardly doing any sniping himself as he could post the good shots amongst the men.[34] Reports from 139 Brigade were obviously couched in more military terms as the Divisional War Diary records:

> Nottingham and Derby Brigade reported that our patrols and snipers are gradually establishing superiority over the enemy.

Even those battalions whose diaries contain a lot of detail on individuals do not mention sniping except 1/8 Sherwoods who refer to classes for snipers amongst other specialists on 6 and 23 March 1915.[35] Subsequently, during their period of instruction the CO and the Adjutant visited the trenches of the Royal Irish Fusiliers and noted that they discouraged sniping until the trench works were strong.[36] Presumably, this approach was based upon the idea that there was little to be gained by initiating a 'sniper war' for which one was unprepared.

The positive reports submitted to Divisional HQ are not matched by entries in the battalion diaries of 139 Brigade. However, by 21 May 1/8 Sherwoods had secured Brigade's permission to establish a mini-range and the battalions's snipers were using it.[37] Even so, three days later a German sniper was able to shoot two soldiers through the head. In July, however, 1/5 Lincolns reported that their snipers had forced the

31   LRO: War Diary 1/5 Leicestershire, 24 April 1915.
32   Letters, ibid.
33   T. Ashworth, *Trench Warfare 1914-1918: The Live and Let Live System* (1980), p.24
34   LRO: March op.cit. letter 101, 2 June 1915.
35   WSF: War Diary 1/8 Sherwoods, 6 March 1915 and 23 March 1915.
36   Ibid., 28 March 1915.
37   WSF: War Diary 1/8 Sherwoods, 21 May 1915.

cessation of work on a German sap and silenced the three German snipers opposite their trenches.[38] Sniping was a specialist activity with victims being more numerous than practitioners.

Another weapon was the focus of much greater attention and that was the hand grenade still generally referred to at the time as a 'bomb' except where it was being used as a 'rifle grenade'. Whereas the GOC had had to procure sniper rifles the Divisional diary does not mention grenades until 8 July 1915, when it records that there was an accident in the clerk's office when "Mr Randall dropped a German grenade whilst examining it" resulting in serious injury to Lieutenant Black (OC Divisional Cyclists) and 2 clerks from 'G' branch. Sergeant John Chambers died the following day of the wounds received in the explosion.[39]

The priority given to grenades is evident in 139 Brigade's order that during the period of trench instruction the battalions are to use their time out of the line to practice grenade throwing and trench work.[40] The diaries of the 1/5 and 1/6 Sherwoods do not mention training sessions but on 6 March 1915, 'A' and 'B' companies practice Bomb Throwing, which the Officers and NCOs of the battalion had practised the day before, the Adjutant recording, "a very important operation just at present".[41] Subsequently, 'bomb throwers' were given a period of instruction during which an officer of the Seaforth Highlanders demonstrated how the German stick grenade worked and concluded that the British bomb was more useful. It is difficult to imagine that any other verdict could have been given at this stage of the war to a newly arrived battalion. The focus on bombing at this stage in the war was general and therefore 46th Division was typical in its position on the learning curve.[42]

By May, 1/8 Sherwoods were holding classes for reserve bomb throwers and the Bombing Officer was lecturing the NCOs of the 8th (Service) Battalion King's Royal Rifle Corps on the use of bombs. Similar instruction was given in June to men of the King's Shropshire Light Infantry.[43] Thus was knowledge disseminated in the British Army in 1915.

46th Division's appreciation of grenades was still largely theoretical, as they had not yet had to carry out an attack. Appendix D of Brigadier General Clifford's Standing Orders to 138 Brigade is headed "Organisation and Handling of grenadiers".[44] This named Lieutenant A.A. Ellwood as the Brigade Grenade Officer with overall responsibility for training. Ellwood was given authority to inspect the battalion grenade sections and to give advice on their tactical deployment in the trenches.

---

38   MLL: War Diary 1/5 Lincolns 3 July 1915.
39   TNA: WO95/2662 46th Division War Diary 8 & 9 July 1915.
40   TNA: WO95/139 Brigade Diary 5 March 1915.
41   WSF: All References are to the War Diary 1/7 Sherwoods, March 1915.
42   Rawling refers to whole companies leading bombing assaults, *Surviving Trench Warfare* (1992), p.43.
43   WSF: War Diary 1/8 Sherwoods, 29 May 1915, 30 May 1915 & 9 June 1915.
44   All References in this section are to this document.

The Standing Orders specified the establishment of a Battalion Grenade Section as a distinct detachment "similar to the Machine Gun detachment" in that it was to be relieved of company duties and to be billeted together. The section, to be led by an officer, was to consist of 1 Sergeant, 1 Corporal and 28 men. With due deference to the politics of the situation, the Battalion Grenade Officer was to be chosen by the battalion 'with the advice of the Brigade Grenade Officer'. Given that the latter was a Lieutenant and that Adjutants were usually Captains one can reasonably assume that effectively battalions made the choice. Battalions, too, had the role of selecting the men for the section and were allowed to train reserve grenade officers. The latter would continue to serve with their companies until needed but their existence would have further restricted the Brigade Bombing Officer's role in selection.

When the Battalion was in the trenches half of the section was to be deployed in the fire trench whilst the remainder under the Grenade Officer would be at a central point. The section in the fire trench would be under the tactical command of the officer commanding the trench whilst the rest of the section came under the Battalion commander for use as a resource. Out of line, however, the Grenade section was to be deemed to be under the control of the Brigade Grenade Officer and at the tactical disposal of the Brigadier. The Brigade Grenade Officer was also to receive a copy of the inventory of grenade store drawn up by the Battalion Grenade Officer on the last day of each trench tour and handed to the incoming Grenade Officer. At the end of each trench tour the Grenade Officer of each battalion was to submit a report to the Brigade Grenade Officer stating what grenades had been used and for what purpose and to what effect. Perhaps because it was felt that these reports to a Lieutenant might not always be forthcoming so the orders stated that these reports were 'for the information of the Brigadier'.

The orders went on to detail that the men in the fire trench should stand to with the trench garrison having with them four grenades each ready for firing but with the safety pins in. This organisation was no doubt intended to avoid the situation recorded by 1/5 Leicesters, who came under rifle grenade and trench mortar fire but could not reply "owing to lack of grenades in trench". Assuming the reason given by 1/5 Leicesters was entirely accurate there was still some way to go towards implementing Brigade Orders. A week later Second Lieutenant R.B. Farrer and 34 Other Ranks returned to the Battalion from a grenade course which would suggest the Battalion would then be able to furnish the required grenade section.[45] On 3 July 1915, Second Lieutenant Binns is noted to be the Bomb Officer of 1/5 Lincolns.[46] Ten days after the Standing Orders were issued to 138 Brigade, 1/6 South Staffords were still undertaking "company" training in "wire erection and bombing".[47] None of the Staffords'

45   LRO: War Diary 1/5 Leicesters, 14 June 1915.
46   MLL: War Diary 1/5 Lincolns, 3 July 1915.
47   SRM: War Diary 1/5 South Staffords, 22 May 1915.

battalions record the appointment of a Grenade Officer but this may simply reflect the fact that individual responsibilities are rarely mentioned at this time.

So far, only brief mention had been made of rifle grenades. Paragraph (e) of Appendix D to the Standing Orders, laid down that at least three lines of fire should be prepared for the rifle grenades. These lines of fire should be oblique and where possible be designed to enfold the enemy. In this way, the rifle grenades were being treated as a defensive weapon in the same way as machine guns. The offensive impact of these weapons was evident when German rifle grenades wounded Captain R.A. Faire and Lieutenant J.G. Abell of 1/4 Leicesters on 30 May 1915.[48] Subsequently, the battalion lost Lieutenant H.C. Brice when a Hales Rifle Grenade prematurely exploded mortally wounding him.[49] Using a new weapon could simply lead to retaliation. The diary of 1/5 Leicesters records that early trials with rifle grenades led to retaliatory mortar fire and that on a subsequent occasion eight rifle grenades were fired and that the Germans replied with ten.[50]

1/5th South Staffords carried out a combined attack using bombs and rifle grenades on 8 July 1915.[51] The same battalion used rifle grenades against "some German trenches" in September whilst patrols were put out. Presumably, this was designed to distract the Germans from the activity of patrols. Whatever the exact purpose was these accounts suggest that at least some elements of 46th Division were aggressive trench holders as discussed by Ashworth.[52] This view is borne out by the comment in the history of 1/8 Sherwoods that the CO was urging on the officers a more aggressive attitude and that they were finding their feet by May.[53]

A less novel but no less potent threat to life was posed by trench mortars and artillery. Thus whilst on Hill 60 in August, 1/5 North Staffords suffered 'considerable' casualties from 'whizzbangs and trench mortars' recording 24 men wounded. The same battalion lost four killed and 20 wounded three weeks later following three days of such fire including two aerial torpedoes, which killed two of the men.[54]

Often the war diaries record lots of shelling with few casualties and yet one 6" shell struck the parapet and wounded 6 other ranks of 1/5 Lincolns.[55] One of the most senior casualties to shellfire in this period was Lieutenant Colonel J.W. Jessop, commanding 1/4 Lincolns. On 4 June 1915 he rode over to the Headquarters of the 1/5 Leicesters and an eagle eyed German observer and battery delivered a shell into the group outside the Headquarters. Colonel Jessop was killed and Colonel Jones

48   LRO: War Diary 1/4 Leicesters, 30 May 1915.
49   Ibid., 9 June 1915.
50   LRO: War Diary 1/5 Leicesters, 27 May 1915.
51   SRM: War Diary 1/5 South Staffords, 3 July 1915.
52   Ashworth, *Trench Warfare, p.???*
53   W.C.C. Weetman, *The 1/8 Battalion Sherwood Foresters in the Great War 1914-1919* (1920), p.54.
54   SRM: War Diary 1/5 North Staffords, 21 August 1915 and 23 August 1915.
55   MLL: War Diary 1/5 Lincolns, 13 June 1915.

Listening post of the 1/6th South Staffs, Hill 60, 1915. (6th South Staffs)

of 1/5 Leicesters was wounded. There were ten other casualties, two of which were fatal. A month later a wiring party of 1/6 Sherwoods, led by Captain Heathcote, was shelled as it returned and lost nine killed and 21 wounded.[56] The danger from artillery was common to the whole of the Western Front but as they were serving in the Sanctuary Wood the cost could be very high. For example, 1/5 Sherwoods lost seven killed and twelve wounded three days later.[57]

56   WSF: War Diary 1/6 Sherwoods, 4 July 1915.
57   WSF: War Diary 1/5 Sherwoods, 26 & 29 June 1915.

Bomb Corner, Ypres, 1915. (Hills)

Barracks in Ypres, 1915. (Hills)

In the sector south of Ypres there was mining and counter mining. On 25 March 1915, II Corps issued instructions that when mining was suspected a 2' picket post was to be driven into the ground and then having placed one's ear to the picket one was supposed to listen to see if the Germans were working. If so, the section of trench between the two nearest traverses was to be evacuated and those traverses strengthened. In the meantime the suspected mining should be reported to battalion HQ and the Royal Engineers. Given the potential for mistakes it is not surprising to find

Corps urging caution and relaying an example of how a few frogs had been mistaken for German mining.[58] At 9 p.m. on 15 June the Germans blew a mine under trench J3 ,near Petit Bois, occupied by 1/8 Sherwoods who were just preparing to be relieved by the Robin Hoods [1/7 Sherwoods]. In the shock created by the mine and under covering fire from artillery, mortars and machine guns the Germans succeeded in occupying the crater before being driven out by 'C' Company at bayonet point. 1/8 Sherwoods lost Lieutenant A.F.O. Dobson and Second Lieutenant W.H. Hollins, who were killed whilst with the machine gun and bombing sections respectively, as well as seven men killed and two missing. For the attached men from the 6th (Service) Battalion King's Own Yorkshire Light Infantry it was an object lesson in what would be expected of them, especially as they suffered casualties too.[59] The success of the counter-attack nevertheless suggests the battalion was holding its own.

The two-way nature of the mining activity is exemplified by 23 July 1915. At 6.55 p.m. 1/5 Leicesters saw the engineers blow a mine under a German gallery and follow this up with a large mine, which they exploded at 7 p.m., supported by artillery fire commencing at 7.01 p.m. 1/5 Leicesters judged the German redoubt to have been destroyed and approximately 40 casualties to have been suffered by the Germans. However, at 9.22 p.m. the same evening the Germans exploded a mine in front of Trench 50 inflicting 42 casualties on 1/5 Leicesters. The fact that the mine was exploded so quickly and in front, not under, Trench 50 may reflect German concerns that it might be discovered but it reflects the stalemate on the Western Front very clearly.[60] It also confirms the point, made above, regarding the 46th Division being an aggressive trench holding force.[61]

Unknown to 46th Division, the Germans were also preparing to try out a new weapon – the flame-thrower, although contemporaries referred to it as liquid fire. On 29 July 1/8 Sherwoods had relieved the Robin Hoods and consequently found themselves on the flank of the front attacked by the Germans at Hooge on 30 July.[62] The German attack caused 7 King's Royal Rifles to retreat but Lieutenant James and Second Lieutenant Vann held onto Trench B8 with 'D' company of 1/8 Sherwoods. Subsequently, the Robin Hoods under Lieutenant Colonel Brewill (who had himself only just replaced Lieutenant-Colonel Birkin, who had been wounded that morning) successfully constructed a flank to protect the position held by 1/8 Sherwoods and therefore secured the British line despite continuous heavy German fire. The Robin Hoods received a commendation from the GOC Second Army and Second Lieutenant Vann (1/8 Sherwoods) was awarded the MC. The performance of the Sherwoods suggests they were good rather than average troops.

58   LRO2 D63/168: 1/4 Leicesters.
59   WSF: War Diary 1/8 Sherwoods, 5 June 1915.
60   LRO: War Diary 1/5 Leicesters, 23 July 1915.
61   See note 51 above.
62   WSF: All references are to the respective War Diary of 1/7 and 1/8th Sherwoods 20 July 1915.

Men of C Company, 1/6th Staffs, in the trenches at Wulverghem, 1915. (6th South Staffs)

The Flammenwerfer attack was, however, very much a break from the normal routine. The Divisional Diary records the pressures placed on the battalions by the GOC Second Army's requirements for digging. A battalion of 138 Brigade was provided for Army digging on 17 days in July.[63] The impact on the men is obvious when one considers that in the second half of July 1/4 Lincolns and 1/5 Leicesters only spent eight days and seven days,[64] respectively, in Divisional Reserve and so if eight days of Army digging were required (i.e. half the month's total) then these soldiers would have spent 50 per cent of their time out of the trenches carrying out large-scale digging projects. Anyone who has read Bill Mitchinson's *Pioneer Battalions in the Great War* will appreciate that however good these specialists were a lot of the standard digging of Corps and Army reserve lines was undertaken by the line battalions.[65]

Not all battalions shared equally in the digging. For example, 1/4 Leicesters were not available in Divisional Reserve for digging, as they spent the second half of July either "in the trenches" (seven days) or in Brigade Reserve (ten days).

63   TNA: Divisional War Diary 1915, Appendix 2.
64   Ibid. See Appendix 12.
65   K.W. Mitchinson, *Pioneer Battalions in the Great War: Organized and Intelligent Labour* (1997), *passim*.

The 46th Division calendar for August 1915 contained between 30 and 37 days if one is to believe the Duty Rota recorded by the staff.[66] Clearly, the reality was that battalions reflected reliefs by double counting but it perhaps reflects a lack of oversight that even within brigades the returns were not standardised. Admittedly, in 137 Brigade three battalions recorded 36 days as did three battalions of 138 Brigade. However, no two battalions of 139 Brigade submitted a return giving the same number of days in the month.

That paperwork was an issue in 139 Brigade is also reflected in a note for the GOC to speak to Brigadier General C.T. Shipley concerning inaccurate strength returns.[67] Devotees of the Sherwoods will doubtless argue that their qualities as fighting troops had only recently been proven during the flammenwerfer attack but the British Army of 1915 needed lions that could count. The requirement to balance martial endeavour with clerical correctness is also evident in the Minutes of the GOC's Conference on 26 August, in which the "Non Compliance with Divisional Orders" and the "unpunctuality of rendering returns and reports" are recorded as matters of concern.[68]

The variability of returns is borne out by 137 Brigade, where the battalion war diaries of August 1915 do not include strength returns except in the case of 1/6 North Staffords.[69]

According to the Staff Record, 1/6 North Staffords spent eight days in Divisional Reserve. In fact the battalion's diary shows it was relieved on 10 August and then spent 11-16 August in Divisional Reserve before returning to the trenches. Only if one counts 10-17 August inclusive does one reach a total of eight days. Given that the battalion was relieved after dark on 10 August and therefore spent the early hours of 11 August making its way to the rear it was not really available during that time. Although the tired men could then have then been sent on a night's digging their final evening in Divisional Reserve would have been spent returning to the line after an afternoon spent carrying out the detailed preparations for the return to the trenches.

The routine which now characterised "trench holding" is fully evident in the itinerary followed by 1/6 North Staffords during August 1915:

---

66   TNA: Ibid., Appendix XIII.
67   TNA: Ibid., Appendix IX a.
68   TNA: Ibid., Appendix IX.
69   SRM: War Diaries of 1/5 & 1/6 South Staffords and 1/5 & 1/6 North Staffords.

August	Duty
1-2	in Brigade Reserve at Railway Dugouts
2 (after dark)	relieve 1/5 South Staffords in trenches
3-9	in trenches
10 (after dark)	relieved by 1/5 South Staffords, proceed to Divisional Reserve
11-16	in Divisional Reserve
17 (after dark)	relieve 1/5 South Staffords in trenches
18-22	in trenches
23	relieved by 1/5 South Staffords, proceed to Brigade Reserve at Railway Dugouts
24-29	in Brigade Reserve (Railway Dugouts)
30 (after dark)	return to trenches
31	in trenches[70]

As the present day memorial testifies, Railway Dugouts often proved to be as dangerous a billet as some front line trenches in other sectors and therefore the strain on the men's nerves would have been severe. One could summarise 1/6 North Staffords' August 1915 as "all quiet on the Western Front". As long as this description assumes the irony intended by Remarque then it would have been acceptable to the men of 1/6 North Staffords and the other battalions. At the end of July 1915, 1/6 North Staffords' Adjutant recorded the Battalion's strength as 26 Officers and 845 men, whilst a month later he recorded the battalion's strength as being 32 Officers and 824 men.[71] The nature of a war of attrition is brought out in these figures as the battalion has lost 2.48 per cent of its Other Ranks in one month without attempting any offensive operations. Battle casualties will be much higher and therefore demand attention but the insidious cost of industrialised siege warfare is very real.

The War Diary does not record any officer casualties but it does record their numbers as follows:

Date	Officers with Battalion	Officers with Details	Total Officer Strength
31/07/1915	21	5	26
06/08/1915	20	5	25
13/08/1915	22	6	28
20/08/1915	23	7	30
27/08/1915	26	4	30
31/08/1915	28	4	32

70   SRM: War Diary of 1/6 North Staffords, August 1915.
71   Ibid.

Unfortunately, there is no record of the arrivals so one has to assume the total is accurate. The only apparent discrepancy is therefore the return for 6 August. This is probably due to an error at the end of July when the number of officers on details is unchanged at five even though the diary records that an Officer of 'B' company was left in the trenches when the battalion was relieved on 27 July.[72]

Turning to the 'Other Ranks', the figures are as follows:

Date	Other Ranks with Battalion	Other Ranks with Details	Total Other Ranks Strength
31/07/1915	809	36	845
06/08/1915	779	47	826
13/08/1915	767	74	841
20/08/1915	745	91	836
27/08/1915	765	66	831
31/08/1915	749	75	824

Again, there is no record of arrivals but we can see that the sharpest rise in men on detail, from 47 to 74, coincides with the period in Divisional Reserve. Casualties were sustained on 13 of the 25 days on which the battalion was not wholly in Divisional Reserve. During August the battalion lost three men who died of wounds, five killed and 20 men wounded as well as one man accidentally wounded. The loss of 29 men, or approximately 3.5 per cent of the battalion's opening strength, would never grab the headlines in the way that 19,000 killed on 1 July 1916 did, but it does a lot to illustrate the concept of attrition. At this rate, a battalion would effectively need replacing every 2½ years since returning wounded would easily be matched by the accelerated losses associated with 'big shows'.

During August 1915 1/6 North Staffords rotated duties with 1/5 South Staffords. Their casualties amounted to ten Other Ranks killed and four who died of wounds as well as 25 wounded. In addition, 1/5 South Staffords had one officer wounded and seven Other Ranks who, though wounded, remained with the battalion. Even if those remaining at duty are excluded then 40 casualties probably represented 5 per cent of the battalion. With a 1 in 20 chance of becoming a casualty during a 'quiet' period the discipline of the troops is commendable.

The Adjutant of 1/5 South Staffords actually records the casualties individually. The case of Corporal W.H. Green is not untypical in that he was wounded on 14 August but remained on duty only to be killed on 25 August. His death came between the wounding of Company Sergeant Major A. Moseley and the death of Company

72   Ibid.

Lt. Col. Goodman and other officers of 1/6th Sherwoods at Kemmel, 1915. (Wylly)

1/6th Sherwoods rest after a tour in trenches, 1915. (Wylly)

Sergeant Major H. Gee, the latter on a day noted for heavy shelling.[73] The loss of two senior NCOs helps to illustrate the constant re-organisation required as regular casualties were sustained and why the need for "promotable" NCOs was so great.

The strain on battalions was also reflected at the GOC's conference on 15 August when it was decided to put three brigades into line because "2 up" was resulting in the men being "overworked". Two days later another conference looked at siting field guns in the forward areas of each brigade.[74] These progressive responses to the problems of trench warfare need to be recognised if we are to obtain a balanced picture of the Division in 1915. The issue of artillery support, for example, was also exercising the mind of Lieutenant Colonel Leveson-Gower, as reflected in the War Diary of 232 Brigade, Royal Field Artillery. Leveson-Gower begins by asserting that the Germans have established an apparent superiority by responding to British battery registration fire with heavier artillery. He goes on to argue that this causes animosity on the part of the infantry, a clear example of Ashworth's description of each side diminishing "the other's risk of death, discomfort or injury"[75] even though the officers of 138 Brigade, to whom his brigade provided support, were ignorant of the means by which they could call for retaliation against German fire. Leveson-Gower identified, almost certainly correctly, that the value of retaliation depended upon its promptness. He therefore advocated that the infantry must take a more direct interest and that:

> communications between the Field Artillery and Heavies and between the Trenches and the Heavies should be direct instead of circuitous.[76]

This appears to demonstrate that the need for close integration of infantry and artillery is recognised. However, control of the heavy artillery was to remain the preserve of senior commanders largely due to their scarcity. The difficulty in deciding upon the role of the artillery bears out Bidwell's argument regarding the lack of an agreed doctrine for the artillery.[77]

To the 'rear' of the divisional artillery were to be found the Divisional Ammunition Column (DAC). The War Diary for 1915, perhaps because it did not have the same daily detail to report contains numerous references to its own learning curve. In the early months there are numerous references to poor discipline. For example, in February, it notes that whilst at Luton the men had accepted vaccination because it was thought to carry a week's leave and that even now the possibility of service overseas was not causing them to stir themselves. Lieutenant Colonel Leach went on to note in March that the DAC was benefiting from working under different conditions

73 Ibid., 26 August 1915.
74 TNA: WO 95/2662, Divisional War Diary, Appendix IX h.
75 Ashworth, *Trench Warfare*, p.19.
76 TNA: WO95/2674, War Diary, 232 Brigade Royal Field Artillery, July 1915.
77 Bidwell & Graham, *Firepower*, Book 1, passim.

CSM Hunt and Sergeant Burdett,
1/4th Leicesters, Ypres trenches,
1915. (Milne)

Trench 47, held by the 1/4th Leicesters, Ypres, 1915. (Milne)

to home – they were now in France. He went on to record that there was no drunkenness but that there had been a small amount of insubordination to NCOs.[78] This last comment would appear to support the general contention in the BEF that the weakness of territorial units lay in their NCOs.

That Colonel Leach's problems were not over is reflected in an entry in April 1915 when he says that discipline has been up to standard as a whole but that "There have been several cases of serious crime but the sentences awarded will it is hoped prevent a recurrence". This tougher approach probably reflects Leach's other note on the benefits of having a regular officer as his Adjutant – a practice that he believed would benefit all Territorial DACs.[79] Leach goes on to record that by August discipline was better, having noted in July that "NCOs have now a better sense of the responsibilities of their position".[80] Clearly, it had been necessary to shake up the comfortable pre-war relationship between NCOs and men.

Much of the diary for March 1915 is devoted to Leach's own appreciation of the guidance he had received from the Adjutant of the 6th DAC. Leach recorded that it was now possible to operate on lines, which that unit had found to work under active service conditions. Leach concluded that "more can be learnt in a few days from an officer who has had experience than from any amount of study of books".[81]

The reality of war was that in September Leach's heavy wagons, used especially for moving artillery ammunition, were reduced by 50 per cent. He noted this would increase the burden on the men in the event of heavy fighting.[82]

On 1 October 1915, 1/5 South Staffords were relieved by elements of 17th (Northern) Division and proceeded to join General Sir Douglas Haig's First Army with the rest of the division to join the Battle of Loos.[83]

Having passed its basic training sine laude the Division had proved adept at learning the arts of trench warfare, though it had in the process suffered numerous casualties since this was essentially a process of trial and error. The more perceptive officers had begun to think more strategically in seeking solutions to problems such as artillery control but were hampered by material shortages. For example, a threatened attack at Hooge led the BGRA V Corps (Brigadier General S.D. Browne) to allocate 100 High Explosive shells as a precaution. One of the major drawbacks of the revised view of 1918 through the "learning curve" paradigm is that the BEF of 1915 was not good enough to secure victory. Whilst this provides evidence of the developments in operational method of the BEF between 1915 and 1918 it is very important to recognise that not only did the BEF of 1915 lack the tactical awareness necessary for

---

78 TNA: WO95/2675, War Diary 46th Division, Divisional Ammunition Column, February and March 1915.
79 Ibid., April 1915.
80 Ibid., July and August, 1915.
81 Ibid., March 1915.
82 Ibid., September 1915.
83 SRM: War Diary 1/5 South Staffords, October 1915.

Field Marshall Sir Douglas Haig, C-in-C BEF 1915-1918. (Author's collection)

victory but it was also not equipped for victory. The control of "Heavies" could not be devolved downwards whilst those guns were in short supply and the ammunition for the artillery was both relatively scarce and of variable quality. The work of thousands on the Home Front to create the abundance of materiel available in 1918 is as essential to victory as the learning curve itself. For example industrial mobilisation meant that the number of heavy artillery guns produced rose from 94 in the ten months to June 1915 to 894 in the twelve months ending in June 1916.[84]

The response of 139 Brigade to the liquid fire attack had shown that territorial troops could be relied upon where neighbouring New Army troops could not be despite the contemporary perception that territorial NCOs lacked the authority they enjoyed in other units. The problem with NCOs was real, as was admitted by line and

84   J.M. Bourne, *Britain and the Great War*, (1989), p.188.

support units, but was remediable. Ironically, this was a function of the inadequacy of pre-war planning by Regular officers who were to complain the most. Given that Territorials were designed for home defence no plans had been made to stiffen them with a cadre of regular NCOs and when war came the decision to raise completely new battalions with no previous training meant the scarce resource of trained NCOs was diverted to them.

French had chosen to use Kitchener divisions rather than summon 46th Division south for the opening of the offensive at Loos. Given the growing rivalry between the two men it is interesting that 46th Division should now be selected. The clear impression given by the post war correspondence contained in his file is that Montagu-Stuart-Wortley saw Sir John French as a patron.[85] It could be reasonably be argued that by 1920 there was no one else to turn to. However, Montagu-Stuart-Wortley's subsequent posting to French's command in Ireland suggests that there was a "network" and Montagu-Stuart-Wortley was not in Haig's. The Major General, if not his Division, was now to be tested in a personally as well as militarily hostile environment. A period in which Haig's eye, following the failure of the opening of the offensive, was at least as much on the opportunity to become Commander in Chief of the BEF as it was to defeat the Germans.

Apart from the endemic weakness in its NCOs, the 46th Division showed no particular signs by September 1915 that it was not following the normal path of British divisions in acquiring experience and progressing along the learning curve. However, it had acquired its experience to date in a defensive role in a defensive sector and it was now to be used in an offensive capacity.

85   TNA: WO138/29, Personal file WO138/29: Major General E.J. Montagu-Stuart-Wortley.

3

The Hohenzollern Redoubt: 13 October 1915

In this chapter the focus will be on assessing the performance of the 46th Division in its first offensive operation, an attack on the Hohenzollern Redoubt on 13 October 1915. The outcome was to play a major part in determining the Division's reputation right up to the breaking of the Hindenburg Line in September 1918. The contrast between the failure at the Hohenzollern, and later at Gommecourt, and the success at the Hindenburg Line is itself prima facie evidence for the existence of a learning curve.

The recriminations that followed the assault provide further insight into the politics of high command in the BEF and the reasons why the commander of 46th Division, Major General Hon. E.J. Montagu-Stuart-Wortley, was "de-gummed" after 1 July 1916. Although Montagu-Stuart-Wortley's fate does not appear to be connected to the learning curve it is in practice. The arguments between Montagu-Stuart-Wortley and his superiors have their origins in operational method which throws light on the early developments of the learning curve outlined by Prior and Wilson.[1] The impact of the events of 13 October on the reputation of 46th Division may well stem from the "political" context in which they occurred. Such an argument can also be made in relation to September 1918. This sub-thesis will be returned to again when we come to consider the debate over the outcomes. The brief departure from the Western Front at the close of 1915 will also be briefly discussed as to the impact this had upon the Division's progress along the Learning Curve.

Following the failures of First Army on the opening day at Loos, 25 September 1915,[2] and subsequent operations 46th Division was relieved by 17th Division on 1 October 1915 and ordered to march south where it was to join XI Corps commanded

---

1   R. Prior & T. Wilson, *Command on the Western Front: The Military Career of Sir Henry Rawlinson* (1991), passim.
2   The controversy surrounding these events ultimately led to Haig replacing French as BEF C-in-C.

by Lieutenant-General Sir R.C.B. Haking[3] in General Sir Douglas Haig's First Army. Lieutenant-General Haking intended to use 46th Division to attack the heavily defended German strongpoint known as the Hohenzollern Redoubt. It was on the evening of 7 October that Haig called on the HQ of 139 Brigade (Brigadier General C.T. Shipley[4]) noting that the men seemed very fit and "say they are delighted to have joined the First Army." Clearly, the men knew how to address an Army commander![5] The Diary of 1/4 Lincolns records that Haig had visited 138 Brigade HQ for 15 minutes on 4 October during a meeting run by the GOC.[6]

The Official History records that Montagu-Stuart-Wortley wished to proceed by siege methods, "by bombing attack and approaching the position trench by trench: but in this he was overruled".[7] Whilst accurate, this note in the Official History hides the depth to which the disagreement between Corps and Division ran. On 7 October 1915 Montagu-Stuart-Wortley submitted an outline plan in which he proposed to attack with two brigades but to a point less deep because "the objective would be more easily held when captured, and, as far as I can judge, it would give us all we want".[8] That he knew this would probably not be well received is indicated by his acknowledgement that his proposed objective was "not quite so far forward as that outlined by the Corps Commander at yesterday's conference".[9]

Given that Robin Prior and Trevor Wilson and others have defined progress along the learning curve in the Great War as moving away from offensives with a strategic breakthrough as their aim to the concept of 'bite and hold',[10] one is bound to ask the question why this divisional commander had stumbled upon the 'holy grail' so quickly and so early in the war. Montagu-Stuart-Wortley provides the following answer:

I have been informed by Staff and other officers who took part in the late attacks.

The officers referred to here are Lieutenant Colonel S.E. Hollond, GSO1 9th (Scottish) Division, and Captain J.S. Drew of the Cameron Highlanders, who had visited 46th Division HQ on 6 October 1915.[11] The reason for their visit was that the Cameron Highlanders had attacked and captured Fosse 8 on 25 September 1915.

---

3   Lieutenant General Sir Richard Cyril Byrne Haking (1862-1945) supported Haig in the dispute over the reserves at Loos. He later earned an unenviable reputation as a 'butcher', principally by organising pointless 'stunts'. He was the leading supporter of trench raids.

4   Promoted to Brigadier General on 5 August 1914 to command 139 Brigade, he continued in that role until 27 May 1917 and was therefore the longest serving Brigade commander in 46th Division during the war.

5   TNA: 139 Brigade War Diary.

6   MLL: War Diary 1/4 Lincolns.

7   Sir J.E. Edmonds, *Military Operations – France and Belgium, 1915* (1932), p.384.

8   TNA: WO95/2662, 46th Division War Diary, 7 October 1915.

9   Ibid.

10 Prior & Wilson, *Command on the Western Front*, passim.

11 TNA: WO95/2662. 46th Division War Diary October 1915, Appendix IV.

Lieutenant General Haking, a Haig
loyalist. (Author's collection)

Lieutenant Colonel P.W. Game, who had served under Lieutenant General Sir Henry
Rawlinson, may have reinforced their advice, as Prior and Wilson cite Rawlinson's
attack at Neuve Chapelle as an early model of success.

Montagu-Stuart-Wortley's concerns about the attack and his subsequent proposal
to Haking are evident in the notes of this meeting.[12] It is recorded that the Cameron
Highlanders had set out 800 strong but that only 80 reached the other side. Notes
were made of the various strong points and the conditions of the trenches, in particular, the fields of fire and the work required to consolidate the positions once captured.
For instance, the soil was identified as not chalk and therefore a proportion of one pick
to three shovels would be required. The advice was not restricted to topography. As
well as general points on the need for counter-battery support and using gun cotton to
blow down traverses, Note 14 says:

> 95 mm guns might well be taken forward to consolidate the position. Phosphor
> bombs fired from these would be of value against the enemy's bomb parties.[13]

12   TNA:WO95/2662, 46th Division War Diary, October 1915.
13   Ibid.

The learning curve of the British Army may be difficult to chart but it does seem that here we have clear evidence of a New Army division passing on its acquired experience.

Hand grenades were a key weapon in trench fighting and the overall advice was to organise large squads of bombers "25-40" with about 40 men to carry as:

> The experience was that the small bombing parties soon ran out of bombs and so were defeated.[14]

Evidence was also provided regarding the relative efficacy of British and German bombs. It was noted that the Germans were likely to have more bombs and so it was important to be able to throw the bombs a good distance. To achieve this extra range "rifle grenades are consequently useful".[15]

Note 17 recorded that the Camerons had also established machine gun batteries in the rear that had continually swept the German Communication trenches during the nights before the attack.[16] This was another way in which the delay in inserting 46th Division into the line was to reduce the effectiveness of the assault. Given this advice from these experienced officers, Montagu-Stuart-Wortley argued that most of the casualties during the assault on the Corons occurred because of heavy enfilade and artillery fire.[17] This experience lead him to propose his revised objectives, as otherwise the enemy would be too close to the new line for proper artillery support to be available. It has to be remembered that given the proximity of British trenches the artillery would tend to overshoot to avoid hitting their own men. In this case, the artillery would not be able to lay down a proper defensive barrage as the need to overshoot might well take their shells beyond the German first line and therefore would not inhibit any small arms enfilade fire. The division was still equipped with the obsolete 15-pounders, which were less effective than the 18-pounder field gun standard in Regular units. The main field howitzers supporting the attack had a 50 per cent zone 29 yards long and two yards wide at 3,000 yards.[18] By 5,000 yards this had increased to 52 yards long and 8.8 yards wide. Thus the front troops trying to consolidate the position would have run a strong risk of suffering from friendly fire.[19]

Montagu-Stuart-Wortley reinforced his proposal by arguing that on the left of his proposed objectives there was an existing trench, which could be consolidated more quickly than the time it would take to dig a new trench if Mad Point were to

---

14   Ibid.
15   Ibid.
16   Ibid.
17   Corons were rows of miners' cottages.
18   This means 50% of shells would land within this rectangular area.
19   The historian of 1/5 Sherwoods says they were told it was the largest artillery concentration to date, L.W. de Grave, *The War History of the Fifth Battalion the Sherwood Foresters* (1930), p.44.

remain an objective.[20] It would appear that in connection with Mad Point, at least, Montagu-Stuart-Wortley was listened to. When he urged that it should be entrusted to I Corps[21] because on 13 October 1915 Mad Point was attacked by 1 Queens, 2nd Division, I Corps.[22] In requesting that Mad Point be excluded from his objectives Montagu-Stuart-Wortley did refer to the relative numerical weakness of Territorial Divisions:

> having an establishment of 800 only instead of 1027, the difference being of course entirely of fighting men.[23]

Montagu-Stuart-Wortley's only specific reference to the timing of the attack was that it should be simultaneous, subject to a decision whether the left battalion in the assault should attack a few minutes ahead of the main assault in order to rush the West Face of the Hohenzollern Redoubt.[24] In requesting artillery support, Montagu-Stuart-Wortley was much more specific. He identified the key targets and singled out the "main telephone dugout just E. of the Manager's house" for bombardment by the "heaviest" artillery available as it "is said to be strongly built".[25] Thus we can see as early as October 1915 that the value of destroying enemy command and control systems was appreciated. Montagu-Stuart-Wortley also correctly identified the strength of the defences that faced his men when he asked that in preparation for the assault the "machine guns which are said to be located in the dump should be destroyed by artillery fire".[26]

Montagu-Stuart-Wortley submitted his proposals to Haking on 7 October 1915 and on the same day at 3 p.m. accompanied Haking on a visit to the Forward Observation Officers of the Guards Division and 12th Division. On 8 October 1915 Montagu-Stuart-Wortley gave orders that as many officers as possible should visit the trenches each day. Later, on 8 October, Montagu-Stuart-Wortley and Lieutenant Colonel Game, his GSO1, went to a conference at Corps HQ.[27] This would seem to have been the decisive meeting in shaping the attack since no further meeting is recorded for 9 October and the Divisional Orders were issued on 10 October.

The plan seems to have incorporated some of the advice received in that 100 and 125 'grenadiers' drawn from 139 Brigade were to support the attacks by 137 and 138 Brigades respectively.[28] Detailed instructions were given for "telling off" the bombing

20   TNA: WO95/2662, 46th Division War Diary, ibid.
21   Ibid.
22   Edmonds, *Military Operations 1915 Vol. 2*, op. cit., Sketch 41.
23   TNA: 46th Division War Diary, ibid.
24   Ibid.
25   Ibid.
26   Ibid.
27   TNA: 46th Division War Diary, entries for 7 October 1915 and 8 October 1915.
28   Ibid., Divisional Order No.20 issued 10 October 1915.

parties from what is to become known as mopping-up as the battalions advance. It was stressed that no dugouts must be left unsearched.[29] Therefore, it would be reasonable to conclude that in preparing for the infantry assault Montagu-Stuart-Wortley had made constructive proposals to his senior officer and that even where these were rejected he had sought practical advice from experienced officers and incorporated that knowledge where possible.

Haking's role in insisting upon a daylight assault upon a heavily entrenched position should be contrasted with Bidwell and Graham's description of him as a "reputable tactician" in describing his contribution to the Staff Conference of 1911.[30] They argue that Haking believed in infantry firepower and that he argued for selecting objectives according to the support available otherwise the infantry would fall to enemy fire. At the Hohenzollern, Haking appears to insist upon the very scenario he had foreseen and with the dire results for the infantry he had anticipated. It is important, however, to understand that Montagu-Stuart-Wortley's disagreement with Haking did not necessarily arise entirely from differences in military judgement. The Division now came under the command of General Sir Douglas Haig's First Army and Sir John French was putting great pressure on Haig to mount an early attack. Haig's diary for 5 October 1915 remarks on Field-Marshal French's inability to realise:

> the difficulties of getting fresh troops and trench stores forward until adequate communication trenches have been dug.[31]

As a further pre-condition for success, Haig's diary records his proposed schedule for the attack, which includes a day for "Reconnaissance by troops in position."[32]

As the Official History explains this was not possible because of the successful attempts by 2 Grenadier Guards at capturing "The Loop" on the night of 10 October and their successful repulse of repeated German counter-attacks right up to the afternoon of 12 October.[33] It was therefore at Midnight on 12 October that 1/5 South Staffords took over the positions opposite Big Willie from the Grenadiers.

Whilst all this fighting was going on the planning of the assault on the Hohenzollern Redoubt had been continuing. In the light of Prior and Wilson's study of Rawlinson, Haig's diary entry for Wednesday, 6 October 1915, is of interest:

> Every available gun will be placed under Haking's orders for the attack on Fosse 8 and the Quarries, instead of "having the call" on certain batteries as has sometimes been arranged.[34]

---

29   Ibid.
30   Bidwell & Graham, *Firepower* op.cit., p.24.
31   TNA: WO95/56, Diary of Field Marshal Earl Haig.
32   Ibid.
33   Edmonds, *Military Operation 1915 Vol. 2*, op.cit., p.379.
34   TNA: WO95/256, Haig Diary, op. cit.

And in the evening the Divisional CRAs were included in the 6 p.m. conference that Haig held at Hinges. The Official History records that on the day of the attack First Army's assault was supported by the following artillery: 56 Heavy Howitzers; 86 Field Howitzers, 19 Counter Batteries; and 286 Field Guns, though it needs to be remembered that the field guns of 46th Division were obsolete 15 pounders.[35]

Using Prior and Wilson's methodology, and therefore including all the trenches to be taken on the 46th Divisional front, the total amounts to 3,680 yards of trench. Haig's diary for 13 October 1915 records that all the above artillery strength was devoted to "the assault on the Quarries and Fosse 8".[36] The orders issued for the attack contain a detailed breakdown of the artillery support available to 46th Division for its assault but make no mention of its own Divisional artillery, simply that of 28th Divisional Artillery.[37] For the initial assault he details the work of nineteen batteries (three with Howitzers and sixteen with Field Guns).

Using the official figures for artillery support we can then add the nine field gun batteries and two howitzer batteries belonging to 46th Divisional Artillery to reach a figure of 25 field gun batteries and five Howitzer batteries. It should be noted here that the Division's Heavy Howitzer battery, the North Midland Heavy Battery RGA, based at Stoke-on-Trent, was withdrawn from the Division on 18 April 1915 to form part of XIII Heavy Brigade RGA. The Official History refers to Heavy Howitzers and Counter Batteries and the orders note that three Groups of Heavy Artillery would be under the control of the Corps Commander.[38] Thus it would appear that the Divisional assault was supported by 100 field guns and 20 howitzers, plus a share of the heavy howitzers. Since 100 field guns represents a little over a third of those available and the howitzers approximately a quarter we can estimate that one-third of the heavy howitzers were supporting 46th Division. Therefore, the division had the support of some 140 guns in total, of which 36 were 15-pounder field guns that would soon be replaced.

If we assume that Haig was correct then we must add the yards of trench to be gained by 12th Division in order to determine the intensity of the preliminary bombardment. 12th Division's objectives amounted to some 1,800 yards. Thus the total objectives for Haking's Corps can be put at 5,480 yards. If we relate the guns to the objectives we see that there were 445 guns to over 5,480 yards at a ratio of one gun to every 12.31 yards. If we accept Prior and Wilson's figures then this is almost precisely half the concentration achieved at Neuve Chapelle in March 1915. However, it has to be noted that XI Corp's bombardment would last two hours compared with 35 minutes at Neuve Chapelle.

---

35   Edmonds, *Military Operations 1915 Vol. 2*, p.379.
36   TNA: Haig, ibid.
37   TNA: WO95/2662 46th Division War Diary, Div. Order No.20, 10 October 1915 Appendix A.
38   Edmonds, ibid.

On the down side, however, it has to be remembered that since 46th Division were Territorials their Divisional artillery was still equipped with the obsolete 15-pounders as Blore and Sherratt recall:

> 12 November [1915] Armentieres Sector – Rue Dubois. From here the Brigade [231st, RFA] said a final goodbye to the old 15 pdrs. which were getting very worn and inaccurate. [39]

These guns were amongst those allocated to the bombardment of the Redoubt itself.

If, however, we adopt the recalculated total of artillery support available to 46th Division, as detailed above, then we can take the trench frontage figure for 46th Division of 3,680 yards and divide it by 140 to reach a figure of one gun to every 26.28 yards. Although this was much better than the one gun to every 141 yards achieved at Loos[40] it was considerably worse than that achieved at Neuve Chapelle (one gun to 6 yards).[41] And, in addition, with 36 15-pounders the weight of shell was also less favourable. Furthermore, given the known strength of the target and the lack of surprise, given that this was the final phase of a big battle, it seems appropriate to conclude that the available artillery support was inadequate. Once again British infantry would pay the price of Britain entering an industrial war for which she was not prepared.[42]

If the artillery was to prove inadequate what other technology was Haig intending to employ? This question was one that concerned Haig and Haking at a meeting on the afternoon of 7 October according to Haig's diary. The diary records Haig posing these questions to Haking:

(a)   Will all arrangements for attacking (gas, smoke, etc.) be complete by 10th?
(b)   If not, can you attack on 10th with artillery preparation only, with fair chance of success?[43]

The second question reflects the continuing pressure from Sir John French.

According to Haig's diary, Haking responded by sending a written reply enclosing a report drawn up by Lord Cavan (GOC Guards Division)[44] arguing that he would have completed the gas preparations by 13 October and that he opposed attacking on

---

39   J.E.Blore & J.R. Sherratt, *A Commemorative History of the Old Leek Battery 1908 to 1919* (1991), p.79.
40   Prior & Wilson, op.cit., p.111
41   Ibid., p.112.
42   See Bidwell & Graham, op.cit., pp.13-14, for a brief summary.
43   TNA: WO 256 Haig Diary, op.cit.
44   Frederick Rudolf Lambart, 10th Earl of Cavan (1865-1946) had become GOC Guards Division in August 1915. He was GOC XIV Corps (January 1916-March 1918) and then GOC-in-C British Forces, Italy.

10 October. Haig noted: "I fully agree with this opinion". This comment by Haig is important because it recognises the merit in Montagu-Stuart-Wortley's views that an immediate assault was inappropriate but shows that Haig did not feel able to argue for a significant delay. Given the long historical debate over Haig's qualities as a senior commander it is perhaps relevant to note his use of a Socratic approach with his subordinates and Haking's decision to submit a formal written reply rather than engage in a face-to-face debate with Haig. There is an abiding feeling that Haig frequently asked the right questions but is unable to take the answers to their logical conclusions. Certainly, it may be that Haig, having put pressure on Sir John French over the events of 25 September, was reluctant to give the Field Marshal any ammunition with which to counter-attack.

The continuing debate over the date of the assault is again reflected in Haig's Diary for 5 October, when he records a meeting with Sir John French at which French accepted 13 October but asks for the attack to be made on 12 October if possible. It is clear from Richard Holmes' biography that French was by now coming under more direct assault both within the army and from within the political class and was therefore badly in need of a victory.[45] Haig's diary for 8 October also records Major General Sir Frederick Maurice,[46] deputising for Sir William Robertson (CGS) at GHQ, sending him a copy of OAM 48, which included this injunction:

> You should be prepared to make the attack without the use of gas so that it may in any case be carried out no later than the 13th

Haig responded by expressing this view to his Diary:

> (The success of our last attack was due chiefly to the use of smoke, and to some extent, the use of gas, I therefore think it an error to attack without their assistance until we are provided with a more numerous artillery and an adequate supply of ammunition for it.)[47]

Obviously, there will be those who question whether this entry has simply been made to protect Haig's reputation and prepare the ground for an assault on Sir John for ordering attacks without adequate preparation. Others may want clarification as to which successful last attack he is referring to given the very mixed results achieved with gas at Loos on 25 September 1915. Nevertheless, the above quotation tells us an important fact, namely that the commander of First Army knew that the artillery

45   R. Holmes, *The Little Field Marshal: Sir John French* (1981), p.306.
46   Major General F.B. Maurice (1871-1951), Director of Military Operations at the War Office, and – in May 1918 – author of the notorious 'Maurice Letter' that accused Lloyd George of lying to parliament about the strength of the BEF prior to the German offensive of 21 March 1918.
47   TNA: WO 256, Haig Diary.

available to him was inadequate and that he was therefore relying on gas and smoke. This would appear to support Travers's view that Haig had a clear idea of the concept of the "killing ground" and was therefore looking for ways to mask the advance of his highly vulnerable soldiery.[48] This concern to create smoke further reduced the weight of the field gun bombardment but the howitzers of 130 Brigade, and other 'heavies" spent 12.00 noon–1 p.m. on 13 October 1915 firing at key strongpoints in an effort to destroy them, using lydite.[49]

This desire to minimise casualties throws up a further question – why was the time of the attack set for 2 p.m.? According to Haig's Diary this had been debated as early as 6 October: "We discussed the hour of attack (Haking wishes it to be about 2 p.m.) and the arrangements for gas (50 minutes of it) and smoke".[50]

The time but not the date is given in the orders issued on 10 October 1915 so presumably this aspect had been decided at the meeting between Haking and Montagu-Stuart-Wortley on 8 October. The diary yields no evidence about how the decision was reached and in pinning responsibility on Haking there is inevitably some suspicion that Haig was trying to distance himself from any possible mistake. There is also evidence of the way in which later, at the Somme and Passchendaele, Haig was to allow his subordinates to make the key tactical decisions. Charteris, and Haig's biographers since, have been so taken up with the story of the reserves at Loos that they make no comment upon the Hohenzollern Redoubt.

Another aspect of the plan that has not yet been noted by commentators is the way in which the two divisions of XI Corps, 46th and 12th, do not form a continuous line of attack. There was in fact a gap between 1/5 South Staffords on the right of 46th Division and 7 Suffolks on the left of 12th Division of some 280 yards. This stemmed from the decision to direct 46th Division at the Hohenzollern Redoubt and the "Dump" whilst giving 12th Division the objective of the quarries. This omission was particularly serious since to the right of Big Willie, as the Staffords approached it, the German line bent south-eastwards allowing the Germans there to enfilade the advancing Staffords. This topographical issue may well help to explain some of the events of 13 October.

It was not possible for 46th Division to relieve the Guards before the Hohenzollern until 6 a.m. on 13 October. Thus the men going into action that day had not been rested beforehand. As the diary of 1/4 Lincolns noted for 12 October: "7.10 p.m. to Vermelles to collect bombs, shovels etc." To overcome the problems to be associated with lack of time to reconnoitre once in position the preceding days had seen parties of officers from the attacking battalions visiting the trenches held by the Guards. The diary of 1/4 Lincolns tells us the following reconnaissance were undertaken:

---

48   T. Travers, *The Killing Ground*, Chapters 3 and 4 et passim.
49   TNA: 46th Division War Diary, Order 20, 10 October 1915.
50   Ibid.

The Water Tower and Railway Track, Vermelles, 1915. (Hills)

8/10/15 – CO, 2ic, Adj., MGO and Company Commanders
9/10/15 – Subalterns
10/10/15 – Senior NCO's & Warrant Officers.[51]

The entry for 10 October also says that a model of the Hohenzollern Redoubt was viewed at Divisional HQ. These efforts represent thorough preparation given the time constraints.

Apart from officers and NCOs being able to assess the task ahead of them the battalions in the Division continued final training. For 1/4 Lincolns, from 7-11

---

51   MLL: War Diary 1/4 Lincolns, 7-11 October 1915.

October, there was "bombing instruction" for at least some of the men each day. The War Diary of 1/6 South Staffords records a broader diet, including "P.T", "bayonet fighting" and marching at the double as well as "bomb throwing". This is borne out by de Grave who notes the arrival of new mills bombs by the hundred thousand.[52] On 10 October 1/6 South Staffords were shown how to block communication trenches and the signallers practised their trade. All this training culminated on 11 October in:

> Battalion bombing parties paraded under bomb officers for special instruction. Machine guns tested. Practising advancing over open ground in fighting kit. Rapid loading and muscle exercises.[53]

The reference to advancing over "open ground" seems rather out of keeping with the task before the division of storming a complex set of trench positions, but it does tie in with Haig's concerns regarding the need for chemical weapons to mask the attacking battalions.

As the men advanced towards their assembly positions and up into the front line their army commander was very concerned about the weather, especially the wind. Haig's diary records the pressure he believed French was applying for the attack to go ahead on 13 October and Haig's own concerns: "There are indications of the wind now changing round to the West". The diary goes on to record:

> I told him [Haking] to be prepared to cancel the operations ordered for tomorrow if the weather conditions are unfavourable...General Montagu-Stuart-Wortley has completed all arrangements for the attack of Fosse 8 tomorrow. I thought it best not to tell him that if the weather was not favourable for gas and smoke, I intended to postpone operations, because I think it unsettles people before an attack to feel it is uncertain.[54]

Montagu-Stuart-Wortley therefore opened his advanced HQ at Noon on 12 October.[55] The GHQ Intelligence Summary on 11 October 1915 estimated German losses in their failed attack between the Double-Crassier and the Quarries at 7-8,000. More ominously for 46th Division, it noted that amongst the dead found in the south-east corner of the Hohenzollern Redoubt were members of 13 Regiment, which had not previously been in the area south of the La Bassée Canal. 46th Division was apparently facing an already reinforced opponent.[56]

---

52   de Grave, *The War History of the Fifth Battalion The Sherwood Foresters*, p.44.
53   Dates as within text, War diaries of battalions cited.
54   TNA: WO95/256, Haig Diary, 12 October 1915.
55   TNA: WO95/2662, 46th Division War Diary, entry for 12 October 1915.
56   TNA: WO157/3, GHQ Intelligence Summary, entry for 11 October 1915.

Subject then to the wind, which Haig said he had decided to take a decision on at 10 a.m. on 13 October, the plan was as follows:

12 noon – Artillery bombardment begins (incl. Smoke)
1.00 p.m. – gas released
2.00 p.m. – Artillery bombardment to cease
2.05 p.m. – Assault to begin

All that remained now was for the plan to be put into action.

As noted in the plan for the attack there was a serious shortage of modern artillery available to support the assault. This is borne out by the diary of 1/5 South Staffords for 13 October 1915:

the bombardment did not appear to affect the "South Face" or the "Dump Trench" south of G.5.a.3.5., as a great deal of sniping from these trenches took place between 12 Noon and 2.00pm three of our periscopes were hit between 1.40pm and 2.00pm.

That this situation was not unique to 137 Brigade Front is evident from the account given in the history of 1/4 Leicesters:[57]

At 1.50pm the smoke and gas stopped and the enemy began merrily to snipe the top of the parapet with machine guns.

The chronicler of 1/6 South Staffords confirms the seriousness of the situation:

As the artillery preparation grew more intense and the time for the advance approached, the enemy machine gun fire was playing with such effect upon the assembly trenches that the C.O. was compelled to report to Brigade the apparent futility of any movement.[58]

It could of course be argued that these are post-war documents and therefore susceptible to having been written up after the event when a shared common perception had come to prevail. However, in his report on the operations on 13 and 14 October, undated but with references to 16 October so probably written on 17 October, Montagu-Stuart-Wortley specifically states that "there were continual bursts of

57   J. Milne, *Footprints of the 1/4 Leicestershire Regiment* (1935), p.54.
58   A Committee of Officers, *The War History of the Sixth Battalion the South Staffordshire Regiment (T. F.)* (1924), p.97.

The British attack on the Hohenzollern Redoubt, 13 October 1915. (Milne)

machine gun and rifle fire from the above mentioned trenches and the Dump" during the bombardment.[59]

The battalion diary of 1/4 Lincolns, who advanced in support of 1/5 Lincolns and 1/4 Leicesters, records the view that the gas and smoke did little to damage the enemy. Indeed, if the time recorded "12.50pm" is correct then Major Cooper had both arms broken by German shrapnel fire whilst in the reserve trenches in the middle of the British bombardment. The evidence for this point has been emphasised given the controversy that is to follow regarding the courage of the Division in pressing home the assault. The history of 1/4 Leicesters states that the smoke as well as gas stopped at 1.50 p.m.[60] If so, this would have left the advance very exposed. Some corroboration for this can be found in the history of 1/5 North Staffords, which records "clouds of gas and smoke were sent over at intervals until 2 p.m."[61]

The Official History says of 137 Brigade's attack:

> The attacking troops left their trenches five minutes before zero hour, and started with the greatest confidence, but immediately began to suffer heavy loss from terrific machine gun and rifle fire. The great mass of this fire came from a number of machine guns in concealed shelters both near the foot of the Dump and in the

59   TNA: WO 95/2662, Div. War Diary Appendix XV.
60   Milne, *Footprints of the 1/4 Leicestershire Regiment*, ibid.
61   W. Meakin, *The 5th North Staffords and The North Midland Territorials (The 46th and 59th Divisions) 1914-1919* (1920), p.37.

south-west and south-east sides of the Corons, and also from parties of Germans who held out stubbornly in Little Willies and Dump Trench.[62]

It goes on to record that the leading battalion on the left of the Brigade, 1/5 North Staffords, was "practically annihilated". Having gone on to detail the gallantry of the attacking troops who tried to press home the attack the Official History concludes:

> Attempts were made by bombing westward along Big Willie to gain touch with the 138th Brigade, and a few yards of trench were secured; but otherwise the advance of the 137th Brigade ended where it had begun.[63]

By order of the Divisional Commander, 137 Brigade attacked at 2.05 p.m. in order to have its flanks covered by the attack of 138 Brigade. This reflects Montagu-Stuart-Wortley's original idea that the left should lead, but instead of one battalion leading off now it would be the whole brigade. The time of the Brigade's assault had become the main time of attack not a preparatory blow. Once again Montagu-Stuart-Wortley's thinking was sound but unheeded.

Although 138 Brigade did reach the German positions with fewer losses than 137 Brigade, once in Fosse Trench its leading units came under enfilade fire from the Dump and Mad Point. The resulting casualties amongst officers were severe, including three of the four battalion commanders. The history of 1/4 Leicesters records this picture of their wounded commander, Lieutenant Colonel R.E. Martin:

> he is in great pain but still directs operations, receiving reports and giving orders. He reads the bible to Clive Harvey, one of the youngest subalterns, who is mortally wounded, and comforts him as he dies. He remains at his post until ordered to the dressing station by the Brigadier twenty-four hours after the attack.[64]

For the men in the assaulting battalions the reality of failure was all too clear. Despite almost all officers in the first two lines becoming casualties 1/5 Leicesters did occupy half the North Face of the Redoubt, but the key trenches named Big Willie and Little Willie, an irreverent reference to the Kaiser and his son, were still held by the Germans.[65] The result was that the assault became a series of hand grenade battles, which meant that the gains could only be tactical and therefore in a strategic sense the operation had already failed.

---

62   Edmonds, *Military Operations 1915 Vol. 2*, ibid.
63   Ibid.
64   Milne, *Footprints of the 1/4th Leicestershire Regiment*, ibid.
65   LRO: 22D63/137, War Diary 1/5 Leicesters, 13 October 1915.

In the case of 1/5 Leicesters the advice given to Montagu-Stuart-Wortley regarding grenade parties was borne out by Lieutenant C.H. Wollaston's attempts to bomb his way along Little Willie only to be driven back due to a shortage of grenades.[66] It should be noted that this was probably due to a vicious circle since the relative strength of the trench forces was heavily weighted in favour of the defenders due to the casualties sustained by the attackers in crossing No Man's Land. The success of the British Army in 1918 can partly be explained in that the artillery were able to deliver whole trench systems to the infantry's assault thus enabling them to establish strategic gains at an operational level. But on 13 October 1915 these successes would have seemed unimaginable as would the Australian use of aerial re-supply at Le Hamel in 1918.

Having been shelled in the support trenches, 1/6 North Staffords advancing in the third and fourth lines of 137 Brigade's attack found that the first two lines were held up by heavy machine gun and rifle fire and so they established their line in the old fire trench.[67] Given that the leading waves were unable to advance this would appear to be sensible but it was susceptible to misinterpretation later by those wishing to allege that the men did not go forward at all. That some of the men did go forward is shown by the experience of Sergeant Norton, 1/6 North Staffords, who was wounded in the assault. In his letter to his brother, dated 30 October 1915, he gave a graphic account of the attack. He described how in advancing his platoon lost its Corporal immediately and then several others. He expressed the view that it was safer to make a single rush to each trench and that his platoon lost no one rushing the second trench when they did this. He described the usual fog of war where the four attacking regiments were all represented amongst those in the trench, where Lieutenant Colonel Ratcliffe, CO 1/6 North Staffords, was organising the consolidation. In his account Sergeant Norton refers to one of the unsung heroes of the war, Lance Corporal F.H. Mallet, who was killed trying to rescue a wounded man – he had already brought two men in despite the hail of fire.[68]

Another survivor, though badly wounded, was Private J.W. Moore of 11 Platoon, 'C' Company, 1/6 South Staffords. His diary records that following the casualties being sustained by 1/5 South Staffords, they went over the top 'like larks' and that although many immediately became casualties he reached within twenty yards of the German third line before his left leg was shattered by an explosive bullet. Subsequent shrapnel wounds to the leg meant that even though he was carried to safety by his 'pal' he was discharged from the army on 23 August 1917 after a long period in hospital.[69]

These detailed accounts by individuals therefore confirm the overall view in the Official History and battalion histories that each attacking battalion did advance, albeit with extremely limited success in some cases, against the enemy positions. They

66   Ibid.
67   SRM: War Diary 1/6 North Staffords, 13 October 1915.
68   SRM: All references are to letters of Sergeant Norton, letter dated 30 October 1915.
69   SRM: Diary of Private J.W. Moore.

were then beaten back by heavy small arms fire and the German artillery's defensive barrage that contained a significant proportion of shrapnel. In the face of these losses 139 Brigade was then brought up to take over the positions held from the assaulting brigades.

Although they had not taken part in the assault, 139 Brigade found themselves in trenches for which the Germans had the range and apparently no shortage of ammunition. The Germans persisted in making bomb attacks against the captured trenches. At 5.30 a.m. on 14 October 1915, Temporary Captain C.G. Vickers of 1/7 Sherwoods (The Robin Hoods) was sent with 50 men to relieve Captain J.C. Warren and the survivors of his team, who had been engaged continuously by the Germans for some twelve hours. The German pressure continued and Vickers proceeded to defend the barricade single-handed and when it was blown up he continued to defend the gap until the new barricade had been constructed behind him. For his bravery the wounded Vickers was awarded the Victoria Cross – the first to be won by a member of the Division.[70] With the attack at a standstill in the original line it was judged a failure and at midnight on 14-15 October 3 (Guards) Brigade relieved the Staffords and the whole Division was withdrawn to billets.

As 46th Division began to recover, it had to come to terms with a failure bought at enormous cost. The official casualty figures are recorded as:

	Officers	**Other Ranks**	**Total**
137 Brigade			
1/5 South Staffords	13	306	319
1/6 South Staffords	18	389	407
1/5 North Staffords	20	485	505
1/6 North Staffords	17	298	315
Total	68	1,478	1,546
138 Brigade			
1/4 Lincolns	10	387	397
1/5 Lincolns	22	461	483
1/4 Leicesters	20	453	473
1/5 Leicesters	12	175	187
Total	64	1,476	1,540

70   WSF: War Diary of 1/7 Sherwood Foresters, 14 October 1915.

	Officers	Other Ranks	Total
139 Brigade			
1/5 Sherwoods	1	48	49
1/6 Sherwoods	2	58	60
1/7 Sherwoods	11	140	151
1/8 Sherwoods	11	159	170
Total	25	405	430
Divisional troops	23	224	247
Total 46th Division	180	3,583	3,763

To put such casualties in perspective, 1/5 South Staffords recorded their trench strength on 13 October 1915 as 34 Officers and 721 Other Ranks. Thus, on 13 October the assaulting troops suffered a 54 per cent casualty rate amongst officers and 42.5 per cent casualty rate among other ranks and still had the second lowest losses in the Brigade.

Given the high cost and signal failure of the assault on the Hohenzollern Redoubt it is not surprising to find that an immediate post mortem was begun. The Official History, without apportioning any blame, offers the following points of explanation:

> On the 46th Division front the gas though the wind was favourable, did not have the expected effect on the resistance – it settled down into the shell holes and the remains of trenches in the open, and very little of it reached the enemy. In fact, it merely gave them warning that an attack was about to be launched, and drew down an artillery barrage before the 46th Division could leave the trenches. The British bombardment, being of small volume, was not effective on the difficult targets offered, and the German portions of Big Willie and Little Willie were almost untouched.[71]

Since we have already seen the Official Historian's comments on the gallantry of the Division in pressing home the assault it might seem that we have arrived at a definitive verdict, namely, death by misadventure; an inexperienced division, assaulting an extremely tough enemy position, with artillery support, which though heavy by 1915 standards was inadequate for the task, and largely without the benefit of surprise, in broad daylight.

The historian of 1/5 North Staffords concluded his account of the attack by detailing the deficiencies in materials and technology, then added, "But there has never been a word of criticism of the behaviour of the officers and men. That was simply sublime."[72]

---

71   Edmonds, *Military Operations 1915 Vol. 2*, ibid.
72   Meakin, *The 5th North Staffords and The North Midland Territorials: (The 46th and 59th Divisions) 1914-1919*, op.cit., p.40.

Within two weeks of the assault there had indeed been criticism of the men's behaviour by none other than General Sir Douglas Haig, their Army Commander and soon to be Commander in Chief.

The day after the assault Haig wrote in his Diary:

> one cause of the failure of Haking's last attack seems to me that his starting trenches were not adequate, nor square opposite the points to be attacked.

So far, then, the analysis is technical, but on 27 October 1915 a new view has emerged:

> In the attack on Fosse 8 on 13th men of this [46th] Division never went more than 40 yards from our trenches, though the officer in charge of the gas arrangements states there was scarcely a shot fired by the enemy for an hour after the gas was stopped.

This is an interesting comment by Haig not least because, on the surface, it reveals an appalling ignorance of the plan of attack. We have already seen that the gas was scheduled for 1 p.m. and the attack for 2 p.m. and so presumably the hour after the gas was stopped is the hour between 1 p.m. and 2 p.m. Neither Haig's diary nor 46th Division's records provide any clue as to the source of this assertion. Donald Richter, apparently without knowledge of Haig's diary, cites Pollitt's opinion that 46th Division went over too slowly and that this then enabled the Germans to recover before the assault. It could be argued that here is the evidence of how far the plan was from those of 1918; no surprise and delayed follow through compared with surprise followed by immediate assault in 1918. Richter describes how Major C.H. Foulkes, in charge of the Gas companies, arranged for a denser concentration of gas against the Hohenzollern Redoubt and the Quarries and for the gas cylinders to be opened two at a time. He then goes on to describe how the Gas Officers, Sanders and Garden, knew that they had the authority to cancel the release of the gas if the conditions were unfavourable. This was to ensure that the attack did not suffer in the way that the main offensive had on 25 September.[73]

Richter then makes the assertion that:

> Moreover, the smaller scale of this operation allowed infantry units to accept a flexible zero hour as well. The infantry would either wait for a more favourable wind or advance without gas.[74]

---

73   D. Richter, *Chemical Soldiers: British Gas Warfare in World War One* (1994), pp.95-97. Richter's source on Pollitt is the Papers of Sir Henry Rawlinson in the National Army Museum.

74   Ibid., pp.95-96.

Richter is correct in suggesting that an advance without gas might be attempted since the gas officers were clearly given the final authority on its release. His idea that the infantry had a flexible zero hour is clearly mistaken, since we have already seen that the time of the attack, as opposed to the date, had been issued on 10 October 1915.

One is forced to conclude that either Foulkes and his men were under a complete misapprehension about the timing of the attack or were looking for someone to blame for the repeated failure of chlorine gas clouds to render enemy troops incapable of resistance. The presence of Foulkes's men in the line proves they knew about the attack and the orders were explicit that the gas would be released at 1 p.m. and the infantry would assault at 2 p.m. Perhaps the key to the problem lies in Richter's reference to a five miles per hour wind blowing towards the Redoubt at 1 p.m. The distance from 138 Brigade to the Redoubt was about 200 yards, whilst the distance to be covered by 137 Brigade was about 400-500 yards. At 5 mph the wind should cover 8,800 yards in an hour and therefore the gas would have reached the German lines by approximately 1.02 p.m. at the Redoubt and 1.04 p.m. for Big Willie, i.e. nearly an hour prior to the time of the assault. Even if the gas travelled at half the speed of the wind, the Germans would have had time to recover before the infantry assault and the use of gas would have been a clear indication that the infantry assault was close to being launched. Even in 1918 Bruchmüller[75] betrayed his plans by which type of gas was being used where.

The question is, therefore, why – given the discretion permitted to the gas officers on the spot – was it felt necessary to allow an hour between the discharge of the gas and the infantry assault, since the only rational argument for such a delay was that if the wind was weak the gas might not travel as far as the German lines. However, the authority given to the gas officers covered this eventuality.

Having raised the issue of gas Haig went on to attack the quality of territorial troops:

> The "Dump" was attacked mostly by Officers and N.C.O.s while the men trickled back into our trenches. This shows how some territorial units still require training and disciplining.[76]

As we have seen, the assault depended very much upon the efforts of the NCOs and men since so many officers became early casualties. Those officers that remained in such a difficult situation could only really exercise command over those who happened to be in the same trench or shell holes given the weight of German fire. 1/5 North Staffords, leading the assault, lost twenty officers as casualties and 1/4 Leicesters saw

75   Georg Bruchmüller (1853-1928) German artillery commander who planned the great bombardment of 21 March 1918.
76   TNA: WO 256, Haig Diary, 27 October 1915.

their Commanding Officer and nineteen other officers hit. Sergeant Norton's description of roll call the following day: "The Strengths were A. Company 90, B. 92, C. 112, D. 114",[77] indicates the extent of casualties at all levels. Norton comments on four sergeants being killed and remarks that he, himself, was the only sergeant not killed or wounded.[78] The casualty lists seem conclusive in proving the valour of the attacking troops of all ranks. Not for the first, or last time, Haig was letting his prejudices obscure the facts.

Having discussed gas and the quality of the men Haig then turned to Montagu-Stuart-Wortley and ventured the opinion that "Much also depends on the fighting spirit of the GOC Division".[79] Haig wrote on 2 November 1915 that "I doubt whether he [Montagu-Stuart-Wortley] is fit to command a division"[80] and that Lord Cavan would be Acting Corps Commander whilst Haking was on leave, even though Montagu-Stuart-Wortley was the senior Divisional Commander. Whilst it is easy to recognise that Lord Cavan had to be well connected to have been given the command of the Guards Division there is more to this decision to ignore seniority than mere snobbery. Montagu-Stuart-Wortley was on poor terms with both General Haig, to whom he would have to report if he deputised for Haking, and Haking himself. Major-General Montagu-Stuart-Wortley's already poor relationship with his superiors was then exacerbated by the outcome of the action at the Hohenzollern Redoubt. Montagu-Stuart-Wortley blamed Haking for the plan of attack but found Haig to be supportive of Haking.

Whilst it has now been established that Haig, apparently in the face of all the evidence, was prepared to blame the morale of 46th Division and/or its commander for the debacle at the Hohenzollern Redoubt there is nothing in the diary to show that Haig acted upon his private views. However, in this case it has been possible to see how the changing views in the diary have practical outcomes. In this case the source is a letter from Haig to Prime Minister Asquith, which is a response to a letter Asquith had received from one of his own backbenchers, Josiah Clement Wedgwood PC MP DSO.[81]

On 22 November 1915, Wedgwood, basing his account on the "wounded and the survivors" wrote to Asquith arguing that the generals needed to be changed to restore morale and that this would not happen "unless something is done outside the War Office; therefore I write to you". Thus, a backbencher was arguing that the military establishment in Whitehall would seek to protect the military establishment in France in order to protect the military, as a whole, from scrutiny.

77   SRM: Norton, op cit
78   Ibid.
79   TNA: WO95/256, Haig Diary, op.cit
80   Ibid.
81   IWM: Papers of Josiah Wedgwood.

Having rehearsed a general account of the attack by the Staffordshire Brigade Wedgwood went on to pose a double set of questions:

> Why was it thought to be such a "soft" thing. That an objective far beyond the bounds of possibility was set: & that the supports were moved up in the open instead of up the communication trenches?

> Why were there no responsible people on the spot to stop the attack taking place when the Artillery observation was still obviously incomplete?

Finally, Wedgwood seeks to apportion the blame:

> The destruction of this brigade is only a sample of what has gone on too often. If it were not for the loyalty of the Higher Command to each other both the Army Corps General Haking & the Divisional General Montagu-Stuart-Wortley – would long ago be enjoying their pensions in this country instead of throwing away the lives of heroes.

At first sight, this attack on the subordinate commanders might not be seen to pose a problem for Haig. However, in the highly publicised debate over Sir John French's handling of the reserves at Loos, Haking had endorsed Haig's view of events. Therefore, to accept criticism of Haking was to diminish the value of a key witness in the Loos affair. In addition to the question of Haking's competence we must also take into account the date of Haig's reply to Asquith, which is 26 November 1915. Haig's diary for 24 October 1915 details his dinner with the King during George V's visit to France. At this dinner Haig put forward his views on French's unsuitability for command and Haig's diary records that the King reported having received negative reports on French from Haking and Gough. Haig knew that Montagu-Stuart-Wortley wrote to the king and was an ally of French so royal opinions may have indirectly confirmed to Haig that he could not rely upon support from Montagu-Stuart-Wortley.

By the time of writing his letter to Asquith, Haig was only 12 days away from being offered the command of the BEF he coveted and he needed to retain the support of men such as Haking and, of course, Asquith, upon whom the responsibility for making that choice would devolve. In replying to Asquith, therefore, Haig sought to use two "independent" sources in arriving at his judgement, namely Lord Cavan and "the officer in charge of the gas detachments". It was upon the Gas commander that Haig relied in telling Asquith, "for nearly an hour after the emission of the gas had cleared there was no hostile fire in the ground about "Fosse 8" & the "Dump". Furthermore, the commander of the Guards Brigade, Lord Cavan, was reported to Asquith as having mentioned to Haig the reports of his men detailed to assist in the smoke barrage, "Companies of the 46th Division which had been ordered to attack towards the line of the dump-quarries did not go forward 40 yards."

Haig therefore told Asquith that he had reached three conclusions: that the preparations for the attack with gas & bombardment were highly satisfactory, but that

the troops did not take advantage of the favourable situation created for the attack and that this was due to want of discipline in 46th Division & general ignorance of war conditions. In one respect Haig agreed with Wedgwood: "I do not think much of Major General. Montagu-Stuart-Wortley as a Divisional Commander & have already spoken to the GOC XI Corps (Haking) on the subject". To borrow a modern idiom Haig might here be dubbed the "Teflon Army Commander" – one to whom nothing sticks. In putting the blame upon Montagu-Stuart-Wortley, of whom Wedgwood himself had been critical, Haig sought to deflect any criticism away from both himself and his acolyte Haking at a crucial time for Haig's future.

If Haig's conclusions are subjected to critical analysis then their "departmentalism" becomes obvious. As Richter's work has demonstrated the commander of the special gas detachments, Foulkes, claimed up to his death that the gas had been more successful at Loos than we now know it to have been. This is hardly surprising since if gas was deemed a failure the newly created special units of the Royal Engineers might well have been disbanded.[82] We have already seen that the Official History itself as well as the application of Prior and Wilson's methodology negates Haig's assessment of the artillery bombardment. Even if the Germans were temporarily incapacitated/prevented from firing by the first gas discharge the troops could not have left their trenches given that the artillery bombardment was not due to start until 2 p.m. Even if Cavan's remark that the assault troops only went 40 yards was correct the casualty list would suggest that it was 39 yards further than an untrained, indisciplined unit would have gone. In addition to this it is important to note that Haig omitted his earlier technical assessment of Haking's operation from the judgement given to the Prime Minister, thus once again avoiding the possibility of any blame being attached to the Corps Commander.

Nevertheless, there are some important lessons that can be derived from this initial offensive operation by 46th Division. The primary reason for the failure of the attack was that the plan was flawed. It involved a frontal assault on a heavily defended position by relatively inexperienced troops without adequate artillery preparation or support. This fits with the general view of Bidwell and Graham that in 1915 the BEF lacked the material resources to implement the types of assault which represent the apogee of the learning curve in 1918. Clearly, Haig, Haking and Montagu-Stuart-Wortley were the authors of the plan and must share some of the blame for it though the latter's initial ideas seemed very sound even without hindsight. However, Sir John French must take ultimate responsibility for the attack since he forced Haig to undertake it even though the capture of the Redoubt so late in the battle of Loos would have had no significant effect upon the war, but might have restored French's credibility with Asquith.

---

82   Richter, *Chemical Soldiers*, passim.

That the attack should fail even when all the available artillery support was given demonstrates the weakness of the British artillery in 1915. This is well known but its relative weakness here and its strength at the Hindenburg Line provides a pointer towards one of the key ingredients of success in the formula for victory in 1918. Britain's un-preparedness for the highly industrialised and prolonged war on which it largely unwittingly entered in 1914 is also a root cause of this attack's failure.[83]

The response to the failure is what today's management consultants would see as symptomatic of a 'blame culture'. The need to attribute blame was paramount and an unpopular major-general was the best solution. However, since Montagu-Stuart-Wortley was also well connected there was no immediate move to remove him from his command. Though 46th division was to be, initially, redeployed to Egypt. In Haig's eyes, Montagu-Stuart-Wortley's correspondence with the King could be conducted from Alexandria though Haig – through Haking – had forbidden it whilst Montagu-Stuart-Wortley was under Haig's command.[84]

It is also clear that the issue of blame was made more acute by the proximity of events to the possibility of Haig's replacing French in the aftermath of the carefully engineered public criticism of French over the events of 25 September 1915. The tenderness of this issue was then increased by Wedgwood's letter to the Prime Minister. Asquith would clearly have a key role in the appointment. In replying to Asquith, Haig chooses to criticise those who suffered most in the affair and their commander. It is hard to see how any credit can reflect upon Douglas Haig in this aspect of the affair but perhaps it is all too easy for any one in authority to feel that no one ever writes in a congratulatory way only to condemn your mistakes. What is surprising in one way is that Haig does not criticise French's own pressure on him to attack, even earlier if possible. It may be surmised that with the succession to French apparently so close Haig felt it would appear churlish to make another attack upon French especially as any controversy might draw attention to his own (and especially Haking's) ambiguous role in the 13 October attack.[85]

Some may find it distasteful that senior generals were so concerned with positions rather than performance. But given that politicians like Churchill and Lloyd George were so prone to playing at being generals, any such distaste should be tempered by historians who recognise the politics of common rooms and faculty board meetings. The failure of the political class is also evident in these events. A Prime Minister more in command of his government might have taken a closer interest in the questions of one of his own backbenchers who was himself the holder of a DSO.

83   See earlier references to Bourne et al on this subject.
84   TNA: WO138/29, Personal File of Montagu-Stuart-Wortley, ibid.
85   See I. Beckett, 'King George V and his Generals', in M. Hughes and M. Seligmann, eds., *Leadership in Conflict 1914-1918* (2000) for a wider view of Haig's and Haking's attacks on C-in-C Sir John French.

It would definitely seem that there is evidence here of the deference paid to the expert (Haig) by the amateur (Asquith), and if we accept that Haig was an educated soldier then we can assume that he was reasonably convincing when responding to Asquith on purely military matters. Asquith would also have been aware that Haig's star was in the ascendant and that he enjoyed the support of the King, and that at this time when he was restructuring his government there was no need to rock the boat in an affair of which he could have only an imperfect knowledge. Haig's links to the incoming Conservative members of the coalition would have encouraged the ever pragmatic Asquith to accept Haig's judgement.[86]

The outcome of the Hohenzollern Redoubt was to show that the British Army was as yet ill-equipped to progress along a learning curve and that the 46th Division was therefore no better or worse than other divisions. However, for largely personal reasons, Haig wanted rid of Montagu-Stuart-Wortley so he succeeded temporarily in choosing to release 46th Division for service in the Middle East. The temporary despatch to sunnier climes marks the division's demotion to an outer loop of the learning curve as it was not seen as an assault division by Haig.

---

86   Haig had passively accepted the view of his officers that they should not be used to coerce Ulster – a view shared by his fellow Scot and Presbyterian Bonar Law – leader of the Conservative Party in opposing Home Rule during 1911-14.

4

Interlude in the Sun

On the evening of 14 November 1915, the history of the 1/5th Sherwoods records that they took a major part in repulsing the German counter-attack supported by bombing groups drawn from the Grenadier Guards and elements of the 1/6th Sherwoods. The History goes on to note that they were eventually relieved and subsequently arrived at Lapugnoy where Stuart-Wortley addressed a parade by thanking them for their efforts and said there would be plenty of food provided.[1] The battalion subsequently took part in the relief of the Meerut Division and subsequently there was some limited contact with the Germans regarding water in the trenches and a possible football match.[2]

Meanwhile, the 1/1 Monmouths, the Divisional Pioneers, were also addressed by their divisional commander on 18 October where they were read a letter in which he reported to the Monmouth Territorial Association on their good work.[3] November saw these pioneers alternating between being in Gorse Street and working to improve billets, camp and even the bomb store. The diary does not record how many men attended the voluntary church parade on 28 November but A and B companies were working on a communication trench.

There was good news at Divisional Headquarters on November 16 when they received word that their obsolete 15pdrs would be replaced by 18pdrs between the 19 and 23 November.[4] Such news also indicates that the production of 18pdr guns is beginning to match the basic needs of the army.

However, more dramatic news arrived that the 46th Division was being sent to the Middle East and by 6 December 1915, the men of 1/6 south Staffords were receiving lectures from their company commanders regarding duties on board ship.[5]

---

1   de Grave, *The War History of the Fifth Battalion of the Sherwood Foresters*, pp.49-50.
2   Op.cit., p.53.
3   War Diary of 1/1 Monmouths, 18 October 1915.
4   War Diary 46th Division, 16 November 1915.
5   War Diary, 1//6 North Staffords, 6 December 1915.

Lt. Col. Law, 1/6th South Staffs, 1915. (6th South Staffs)

To facilitate this move, the 1/5 North Staffords were served Christmas Dinner on 24 December and entrained at Berguette on Christmas Day. They spent Boxing Day on the train and arrived at Santi Camp, in Marseilles, on 27th December, alongside the 1/6th South Staffords who had followed a similar routine.[6] On 2 January 1916, the 1/5 and 1/6 South Staffords were embarked, along with two field companies of Royal Engineers, on to HMS Magnificent and sailed for Alexandria where they arrived on 9 January 1916.

Having subsequently been landed and entrained to Shallufa, the Staffords proceeded to cross the Suez Canal and camp on the East bank. Then they underwent a programme of training which included fighting in extended order as well as more familiar aspects such as bayonet drill.[7] However, on 21 January 1916, at 8pm, the 46th Division received the order cancelling the move to Egypt.[8] It was not until 30th January that the Staffords entrained at Shallufa for Alexandria and only on 10th February 1916 did they reach Marseille only to remain on board until 12th February.

L.W. de Grave records the disappointment of the Sherwood Foresters at the news that they would be returning to the Western Front as they had enjoyed the sunshine and the men had used up the credits accrued with the field cashier during long periods

6   War diaries of named battalions on stated dates.
7   War Diary of 1/6 South Staffords, January 1916.
8   War Diary 46th Division.

of service at the front.[9] He also records the amusement of the men on the way past Macon when the train driver set off suddenly leaving the Brigadier to run after the train. Another officer whose journey was different on the train back north was 2nd Lieutenant Brodribb who had travelled south with 1/5th Leicesters as Sergeant AE Brodribb but had now received a commission.[10] That battle hardened men were ready to fill the gaps amongst the officers is also shown by the awarding of commissions to RSM Sheperd and Sergeant Kell of 1/4th Lincolns.[11]

In his file, there is a letter from Haig regarding Montagu Stuart-Wortley which states that Haig never wanted him under him on the Western Front again.[12] Although the letter is dated after his de-gumming, it is very likely that their personal relationship was already sour and that this return to the Western Front had been achieved by Stuart-Wortley "pulling strings". Stuart –Wortley's resolve to be where the decisive battles were taking place would lead to his dismissal and to the deaths of many under his command that were, as de Grave says, disappointed not to be leaving the Western Front.

9   de Grave, *The War History of the Fifth Battalion The Sherwood Foresters* op.cit, p.58.
10   War Diary, 1/5 Leicesters, 25 January 1916.
11   War Diary, 1/4Lincolns, 14 February 1916.
12   Personal File of Stuart-Wortley, letter dated 4 July 1916.

5

Mounting a Diversion on the Somme

Following its brief stay in the South of France / Egypt and a relatively short spell near Vimy, the 46th Division proceeded to join the Third Army and took over trenches opposite Gommecourt. In assessing the progress of the 46th Division along a learning curve the historian is faced with the reality that their initial reputation rests upon a daylight assault of the Hohenzollern Redoubt and the diversionary attack upon Gommecourt on 1 July 1916. General Sir Henry Rawlinson,[1] GOC Fourth Army, had primary responsibility for conducting the British offensive in the Somme region. To the North of Rawlinson was the British Third Army, commanded by General Sir E.H.H. Allenby.[2] To Third Army was entrusted the task of making a diversionary attack on the Gommecourt Salient from which the Germans would be able to enfilade the British left on the northern flank of the proposed Fourth Army attack.

In assessing the performance of the 46th Division it is possible to draw upon the evidence given to the Inquiry into the conduct of 137 and 139 Brigades immediately after the battle. This does make it possible to answer the question; was the 46th Division in line with the development of the British Army at 1 July 1916 or was it significantly worse? In the last chapter it was suggested that it was not now seen as an assault division and therefore may now be beginning to fall behind. Certainly, because

---

1   General Sir Henry Rawlinson Bt. (1864-1925), previously Commandant of the Staff College (1903-6), rose from divisional command in 1914 to GOC Fourth Army in March 1916. He was later British Representative on the Supreme War Council at Versailles. His career revived after the dismissal of General Gough in March 1918 and he led Fourth Army to victory in the second half of 1918.

2   General Sir Edmund Allenby (1861-1936) began the war as GOC Cavalry Division. He was appointed GOC Third Army in October 1915. After the battle of Arras (April-May 1917) he was appointed GOC-in-C Egyptian Expeditionary Force, which he led to victory over the Turks in Palestine. His capture of Jerusalem in December 1917 was a bright spot in a black year.

Prior and Wilson focus their study on Rawlinson the Fourth Army takes centre-stage and the focus is on true offensive operations which Gommecourt was not.[3]

The GOC VII Corps, Lieutenant-General Sir T. D'O. Snow, chose 46th Division to form the northern half of the attack on the salient. The Division was in effect therefore the left hand Division of the whole offensive and would therefore be attacking with one flank supported only passively by the next unengaged division. In any offensive this would be an unenviable role and where the main purpose was to be a diversion then it was clearly likely to be a bloody one. As at the Hohenzollern, Montagu-Stuart-Wortley was serving under a Corps commander who hated him. In the absence of any surviving personal papers other than the complaining post-war letters to French it remains a mystery why he was so widely disliked; certainly Haig felt threatened by his access to the King, possibly both Haking and Snow resented Montagu-Stuart-Wortley's intellect which was definitely superior to theirs as the initial planning for the Hohenzollern operation demonstrated.

In preparing his plans for the new task, or if Lieutenant Colonel P.W. Game is to be believed, in doing the plans for him, Montagu-Stuart-Wortley had a new chief staff officer in Lieutenant Colonel A.F. Home, who had arrived on 9 April 1916 after Game had been transferred to RFC HQ. However, Home too was to leave before 1 July 1916 and on 14 June 1916, Major G. Thorpe, the GSO2, was promoted Lieutenant Colonel and became GSO1. Montagu-Stuart-Wortley also lost Brigadier General Edward Feetham through illness. Feetham had commanded 137 Brigade since the Division came to France and his successor, Brigadier General H.B. Williams, took over on 5 June 1916 only three and a half weeks before the offensive. Both the other brigade commanders, G.C. Kemp (GOC 138 Brigade) and C.T. Shipley (GOC 139 Brigade) had commanded their formations since before mobilisation. Brigadier General H.M. Campbell, commanding the divisional artillery (CRA), had been appointed on 1 August 1914 and Brigadier General C.V. Wingfield-Stratford, commanding the Royal Engineers (CRE), had been appointed on 19 October 1914, when his predecessor was invalided out after mobilisation. Completing this team of reasonably seasoned senior officers was the Assistant Adjutant and Quarter-Master-General, Lieutenant-Colonel E. Allen, who had been in post since 27 October 1914.

This continuity did mean that the importation of new ideas was limited.

On 14 May 1916 Montagu-Stuart-Wortley attended a conference with Lieutenant General Snow at Corps Headquarters. The outline plan called for 46th Division to assault the German trench system north of Gommecourt and to link up in the village with the southern attack to be made by another Territorial division, the 56th (London). The use of two Territorial divisions to mount a diversionary attack well away from where Haig expected the breakthrough to be achieved may seem less than coincidental. However, it has to be said that Snow only had three divisions in his Corps, of which two were Territorials, so he had little choice. When 46th Division was brought

3   Prior & Wilson, *Command on the Western Front*, passim.

Lieutenant General Sir Thomas
D'Oyly Snow, Corps Commander
at Gommecourt. (Author's
collection)

into the line it was allocated part of 37th Division's front[4] as well as taking over from
48th Division who had held the line for over a year with few casualties.[5] 48th Division
was transferred to Fourth Army's northern flank where it provided the inactive link
between the Fourth Army's most northerly attacking division at Serre (31st Division)
and the diversion at Gommecourt. On 1 July 1916 it had two brigades in reserve,
plus two battalions (1/6 and 1/8 Royal Warwicks) detached to join Major General
Hon. W. Lambton's 4th Division in its assault upon Beaumont-Hamel.[6] Given that
the 48th Division was another Territorial division and that it was familiar with the
Gommecourt sector it is difficult to see why it was transferred to Fourth Army and

4   TNA: WO95/2663, 46th Division War Diary 7 May 1916.
5   Meakin, *The 5th North Staffords and The North Midland Territorials (The 46th and 59th
      Divisions) 1914-1919* (1920), p.50.
6   M. Middlebrook, *The First Day on the Somme – 1 July 1916* (1984), p.68.

46th Division substituted for it on technical grounds. As 48th Division lacked the combat experience of 46th Division and that Haig saw the northern sector as the main line of exploitation for the breakthrough then 46th Division would have been better used in Fourth Army. However, if Rawlinson still held the same view of Montagu-Stuart-Wortley that he apparently gave Lieutenant Colonel Game then presumably he would not wish to have had him serve under his command.[7] If operations had progressed as Haig envisaged he would not have wished to rely upon Montague-Stuart-Wortley to exploit the situation. Haig would not have believed that Montague-Stuart-Wortley would have had the necessary drive.[8] Haig had preferred to use newly arrived Kitchener battalions at Loos and his preference for them over Territorials, shared by Kitchener, seems to be confirmed by the order of battle on 1 July 1916.[9] Although there was never a formal distinction between fighting divisions and trench holding divisions in the British Army there does seem to be evidence of a hierarchy emerging one which would put 46th Division on an outer loop.

The general outline for the assault was that the infantry would attack on a two brigade front and the brigades selected were 137, composed of two battalions each from the North and South Staffords, and 139 comprising 1/5, 1/6, 1/7 and 1/8 Sherwood Foresters. In contrast to the limited preparation time available for the Hohenzollern Redoubt the brigades had several weeks in which to train. Haig himself visited 137 Brigade on 25 May 1916 when they were completing the digging of the practice trenches.[10] Meanwhile, 138 Brigade was employed doing preparatory work in the back areas and on 30 May 1916 46th Division dug and wired 250 yards of new fire trench to link up with 37th Division.[11] This raises the question why the digging was carried out by a division preparing for a major assault when the 37th Division with no responsibilities in that assault could have done the work. Given Corps' apparent unwillingness to apportion the workload more fairly it is without surprise that on 11 June 1916 the Divisional War Diary records "problems balancing Corps needs for working parties with Corps requirements to get front trenches in order".[12] The most worrying aspect of this entry is the way in which all these priorities are not related to training, which should presumably have been an issue too.

On the same day 139 Brigade did begin training at Sucheux and on 14 June 1916 it carried out a practice attack. However, on the following day one battalion was withdrawn to provide working parties at Humbercamps.[13] The Brigade was again carrying out practice attacks on 17 June but this time it was in the presence of Montagu-Stuart-Wortley and the Corps Commander, Lieutenant General Snow. The use of smoke was

7   See Chapter 3 for Haig's relationship with Montagu-Stuart-Wortley.
8   Ibid.
9   See Neillands, *The Great War Generals*, p.55.
10   TNA: WO95/2663, 46th Division War Diary, 25 May 1916.
11   Ibid., 26 and 30 May 1916.
12   TNA: WO95/2663, 46th Division War Diary, 17 June 1916.
13   Ibid., 11, 14 and 15 June 1916.

Troops from the 1/6th South Staffs in a support line brewing up, 1916. (6th South Staffs)

clearly an issue since the attack was performed twice – the first time with smoke and on the second occasion without.[14] The availability of smoke was to be a controversial issue on 1 July 1916 and it seems that its effectiveness in screening troops was being judged against their ability to maintain direction and formation.

As is customary in large organisations at this time the emphasis at the end of the training was on what the senior officers believed those involved should have learnt from it. The diary records that Snow and Montagu-Stuart-Wortley addressed the officers afterwards:

> bringing various points to notice especially necessity of carrying through attack with the greatest possible dash and of quickly taking action in unforeseen circumstances which are certain to arise.[15]

These remarks seem to epitomise a command in transition between Haig's 1915 comments on "fighting spirit", which reflect Bidwell's view of Kiggell's emphasis upon élan,[16] and the later emphasis upon initiative, which sees the development of the platoon as a key tactical unit by the end of the war.[17]

14 Ibid., 17 June 1916.
15 Ibid.
16 Bidwell & Graham, *Firepower*, op.cit. p.24.
17 See Chapter 3.

On 18 June the offensive was postponed for four days and therefore a revised schedule of reliefs was drawn up to accommodate this and revised instructions for the coming attack were issued to all Brigades.[18] In these plans notice is taken of German activity. Thus, although the Divisional Artillery fired on a new German trench running north from Gommecourt Wood on 19 June the plan states that as the new trench:

> lies over a ridge. It is, therefore, possible that uncut wire will be found in front of this trench. It has therefore been arranged to keep up the bombardment against this line for 20 minutes after the hour of assault.[19]

That the Germans were taking defensive measures reflects the added difficulty faced by a division making unconcealed preparations. Even though the instructions issued to brigades on 30 May were explicit that "the ground in front of our line must not be broken"[20] the Germans were able to overfly the area. This would not only have revealed the level of preparation opposite Gommecourt but also the inactivity of 37th and 48th Divisions.[21] The Official History notes that the Germans had complete observation over a field of 2,000 yards.[22]

Martin Middlebrook makes clear both Allenby's and Snow's unhappiness with a plan that led to two of their divisions making an isolated attack for purely diversionary purposes.[23] That the attack was intended only as a diversion was not offered as a defence at the inquiry that followed, presumably because the questions which the Board of Inquiry were given were deliberately focused on the brigade level. The High Command knew that any discussion of the divisional objectives would have revealed the dissensions to which Middlebrook refers and shifted the blame away from Montagu-Stuart-Wortley.

Although Middlebrook has become the standard work on 1 July 1916 it has to be noted that it contains no footnotes and only a very general bibliography, which makes it unclear from where the evidence is drawn, though in this case the Official History is the source.[24] The Official History states that Third Army proposed an alternative threat from Arras but this was deemed to be too far away to divert the fire of the heavy guns behind Gommecourt from enfilading the main attack.[25] The Official History was written with drafts being sent out to the surviving participants and this may therefore have led to a favourable view of Allenby's position since his later achievements made

---

18   TNA: WO95/2663, 46th Division War Diary, 18 June 1916.
19   Ibid., 19 June 16.
20   Ibid., 30 May 16, Appendix II.
21   Ibid., 20 June 16.
22   Edmonds, *Military Operations 1916 Vol .1.* p.485.
23   Middlebrook, *First Day on the Somme*, p.73.
24   Edmonds, *Military Operations 1916 Vol. 1*, pp.459.
25   Ibid., p.454.

him a popular figure after the war and Bidwell makes the point that Edmonds became more critical of Haig after 1928.[26]

All this discussion about the overall purpose of the attack was, of course, irrelevant to the average soldier since he was not privy to it, and therefore had to prepare for a 'real show'. The preparations could be very risky, too, since working parties in No Man's Land were hard to conceal especially from an alert enemy as was true in this case. On 24 June, the Division recorded that 107 casualties had been suffered on the previous night during digging and wiring operations.[27] There is a real contrast here with the Hindenburg Line in 1918 where the key assault brigades were held back from the line for as long as possible.

On 26 and 27 June both 46th and 56th Divisions discharged smoke combined with artillery bombardment. On the second occasion the mock attack was accompanied by machine gun fire but was partially thwarted by the wind changing from West to South West and therefore blowing the smoke up between the lines.[28] This use of dummy barrages is interesting, and anticipates Plumer's preparations at Messines, but in this case it probably only served to ensure that the Germans could note the positions of the British batteries. Also, the British had revealed where the attack was to be since no activity would have been evident from neighbouring divisions. It was also unfortunate that verbal warning of the postponement of the offensive came through on the morning of 28 June to be confirmed at the Corps conference at 2.30 p.m. that afternoon since the additional artillery preparation gave the Germans further opportunities to 'spot' batteries and other positions.[29] Given the extra two days of artillery preparation, Montagu-Stuart-Wortley held a conference with his brigade commanders and the CRA to assess what raids needed to be carried out to secure information on the progress in wire cutting.[30] As a result of the meeting it was agreed to give priority to maintaining continual machine gun fire on the German back areas and wire during the night to ensure that they could not carry out repairs.[31]

For the assault itself the division chose to employ four waves at intervals of 50 to 70 yards and with one man to every two yards. The waves were explicitly instructed to push straight on to their final objective leaving the "special clearing parties" following behind the fourth wave to subdue any remaining resistance.[32] The clearing parties were to work North to South and to turn East along the first communication trench they reached and the lower formations were enjoined to ensure that the clearing parties would cover the whole German trench system.[33] The grenade squads for trench

26   Bidwell & Graham, Firepower, op.cit., p.39.
27   TNA: WO95/2663, 46th Division War Diary, 24 June 1916.
28   Ibid., 26-27 June 16.
29   Ibid., 28 June 16.
30   Ibid., 29 June 16.
31   Ibid.
32   Ibid., Divisional Instructions June 1916, Appendix 3.
33   Ibid.

clearing were composed of a leader, three throwers, three carriers (who were also reserve throwers) and two bayonet men. Each of these squads carried a total of 124 No.5 grenades.[34] Whilst this is hardly the most sophisticated approach it is practical and attempts to be thorough which suggests staff work was at least satisfactory, if not good and equal to most other divisions.

Some flexibility of response to circumstances was built into the plan as both brigades were instructed to bomb their way up the communication trenches to Gommecourt Wood if the main attack on that feature were to be held up by uncut wire.[35] Each infantry battalion was to carry 150 wire breakers. The men in the third wave had to carry a pick or a shovel but not the men in the first two waves.[36] Whilst this hardly represents a model of contingency planning it does provide clear guidance in the event of a quite likely event occurring and reinforces the view that the division's staff work was up to scratch.

To provide close support to the attacking infantry three Russian saps were to be blown at the time of the assault and medium mortars were to be positioned in the sap heads.[37] Earlier in June the Division recorded experiments at manhandling an 18-pound field gun over rough ground noting that it caused 'much dust'.[38] It would seem that although the Division had not yet found the answer it was asking the right questions about how to give the vulnerable infantry the close fire support they needed in attacking heavily defended positions. Here we may discern the learning curve in action amongst those who had been pitted against the Hohenzollern Redoubt and a step towards the operational method employed in the "Hundred Days" of 1918 where Stokes mortars were kept in close support.

Another lesson of the Hohenzollern had been the difficulty in maintaining the supply of hand grenades to the assaulting battalions given the intensity of 'hand to hand' warfare, which could develop in contested trench systems. The division arranged for, "special stretchers each capable of taking 6 filled Bucket pattern grenade carriers" to be made.[39] The purpose of this was to "quickly form a reserve of grenades across No Man's Land" by "dumping them against the parapet outside the trench".[40] These grenade carriers were to be carried by "every two men" in the fourth wave. Although this may also reinforce the idea of the overladen infantry on 1 July 1916 it does represent a rational solution to a re-supply problem and is further evidence of a learning process. The purpose of the first three waves was to take the objective and the fourth wave normally included the Lewis guns, which were the first weapon of

34   Ibid.
35   Ibid.
36   Ibid.
37   Ibid.
38   Ibid., 22 June 1916.
39   Ibid., June 1916, Appendix 3.
40   Ibid.

consolidation. Lewis guns and grenades were usually the main weapons used to drive off the standard German counter-attack.

As a further element of close support the Division detailed that rifle grenadiers should be deployed but not as part of the trench clearing parties. Given the greater range they could achieve it seems they were to operate on the flanks – an important position given the overall plan. Each rifle grenadier, they were to work in pairs, was to carry 20 rifle grenades and 120 rounds of ammunition.[41] This method of deploying the rifle grenadiers is reminiscent of the way in which rifles were deployed on the flanks of units in the Napoleonic era and marks a step towards their use in composite platoons later in the war.

Given the fate of the brigades on 1 July 1916 and the subsequent inquiry it might seem irrelevant to look so carefully at the plans that were never to be fully carried out. However, where one is looking for the ways in which an organisation learned/improved then it is necessary to attempt to discern whether they were trying to do the right thing but for some reason not succeeding or whether they were still trying to do the wrong thing. 46th Division was clearly intending to improve upon its operational method in the light of experience gained at the Hohenzollern Redoubt.

It is a central theme of this book that artillery was the key to Britain's ultimate success on the Western front. Whilst artillery support was inadequate the infantry would be unable to succeed and that even well trained and experienced infantry would be unable to succeed without adequate artillery support. Thus the evidence presented here of a standard infantry division seeking to improve its techniques helps us to understand why, when the artillery support is sufficient (or better) in quantity and expert in application, the infantry will be able to take full advantage of it.

The Official History gives the attack frontages of 137 and 139 Brigades as 700 and 600 yards respectively.[42] However, the depths of the objectives were very different. As the Staffords were nearest Gommecourt they were required to penetrate further than the Sherwood Foresters because the latter would form the shoulder of the new British line when the Gommecourt Salient was eliminated. The units were once again obliged to attack at oblique angles. The line opposite the Sherwood Foresters bent away from the British lines so the 1/7 Sherwoods (Robin Hoods) had the shallowest penetration to achieve, 600 yards, but approximately 400 yards of this was No Man's Land.

If we adopt Robin Prior and Trevor Wilson's methodology the total amount of trenches to be captured up to the first objective was some 7,300 yards. However, the battle plan of 46th Division included, according to the official historian, at the request of Montagu-Stuart-Wortley a prohibition on the artillery bombarding the front trench as he required it for his own men. In his subsequent detailed report to the Inquiry, Brigadier General Campbell makes no mention of this and specifically adds

41   Ibid.
42   Edmonds, *Military Operations 1916 Vol 1*, p.454.

to his summary on wire cutting, "the Preliminary Bombardment did much to damage the enemy's trenches, which were almost unrecognisable on Z day".[43]

Since Brigadier General Edmonds does not provide notes on his sources it is difficult to substantiate the Official History, given the above evidence from Brigadier General Campbell, the Divisional CRA. The instructions given by the CRA to his units appear specifically to contradict the idea that the front trenches were to be left untouched. For example, on YI and YII days the Right and Left Groups were to "engage the front system"[44] searching in each case up to the flanks. The map contained in Blore and Sherratt,[45] showing the targets for 231 Brigade RFA, does show shoots on the front line before Z day, but it is unclear whether this means wire on the front line since both wire cutting and registration were tasks for the day. There is, however, the statement that "No front line trenches were to be fired on although they contained dugouts 40 feet deep".[46] The statement is tagged on to the note on 1 July 1916 and it will be seen later that Blore and Sherratt repeat commonly held views but this does not necessarily mean they are accurate.

The evidence becomes more favourable to the official historian if one looks at the orders given for YI – the first extra day due to the postponement – when three batteries were allocated to firing on the "2nd line and the communication trenches leading up to it". In addition three trench mortar batteries are targeted on "strong points and the 2nd line where in range".[47] This then has to be set against the orders to twelve batteries to "sweep and search back to the 2nd line" and 'V' Trench Mortar Battery to fire on Ford Trench and on the very strong point in the German line called the 'Z'.[48]

Both the CRA and the Divisional Diary refer to the survival of the Germans because of the depth of their dugouts and at the Inquiry the alleged failure to bombard the front line trenches is not mentioned either before or after Montagu-Stuart-Wortley was degummed. It would have provided a very strong charge against Montagu-Stuart-Wortley and so, given his fate, it seems unlikely that it would not have been used. As the evidence available is ambiguous it will therefore be necessary to calculate the artillery support both with and without the front line trenches. The basis of the calculation is 7,300 yards if all trenches are included and 6,000 yards if the front line is excluded.

In order to carry out the bombardment Campbell divided his guns into a Right Group supporting 137 Brigade and a Left Group supporting 139 Brigade. There were four artillery brigades (230/231/232/233 RFA), so Campbell had a total of 48 18-pounders and twelve howitzers, giving him 60 guns in total, as 233 RFA did not have howitzers. The Division was to be assisted by a share of the Corps heavy artillery

43   TNA: WO95/2663, 46th Division War Diary, ibid.
44   TNA: WO95/2667, Papers of CRA 46th Division. July 1916.
45   Blore & Sherratt, *A Commemorative History of the Old Leek Battery 1908 to 1919*, map opposite p.92.
46   Ibid., p.92
47   TNA: WO95/2667 46th Division, CRA June 1916, Appx. XIV.
48   Ibid.

which registered on 23 June.[49] With 60 guns, Campbell had 10 guns per 1,000 yards of trench if we exclude the front line and 8.21 guns per 1,000 yards of trench if they are included. Taking Prior and Wilson's yardstick of one gun to six yards at Neuve Chapelle and one gun to 141 yards at Loos the equivalent figures for Gommecourt would be one gun to 100 yards excluding the front line trenches and one gun to 121 yards including the front line. If this had been purely a diversionary action, it would have been well equipped since the ratio was better than that at Loos. However, since an attack was actually to be mounted then the infantry were likely to suffer badly, as the ratio was fifteen to twenty times worse than Neuve Chapelle. In these circumstances, the trench mortars were a very useful additional weapon since they "were more effective than 18 pdrs., as they cleared the wire and stakes away, whereas the 18 pdrs. only cut the wire".[50] Problems with the ammunition supply delayed the introduction of the new Four-Inch Trench Mortar, but on 29 June 1916 the 240mm mortar was noted to have "fired with effect".[51]

In total the artillery fired 115,600 18-pounder shells and 13,100 4.5" Howitzer rounds as well as 2,100 2" Trench Mortar bombs. Of this total, 25,000 18-pounder rounds were devoted to wire cutting in addition to the 2" Trench Mortars.[52] It is interesting to note here that whilst Prior and Wilson[53] suggest that at the Somme approximately two-thirds (1 million out of 1.6 million) shells were devoted to wire cutting only 21 per cent or just over a fifth were devoted to this task on the 46th Divisional front. Even if the Trench Mortar rounds are included the ratio is still much lower than for Fourth Army operations facing similarly fortified points such as Beaumont Hamel and the Schwaben Redoubt. The disproportionate use of 18-pounders to shell trenches suggests the 46th Division was deviating from best practise.

The artillery, too, were part of the learning process. On 19 June it was noted by 230 Brigade RFA that "D/230 in the course of registering strong points etc. found ballistic charges infinitely preferable to N.C.T., which is very erratic."[54] Not all the learning was being done internally. During May 232 Brigade were due to establish gun positions and dugouts behind Fonquevillers:

> these were a new pattern brought out by the VII Corps as shell-proof – all dugouts being 14 feet below the ground and the gun pits having two roofs to them.[55]

---

49   TNA: WO95/2663, 46th Division War Diary, 23 June 1916.
50   Ibid., CRA's report, 7 July 1916.
51   Ibid., 27 June and 29 June 1916.
52   TNA: WO95/2663, 46th Division War Diary, CRA's report, 7 July 1916.
53   Prior & Wilson, *Command on the Western Front*, p.173.
54   TNA: WO95/2673, War Diary 230 Brigade RFA, May 1916.
55   Ibid.

For various operational reasons not all the batteries were able to construct their positions on this pattern, but it does provide clear evidence that Corps organisations were disseminating 'best practice' and whilst Corps did not have a permanent composition this could lead to benefits as units rotated through different corps they would benefit from exposure to new ideas.

For the day of the assault – designated Z day – the plan involved a 65-minute barrage by the field guns immediately prior to the assault with the guns firing 40 per cent shrapnel and 60 per cent high explosive. The rest of the support, in common with that on the Fourth Army front, would then consist of the artillery laying down barrages on pre-timed lifts based on the infantry being able to achieve their objectives on schedule. Two other interesting elements to the orders for 'Z' day are that only one howitzer section is to be assigned to counter-battery work in support of the Corps Heavy Artillery.[56] In common with the rest of the British Army the vital role that this was to play in future successes was as yet unappreciated or beyond their available resources. One step towards the future is, however, evident in that another section of the howitzers in 'D' Battery, 232 Brigade was to pass temporarily under the command of GOC Heavy Artillery at 7.25 am on 1 July in order to fire tear gas shells – presumably as a counter-battery measure. In its own very small way this anticipates the complex battery firing patterns which typify "the hundred days".

In conclusion, therefore, it is possible to regard the plans laid down for the operation at Gommecourt to be adequate to good. In certain respects both the infantry and artillery plans contained innovative approaches, which, even if they did not succeed, demonstrate that the Division was an organic organisation with a sentient leadership. The main flaw therefore must be seen in GHQ's decision to order a well-advertised assault upon a strongly defended enemy salient with one flank in the air and with artillery support which previous experience alone has shown is unlikely to be strong enough.

The overall story of the attack on Gommecourt is well known. 46th Division's attack failed to capture any of the German positions opposite them and the Official Historian puts the Division's total casualties at 2,455, of which 853 were killed (including 50 officers). He put German losses at thirteen officers and 578 men in the units, which were predominantly attacked by 46th Division. The 56th Division suffered 4,314 casualties and caused the Germans some 621 casualties plus 29 officers. The relative scale of these casualties leads Martin Middlebrook to accept the view that Montagu-Stuart-Wortley saved his division from further slaughter by cancelling the afternoon attack and that this was why he was "de-gummed" by Haig on 3 July 1916 never to hold a field command again.[57] This view of Montagu-Stuart-Wortley's dismissal is repeated by Blore and Sherratt.[58]

56   TNA: WO95/2663, 46th Division CRA Orders, 23 June 1916.
57   Middlebrook, *First Day on the Somme*, p.258.
58   Blore & Sherratt, *A Commemorative History of the Old Leek Battery 1908 to 1919*, p.93.

The rest of this chapter will therefore seek to analyse the performance of the Division through the evidence provided to the Inquiry before considering Montague-Stuart-Wortley's fate in a wider context.

The two question that formed the remit of the Court of Inquiry were:

> How it came about that touch was lost with the two leading battalions of the 139th Brigade?

and

> How was it that the 137th Brigade failed to close with the enemy both in the original assault at 7.30 am and in the renewed assault at 3.30 pm?[59]

Given that the Inquiry was in effect conducting a review of the Divisional assault the framing of the questions relating to Brigades is interesting. By focusing the Inquiry at Brigade level a Brigadier could be appointed as President. Given what we know about the controversy regarding the overall plan at Army/Corps level this was one way of ensuring that the involvement of senior officers was not raised but would leave Montagu-Stuart-Wortley in the firing line since any failures on the part of the Brigades were likely to be generally regarded as a failure of his leadership.

The officer picked to preside at the Inquiry was Brigadier General P.M. Robinson CMG, GOC 112 Brigade, 37th Division, which as we know was Snow's only unengaged division on 1 July 1916. He could therefore be relied upon to ensure that there was no criticism of Snow or Allenby. Of the other two members of the Court one was drawn from 46th Division and the other from 56th Division. Lieutenant-Colonel A.S. Bates DSO, CO 1/5 London (London Rifle Brigade), represented those on the other side of Gommecourt on 1 July 1916, and Lieutenant Colonel Sir Hill Child Bt MVO DSO, OC 231 Brigade Royal Field Artillery, represented 46th Division.

The Inquiry dealt with the questions in order and so it looked at the conduct of the 139 Brigade first.[60] The first witness to appear was Lieutenant Colonel G. Thorpe, GSO 1 46th Division. Thorpe was a regular soldier, originally commissioned into the Argyll and Sutherland Highlanders.[61] He was asked whether any arrangements had been made for contacting attacking units that became unable to communicate using normal means. Given the problems incurred here and by Fourth Army one might ask why it was necessary to ask this since the problem usually lay in being able to signal.

---

59   A copy of the records of the Court of Inquiry is to be found in the War Diary of 46th Division for 1916. See TNA: WO95/2663, 46th Division War Diary.

60   Ibid. All references in the rest of the section are to the Inquiry records unless otherwise stated.

61   He eventually retired as a Major General with a DSO and bar. Later in the Great War he was to command 17 Brigade.

Thorpe detailed how the first four waves had been issued with "hand discs, venetian shutters and signalling flags" and that a visual station has been set up at the Gendarmerie, which had observation of all the objectives of the Division. He also informed the Court that between 7.30 a.m. and 9.00 a.m. the "smoke cloud was too dense to admit of visual signalling".

Thorpe also told the Court that each battalion had been issued with 100 red flares as well as blue SOS signals but that the latter had not been intended for use until after the assaulting troops had gained their objectives. He added that carrier pigeons had been given to brigades but that no orders had required battalions to use them in conjunction with the assault. Finally, infantry had been attached to six artillery observation posts to read messages sent by the attacking infantry. Before calling the second witness the Court inspected the orders and instructions produced by Colonel Thorpe and satisfied themselves that they were communicated to 139 Brigade.

Thorpe's evidence had simply proved that 46th Division had put in place all the normal measures for maintaining contact with its assault troops. The Court now needed to ascertain what 139 Brigade had done to respond and so the next witness was the Brigade Major, Major W.G. Nielson CMG DSO, also from the Argyll and Sutherland Highlanders.

Nielson's answers provide a useful insight into the then current thinking on signalling. Nielson began by confirming the issue of the signalling equipment described by Thorpe and that the red flares had been issued for communication with aeroplanes. His evidence on blue flares for artillery communication initially reads "practically certain" that they were issued to the leading battalions. This was then amended by deleting "practically" and reference is made to it being the grenade officer's job to issue them. Nielson went on to confirm that orders were given for pigeons to be taken forward by the battalions and that he, personally, had ordered the Officer Commanding 1/8 Sherwood Foresters to detail signallers to go to the artillery observation posts.

Nielson then provided the Court with a description of the system of runners employed. Not only were the runners lightly equipped and wearing blue brassards but they all "knew our system of trenches and the model made of the enemies trenches at Lucheux". Nielson said that each Battalion Headquarters had 20 runners: eight to carry communications to their companies and eight to take messages to Brigade HQ. The other four were attached to Brigade HQ with the job of carrying messages to their battalion HQ.

In response to the next question about the arrangements Brigade itself had made Nielson cited repeated rehearsals, including those on the life size model trenches that had been dug and, as we know, that some of the rehearsals had included smoke. One potentially damaging admission was that no rehearsals had been carried out with 137 Brigade but given the level of preparations required before the offensive it is easy to see why it would have been impossible to pull two brigades out for training at the same time.

However, we can see that this point leads to one of the successes of Amiens in August 1918, preparing the assault troops behind the line with a thin screen in front.

Since the Germans were attacking at Verdun, instead of the 46th Division being allocated part of 37th Division's front why not hold the front with 37th Division and in this case 138 Brigade whilst the other two brigades train and prepare behind the lines. No one would deny the fighting abilities of the Canadians but there is a sense sometimes of the 'star' divisions being given some remission from the donkey work thus making their success and retention of star status more likely. Hence the view that 46th Division was on an outer loop of the learning curve.

The Court saw no problems with Nielson's answer and he went on to say that platoons were in single ranks on an 80 yard front before introducing a recurrent theme into the evidence by saying:

> The smoke cloud on the day of the attack was so much more dense than that which we had carried out at rehearsal that the difficulty of maintaining touch either laterally or from front to rear had never been properly understood.

The key difference of course on 1 July 1916 was that there was not only the smoke itself but also the smoke from the German barrage, which the Official Historian described as "more severe than in any other sector".[62] The next witness, Brigadier General Shipley simply confirmed the evidence of his Brigade Major when it was read to him. Shipley seems to have been reluctant to commit himself from the beginning, perhaps reflecting the semantics into which some of his officers would seek refuge as the inquiry proceeded.

The Court then called as the fourth witness Captain D.P. Forman, 1/7 Sherwoods, the Brigade Signals Officer. Captain Forman's response to the Court's questions about signals failure was to point to the high level of casualties amongst the signallers citing that the Signals Sergeant of the 1/7 Sherwoods was one of only two survivors from that section. He added that he personally had surveyed the whole line at 2.30 p.m. and that two receiving stations had been manned all day and that the signallers, who had been detailed to go forward behind the sixth wave with battalion HQ had started before their time. Given the intensity of the barrage the Court were not surprised at his evidence that the telephone lines prepared beforehand were run out but did not reach the German trenches. Captain Forman also added that he had established observation posts in the front line.

Captain V.O. Robinson, of 1/6 Sherwoods, was in command of the right support company on 1 July 1916. His description of the appalling congestion in the fire and communication trenches demonstrated clearly the domino effect created by the failure of units ahead to clear the trenches. However, his description of the shelling as neither heavy nor concentrated would have raised a few eyebrows as would his statement that twice when he was in the fire trench between 07.45 to 08.00 and 08.15 to 08.30 he saw no formed body of men leave it. This could have been interpreted as evidence that once

---

62   Edmonds, *Military Operations 1916 Vol. I*, p.460.

the early waves had met with stiff resistance the later waves opted for safety. Captain Robinson next told the Court that an officer and sixteen men of a carrying party did leave the trench but that only the officer reached the advanced trench unwounded due to the heavy rifle and machine gun fire.

Ahead of Robinson, on 1 July 1916, had been Captain A.B. Naylor commanding the right assault company of 1/5 Sherwoods. He described how he, advancing with the third wave, caught up with the officers in the first two and that the smoke was dense. He testified to being one of only six who reached the German trench and that after ten minutes hand to hand combat with the Germans there were only three Sherwoods left so they had returned. He added that he had seen no other British troops in the trenches. Two artillery officers then gave evidence to the Court that they thought they had seen British troops in the German trenches; the more certain of his sighting was Captain Dwerryhouse of 101 Siege Battery who said he had seen twelve men in the Little Z at 2 p.m.

So far, the Court had heard that all the usual methods of communication had been put in place and that the attack had suffered from heavy German fire and that the smoke caused problems for the troops because it was so dense. With the possible exception of Captain Robinson no evidence has been given which would call into question the general conduct of the Brigade and its formations during the battle. Although it will play a large part in the Inquiry into 137 Brigade the next witness raised another of the obstacles facing the troops – mud. Mud is generally associated with Passchendaele and the Somme in its later stages but there had been rain on most days during the three weeks before the attack and so the assaulting troops had to cope with this problem.

In his evidence, Captain Kerr pointed to the problems he had had as OC of the carrying company of 1/5 Sherwoods. He told the inquiry that the break occurred between the third and fourth waves because the first three waves were formed up in the fire trench whereas the fourth wave (carrying wire and screw pickets) was formed up in the communication trench. With the congestion caused by the fourth wave and the mud it was 8.10 a.m. before his company were formed up and by then, he said, the smoke had cleared leaving the enemy trenches 'plainly visible'. Given the visibility his men became casualties as soon as they showed themselves. He said he only got about 70 yards from his trench and, although the right platoon got further forward, that no supplies were carried to the assaulting troops by his men.

Captain Kerr was followed by Company Sergeant Major Mackenzie, whose company had been the carriers for 1/7Sherwoods. He described the heavy artillery, rifle and machine gun fire and the way in which his company commander and the second in command had been hit when only barely out of the fire trench. Although CSM Mackenzie testified that he had reached the German trenches, he stated that the other twelve in his group did not make it so he went back as he could not see any other British soldiers. The next two witnesses, Second Lieutenants Rushton and Pickthorn of the RFC, both reported seeing elements of the Sherwoods in the trenches. Sergeant Birkenhead, 1/7 Sherwoods, told the Inquiry that of the signallers with the second wave only three were not casualties and that they could not get through the German wire. The evidence of these witnesses served to document the inability of supporting troops to cross No Man's Land to reinforce the assaulting troops. This was confirmed by Sergeant Sanderson, Signals Sergeant of 1/5 Sherwoods, who reported nine of the twenty seven signallers in the battalion had become casualties and that they were all with the assault troops. He added that he himself had been at a signal receiving station in the advanced trench and had received no messages.

Brigadier General Shipley was then recalled and gave further evidence:

> At 10.40 am approximately I went to the Headquarters of the 137th Infantry Brigade to consult with Brigadier-General Williams, where I learnt that orders were being given to him to organise a second attack. I then decided not to make any further attempts to advance stores and ammunition until I could do so in conjunction with this proposed attack.

This is a key piece of evidence because in conjunction with what the Court has already heard it makes it clear that the break in contact with the leading battalions was due to enemy action and the mud and congestion encountered by the later waves. Since it was only going to be possible therefore to cross No Man's Land with proper support the last reason offered for the break is the pause whilst the second attack is prepared. The full significance of the evidence, though, is that it is the beginning of the defence, which will be offered to the second charge against 137 Brigade of failing to close with then enemy either in the morning or the afternoon.

By bringing his meeting with Brigadier General Williams into his evidence, Shipley was making it clear to the Court that the order had been given to Williams for the attack. And the only person who could have given that order is Montagu-Stuart-Wortley since only he, or Lieutenant Colonel Thorpe, on the authority of Montagu-Stuart-Wortley, was able to give orders to a Brigadier. Thus, assuming there was documentary evidence, which there was, the Inquiry was on course to exonerate 139 Brigade and with the key point introduced by Shipley any blame which might attach to 137 Brigade would not stick on Montagu-Stuart-Wortley because he had given all the appropriate orders.

Therefore, if the Inquiry continued Montagu-Stuart-Wortley would be exonerated. The Inquiry had opened on the 4 July but had to continue with question 1 on 5 July so Shipley's recall as the last but one witness would have been at some time on 5 July – possibly in the morning since the Court was able to give its written judgement that day. If Haig was to "degum" Montagu-Stuart-Wortley, it was necessary to act quickly. It is unlikely that Haig was unaware of the general trend in the evidence before and views forming at the Inquiry given that the removal of a major-general was hardly a matter for someone else to decide.

Thus it was on 5 July that Montagu-Stuart-Wortley received the orders to relinquish his command. Given the past disputes between Montagu-Stuart-Wortley and his superiors, Haig and Haking, it seems easier to believe that Haig selected

Gommecourt for an Inquiry because of his dislike for Montagu-Stuart-Wortley, in which Snow shared, even though this was supposed to be a diversionary action. As in 1915, Montagu-Stuart-Wortley was in the awkward situation of having been right and his superiors less so. So why was he degummed in 1916 having been sent to Egypt and then recalled in 1915? The answer may lie in the Sudan.

In 1884-85, Montagu-Stuart-Wortley served in the Gordon Relief expedition, in which Sir John French made his name, and was the officer whose gunboat spotted that Gordon's flag was no longer flying and that Khartoum had fallen. This explains his affiliation with French evident in the post-war correspondence. It was therefore unsurprising that in the wake of French's replacement by Haig, he should find himself transferred to where his correspondence with the King could not reflect on Haig. However, Montagu-Stuart-Wortley would have had a further connection to authority as he had commanded the "friendly Arabs" at Omdurman and his commander that day was Kitchener who by 1915 was Lord Kitchener and Secretary of State for War.[63] However, by July 1916, Kitchener was dead, having drowned on his way to Russia, so Montagu-Stuart-Wortley no longer had a friend in very high office. The Omdurman connection is also borne out by Montagu-Stuart-Wortley writing to Churchill as well as French after the war to seek recognition of his services.[64]

If we accept that Haig and Allenby were on uneasy terms then sacrificing Montagu-Stuart-Wortley was probably a price that was affordable and a head which it would be difficult to refuse. To wait for a Court of Inquiry to acquit Montagu-Stuart-Wortley might make Allenby uncooperative so Haig moved quickly and the press at home could see one Major-General sacked and would not be in a position to know whether it was the wrong one or not.

On the evidence before the Court of Inquiry on 139 Brigade Montagu-Stuart-Wortley did not deserve to be sacked. The Court's judgement was delivered on 5 July 1916 and began by saying that satisfactory arrangements for communicating with advanced troops had been made. The Court accepted that the troops who reached the German lines had suffered "a considerable number of casualties" and had fired the red flares seen by the RFC.

In drawing up its fourth summary point the Court clearly was in two minds since the document includes some studied ambiguities and a significant amendment. The statement begins:

> D. Evidence further shows that it is doubtful whether the 4th wave advanced in its entirety; that it is certain that at the most only portions of the fifth and sixth waves ever got beyond their advanced trench.

---

63   J. Pollock, *Kitchener: The Road to Omdurman* (1998), p.127.
64   TNA: WO138/29, Personal File of E.J. Montagu-Stuart-Wortley.

Thus far it is an unexceptional statement of evidenced fact. Then it makes a judgement: "and it is also certain that the 2 supporting companies were unable to advance". Left like this the text would have exonerated the troops from any blame but it was altered to "it is also certain that the 2 supporting companies did not advance".

It might be argued exegetically that the original wording was not in keeping with the simple restatement of the evidence that precedes it. However, by not leaving the original wording alone the Court appears to have balked at removing the implication that more effort could have been made. In his report on the Inquiry to Allenby, dated 10 July 1916, Snow's criticisms of the Division, tempered as they were by his overall assessment of the difficulties faced by them, would have been hard to sustain if the original wording had been retained. Snow's description of the organisation of the rear waves as 'unsatisfactory' puts much more blame on the officers than the Germans. This also raises the issue of the quality of the NCOs which has surfaced before.

Having made this amendment the Court's point 'D' continued.

> A break in the continuity of the advance therefore occurred at some point behind the 3rd wave and in front of the 5th and 6th waves.

Even those like John Laffin or Alan Clark who have attacked the higher command regarding their competence would not accuse them of not knowing what number comes between three and five! Such a refusal to point the finger seems extraordinary given that by going so far no one is left in doubt and so there is an impression of dithering. Also, forming such a judgement means that the purely exegetical arguments for making the previous amendment are undone. If this sentence can contain a judgement, why not the previous one, especially as Point D goes on to conclude:

> The assaulting troops must therefore have found themselves in the German lines without reserves of grenades or ammunition and without any material for consolidation of the trenches.

Few would disagree that this was a frequent occurrence on the northern half of the Fourth and Third Army fronts.

The Court also noted the attempts to regain touch. The members of the Court then gave five reasons for the loss of touch with the assaulting battalions:

- The 'heavy state' of the trenches and the delays this caused the carrying companies
- the congestion caused by the dead, wounded and units delayed in front
- the heavy German barrage immediately in front of the trench and the heavy rifle and machine gun fire sweeping the area between the lines
- the minimal cover provided by the advances and communication trenches [on Shipley's evidence the latter were only 2'6"–3' deep] necessitating crossing 400 yards of open ground
- smoke cover decreased rapidly after 8.10 a.m.

On the basis of these conclusions one could clearly add "why did you bother to hold an inquiry?" given that a similar story could have been told by countless other brigades. It also suggests that 46th Division were no less far down a learning curve than most other divisions on 1 July 1916.

In addition to noting Montagu-Stuart-Wortley's departure the Divisional Diary records on 6 July:

> Court of enquiry continued – question of attack of 137 Bde. At 7.30 am satisfactorily disposed of – appeared to be ample proof that a big effort to close was made, but failed as many others have done in this war of frontal attacks against strong defences.

Naturally, the Divisional diary had a vested interest in stating a positive outcome, but the relative speed with which the Court's inquiry proceeded, and the calling of only nine witnesses, bears this out.

One reason perhaps for the change in pace was the summoning away of Brigadier General Robinson and his replacement with Brigadier General Loch, GOC 168 Brigade, 56th Division. Unavoidable as Robinson's departure may have been, it seems to somewhat offend natural justice that a senior officer of the neighbouring division, which had suffered so heavily, should now head the inquiry. The failure of the 3.30 p.m. attack was the last hope (if there was one) for those leading elements of 56th Division which had succeeded in penetrating the German positions.

However, in looking at the question of the first attack at 7.30 a.m., Loch may well have been a good choice for 137 Brigade, since he would have no reason to minimise the difficulties faced. Only officers were called as witnesses and they painted the by now familiar picture of great endeavour being met by overwhelming resistance. Captain Mander, 1/6 South Staffords, who had been in command of the left-centre company, said the bulk of his casualties had been sustained when the men tried to get through the one 'penetrable' lane cut in the wire which was covered by a German machine gun. The commander of the other left-centre company, Lieutenant J.L. Auden, 1/6 North Staffords, reported that the majority of the men were killed in front of the wire, which was unbroken except for the gaps made by the Germans to facilitate their own patrols. He said three of them reached the parapet and engaged a machine gun, but were bombed away by the Germans.

It was noted above that the topography made wire cutting especially difficult on the 137 Brigade front. Major T.R. Price, Welsh Guards, GSO2 of the Division, told the Court that, in accordance with Corps orders, patrols had been sent out to inspect the wire on the nights of Y/Y1 and Y1/Y2, and that therefore the brigade's machine guns could only fire forward to avoid hitting their own patrols with traversing fire. Major Price advanced the argument that these long pauses during the patrols and whilst the Russian saps were extended "gave the Germans the opportunity to mend the wire".

Major Price also stated that the Divisional Commander was "satisfied" on Y day with the progress of wire cutting. This is true in so far as the Divisional Diary for 28

June records: "all reports show that both trenches and wire are being damaged". It is rather selective, however, given that on 29 June (Y1) the diary records: "Reports from the patrols that visited the German wire last night show that there is a good deal still in various places", and that on 30 June (Y2) despite noting "a good many practicable gaps", arrangements were made for the 2" Trench Mortars to be used to cut sections which were supposed to have been done already. What seems clear is that if the attack had gone ahead on 28 June, the wire cutting would probably have been far less complete.[65]

Rather unsurprisingly, the CRA in his report on the operation purported that "The Infantry could pass almost everywhere up to enemy Front Line". He saw the main problem as smoke, whose use he described as a "doubtful advantage", since it obscured the artillery's view of the infantry. Unable to monitor the infantry's progress, the artillery could only be governed by the timetable for lifts and therefore could do little to assist the infantry when faced with points of resistance. The CRA then went on to address the infantry's own problems including losing direction and added:

> they cannot see, and encourage each other and men who are inclined to shirk, know that they can do so without it being noticed by their officers and comrades.

The report was produced on 7 July and by then the Inquiry had moved on to the afternoon attack. Given the potentially damaging imputations about the fighting spirit of the men it does not seem that anyone felt the need to rush a copy over to the Inquiry. Three of the witnesses did imply to the Court that there was some lack of spirit. Captain C. Lister, 1/5 South Staffords, whose company were leading that battalion forward in its support role, found men in the fire trench from the 4th wave and testified: "I am of the opinion that those men had not left the trench". He also added that he had found an officer and 20 men of 1/6 South Staffords in the advanced trench. The officer told him that they had been forced back, and Lister had then ordered him and his men forward, which order they had followed. Lister did say the wire would have stopped the troops, and the court allowed Major Price that this spot had been given special attention because of the reported problems.

Captain Brown, of 96 Siege Battery, confined himself to describing the German barrage as "never more than moderate" but he was followed by Lieutenant May of 2 Company, Special Brigade, Royal Engineers. Not only did May say that only four 77mm guns were firing on 137 Brigade's front but that only the first wave advanced. One can only imagine the feelings from the infantry in the room at this statement. The Court "immediately" noted that from the earlier evidence of Lieutenant-Colonel Thursfield, commanding 1/6 South Staffords, the other waves had advanced but "were probably invisible to this witness". Whilst undoubtedly correct, this summary passed over Thursfield's own evidence of problems with the 3rd and 4th waves.

---

65   TNA: WO95/2665, 46th Division War Diary 1916, dates as cited.

Lt.Col. Thursfield, 1/6th South Staffs, at Fonquevillers, June 1916. (6th South Staffs)

The last witness on this attack was Major E.H. Tomlinson, 1/6 North Staffords, who said he reached the advanced trench between 10.00 a.m. and 11.00 a.m., where he found that the only unwounded men were the signallers stationed there. He told the Court that of the 23 Officers and 740 Other Ranks engaged 19 and 323 respectively had become casualties. He told the Inquiry the smoke had caused men to stumble into the wire and that he had received many reports of repaired wire. In summary he said:

> I attribute the failure of the men left alive in No Man's Land to push forward to the fact that there were no officers to lead them, and that of the NCOs who went forward some 50% were casualties.

The Court therefore found itself able to conclude that:

> The 137th Infantry Brigade did close with the enemy at the original assault at 7.30 a.m. – 1 July 1916 as far as uncut wire and hostile Machine Gun fire rendered this possible.

It also came to the view that the men of 1/6 North Staffords who had remained in No Man's Land for several hours were leaderless. The British Army in the Great War may have suffered from class distinction but at least the converse of noblesse oblige was recognised too; that without their social superiors to lead them the lower orders were absolved from the requirement to die without any obvious hope of success.

The Inquiry then turned to the issue of the afternoon attack. We know from the Divisional Diary that consideration of this question began on 6 July, probably quite late, took up the whole of 7 July and was not concluded until the evening of 8 July. A further 17 witnesses gave their evidence to the Court. Once again, in contrast to the first day of the inquiry, only officers were called to give evidence.

The issue under examination was, given that everyone agreed that Corps expected the 137 Brigade attack to be renewed, why it had not been carried out? Implicit therefore in the Inquiry was the question of whether the Brigade/Division lacked the necessary fighting spirit. This implied charge had not been made to stick in the case of 139 Brigade or the morning's attack – would it now be more successfully applied? Haig's views on "some territorial" divisions hang over the proceedings.

As the evidence was presented it became clear that because the attack was to be co-ordinated between the two brigades both Brigades had to be interviewed. The last part of Brigadier General Shipley's evidence in the first part of the enquiry was that he postponed any more attempts to reach his forward battalions once he knew Brigadier General Williams was planning a further assault. The question before the Inquiry therefore acquired two inter-dependent parts: why did neither 139 Brigade nor 137 Brigade make an attack that afternoon?

The tenth witness to be called was Major Price, the GSO2, who presented copies of the telegrams and telephone messages received and transmitted by the Divisional H.Q. on 1 July 1916. These agree with the Divisional Diary and, to provide the framework for assessing the evidence, they are briefly summarised below.

Table 4.1: Summary of Messages Received and Transmitted by 46th Divisional HQ on 1 July 1916 regarding the afternoon attack, with relevant diary notes.

8.20 a.m.- from 137 Brigade	Brigade reports 137 held up by wire and machine guns
9.31 a.m. – to 137 Brigade	"The success of the whole operation depends upon your pushing on as soon as possible."
9.40 a.m. – to Corps	Requesting 6 inch guns fire on side of Gommecourt Wood – timing to be agreed with 137 liaison officer.
10.10 a.m. – to Corps	"GOC informed BGGS VII Corps that 137 Brigade has been ordered to take Gommecourt Wood at all costs" – possible artillery arrangements discussed.
11.15 a.m. – from 137 Brigade	Williams telephones that 137 will be ready to attack at 12.15 p.m.
12.11 p.m. – from 137 Brigade	Attack postponed until 1.15 p.m.
12.15 p.m. – visit by Corps GOC	"Corps Commander visited GOC – approved his plan for further attack, told him on no account to use up his reserves so as to have his troops too thick on the front."
1.20 p.m. – from 137 Brigade	Request delay as 139 not ready and want smoke.

1.30 p.m. – to 139 Brigade	Shipley told "attack must start at 2.30 p.m. smoke or no smoke."
1.40 p.m. – to 137 Brigade	Williams told bombardment will be from 2.30 – 2.45 p.m. with smoke from 2.40 p.m. and the attack to go in at 2.45 p.m.
1.45 p.m. – from 139 Brigade	Shipley says he can have smoke from 3.15 p.m. so attack set for 3.30 p.m. – this then was relayed to Williams too.
3.15 p.m. – from Captain Guthrie, GSO3	All smoke arrangements now made. "GOC telephoned orders through Captain Guthrie (who was with Hugh Price GSO II) that General Shipley was to attack at time ordered, whether smoke favourable or not."
3.25 p.m.	Smoke has started
3.26 p.m. – from Brigadier General Williams	5th Leicesters in support will not come forward 5th North Staffords and 5th South Staffords are attacking in four waves.
3.50 p.m. – from Brigadier General Williams	Major Abadie has informed him that 139 Brigade has not attacked and therefore 137 Brigade has not attacked either.
3.53 p.m. – from Brigadier General Shipley	Attack unable to advance, that it had started but was stopped by heavy machine gun and shrapnel fire.

Neither the order of these events, nor their accuracy, was challenged at the Inquiry so they provide a useful measure of the difficulties of command and control at this level at this stage in the Great War. The evidence that provides the tissue for these bones reflects the very real problems experienced from Brigadier Generals downwards.

The key witness for 137 Brigade was the Brigade Major, Major R.N. Abadie DSO, King's Royal Rifle Corps (Montagu-Stuart-Wortley's regiment). He told the inquiry that after 9.00 a.m. he tried to organise fresh attacks as it was clear that the initial assault had failed. In support of his description of the difficulties he encountered he told the Court about the initial dispositions of the support battalions – 1/5 North and 1/5 South Staffords. Each battalion had been given specific tasks for the initial assault at 7.30 a.m. and was equipped accordingly.

1/5 South Staffords	1 company defending flank ½ company organised as clearing parties 1½ companies carrying RE stores
1/5 North Staffords	1 company organised as clearing parties 2 companies carrying

These companies would have to pile stores and draw extra ammunition ct cetera before taking part in an assault. Therefore only the fourth company of each battalion, who were acting as reserve, were immediately available.

At 11.15 a.m., the Brigadier sent Major Abadie forward to take charge of preparations and at 11.50 a.m. he was able to meet with representatives of all four Staffords battalions. One can imagine the pressure on young subalterns, upon whom senior officer casualties were devolving responsibility, when receiving orders direct from the Brigade Major. He ordered an attack in three waves (150 men to a wave) by the 1/5 North Staffords on the left and the 1/5 South Staffords on the right. In each case the 1/5 Leicesters of 138 Brigade would form the 4th wave.

Abadie then encountered further problems as a party of 1 Monmouths (the Divisional Pioneer Battalion) working on Number 2 Sap were blocking the way forward. Having sent the Monmouths to fetch ammunition for the 240mm trench mortar, Abadie then received reports that the 1/6 South Staffords had been held up by uncut wire whilst some of the 1/6 North Staffords had reached the German lines. This information was important in that it gave him a clearer picture of the front ahead of the proposed attack, and so Abadie, having obtained the Brigadier's agreement, issued revised orders at 1.20 p.m. which required the 1/5 North and 1/5 South Staffords to realign their assault by 270 yards.

Clearly, such a change needed to be communicated to 139 Brigade so Abadie went and met with his opposite number Major Nielson and Lieutenant Colonel G.D. Goodman, CO 1/6 Sherwoods. The line of attack was agreed but Abadie testified; "that in the event of there being no smoke provided, their attack would probably not take place". On returning to the Staffords' trenches he contacted the Brigadier who "impressed on me the importance of attacking at 3.30 p.m. smoke or no smoke". With this statement Abadie effectively absolved his Brigadier from any blame for the failure to mount the attack.

Abadie then passed through the heavily congested trenches, which were fifteen inches deep in 'holding mud' to the HQ 1/5 South Staffords where that battalion's adjutant, Captain J. Lamond, said the battalion would not be ready for 3.30 p.m. Appearing later at the Inquiry Captain J. Lamond, Royal Scots, who had been posted to the battalion as Adjutant in early 1915, explained that Lieutenant Colonel Raymer, commanding the battalion, had been wounded and that he had been sent to find Lieutenant Colonel Burnett, 1/5 North Staffords. Burnett too had been wounded but at his HQ Lamond had met the Brigade Major who had ordered him to prepare for an attack at 11.15 a.m. The Inquiry paused over this timing but concluded that this reflected Abadie's statement that he had been trying to organise a fresh attack since 9 a.m.

Lamond said he told Abadie 11.15 a.m. would be impossible but he recognised that he must get his battalion ready as soon as possible. Lamond, on returning to his own battalion H.Q., found Lieutenant Colonel C.H. Jones, 1/5 Leicesters in command and he told Lamond to prepare for 1.15 p.m. This presumably reflects the calls from Brigadier-General Williams to Montagu-Stuart-Wortley. Then, at 1.00 p.m., Major Wistance the battalion's second in command arrived and Lieutenant Colonel Jones handed command over to him with the order to launch an attack in three waves at 3.30 p.m. The written orders were produced for the Court's inspection. Although

Major Wistance regarded 3.30 p.m. as impossible he went off to organise the attack. Upon querying whether, with the problems he was encountering, 3.30 p.m. was still definite; Abadie confirmed the orders with Lamond acting as runner between them.

Lamond testified that he personally communicated the definite order to advance to Wistance at 3.15 p.m. and Major Wistance in his own testimony said:

> As regards co-operation mentioned by other witnesses I am quite clear in my own mind that my battalion was to attack at 3.30 p.m. whatever happened or did not happen on my flanks and that the orders to this effect were quite definite.

Clearly, now the responsibility for the failure to attack by 137 Brigade lay with Major Wistance, since he had made it very clear that Abadie had issued the appropriate orders. However, Wistance had a perfectly solid reason to offer the Court:

> I am of the opinion that had I been in command at 3.30 p.m. I should have given the orders from my position in the 1st wave and the waves would have undoubtedly gone over. I account for their not doing so to the fact that they did not realise I had been knocked out and were perhaps awaiting the executive signal. The 2 officers left in the front trench were both very inexperienced having only been in trenches for 48 hours.

Since Major Wistance had received his orders at 3.15 p.m., and Lamond and the runner bearing news of Wistance being wounded both arrived at the dugout at about the same time, Wistance must have been wounded around 3.20 p.m., barely 10 minutes before the designated time of the planned assault.

Captain Lamond was now in command of the battalion, so he headed back towards the trenches occupied by the first three waves formed for the attack. However, in practice tactical command of the battalion fell on the two surviving officers Second Lieutenants G.E. Cronk and G.H. Ball, both of 'C' Company. Cronk told the Court he had witnessed the order being received by Major Wistance and had asked him if they were to go over at 3.30 p.m. He said Major Wistance had replied: "I will give you the word when you are to go over". Having understood he was to receive a definite order and, having returned to his men, not receiving one he did not advance.

Ball similarly stated to the Court:

> I understood from Major Wistance that he would give a signal when we were to attack and that he would let me know what form the signal would take. At 3.30 p.m. no signal having been given I looked over the parapet to see if anyone else was advancing. Seeing no one was advancing I decided to remain – I concluded that the attack had been postponed.

Given that news of Major Wistance being hit had had time to reach the Battalion H.Q. it is hard to believe that news had not reached the neighbouring trenches. In his written submission to the Court, Brigadier General Williams had completely exonerated Abadie and emphasised that the issue was for Regimental officers to explain, but that it had to be recognised how many had been lost and the inexperience of the remainder.

Sensing, the responsibility which had thus fallen on Cronk and Ball; the Court asked each of them to state their age and experience. Both were 18 and from Birmingham. Cronk, from Handsworth, said he had been in the trenches for four days prior to 1 July, having joined the Battalion about a month earlier. Ball, from Moseley, having only joined on 13 June 1916 had been in the trenches for two days prior to the assault. Given their total inexperience, and the absence of a superior officer, it is hard to believe they would have had sufficient authority to lead the attack, given the events preceding the 3.30 p.m. bombardment, but the Court adjudged that "had any portion of the leading wave on the brigade front set the example the remaining portions would have followed".

The Inquiry had also been investigating 1/5 North Staffords, where Captain F.E Wenger, a veteran of the Hohenzollern Redoubt, was in command from 10.50 a.m. when Lieutenant Colonel C.E. Boote was wounded. At 3 p.m. he conferred with Major E. Hall, the second-in-command of 1/6 Sherwoods and Major Nielson (Brigade Major 139 Brigade), with whom his battalion had to keep touch in the attack. According to Captain Wenger, they said they would not attack without smoke.

Wenger said he sent a runner to Abadie with this information but had not received a reply, only orders that, notwithstanding the unreadiness of 1/5 South Staffords, he was to attack at 3.30 p.m. As a far more experienced officer than Cronk and Ball, who had not yet been called but who were bound to agree with Abadie's evidence, Wenger's reputation was clearly now on the line. Wenger said that at 3.30 p.m. he received a message from Second Lieutenant Lemon on the left of his battalion that 1/6 Sherwoods were not preparing to attack and were not going to. When asked about this, Lemon confirmed he had sent a message to say there was no movement to the left, but denied saying they were not going to attack. Wenger said he responded to this message by inquiring whether he was to take the battalion in alone. This message via a runner sent to ring the Brigade Major resulted in the order to sit tight. Abadie had already explained these final orders by stating that once the units had attacked and the British barrage had lifted to the next point the German barrage was already falling on No Man's Land. On this evidence the Court concluded:

> a desire for co-operation with the 139th Brigade was allowed to over-ride the determination to push on at the clock hour.

At this distance in time it seems evident that Wenger had decided the attack was hopeless, and having seen the wasting of the division at the Hohenzollern, he saw no need to repeat the error.

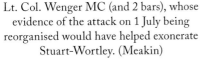

Lt. Col. Wenger MC (and 2 bars), whose evidence of the attack on 1 July being reorganised would have helped exonerate Stuart-Wortley. (Meakin)

By stating that it was at 3.30 p.m. that he received the message, i.e. at the time when he and his men should have been leaving the trenches, Wenger seems to signal this. The Court's interpretation was favourable, and we may surmise from the questions to Ball and Cronk that the Court was reluctant to find junior officers at fault. In passing judgement on 137 Brigade the Inquiry had drawn attention to the failure of 1/6 Sherwoods to advance and the time needed to investigate this partly explains the length of the Inquiry.

In giving evidence Lieutenant Colonel Goodman said that he had spoken to Wenger and that he had been clear that the requirement for smoke did not relate to Wenger. Goodman restated his own view that he had had discretion over the attack with regard to smoke. Under close questioning Major Nielson, the Brigade Major, said that they saw the attack as primarily an opportunity to take stores forward and when asked could he "personally corroborate" Goodman's statement that he was ready to attack at 3.30 p.m. he said that he could as he had personally visited the whole line after 3p.m.

Brigadier General Shipley's own evidence is very interesting in that he did not actually confirm Goodman's discretion regarding smoke. Shipley concluded his evidence:

> At 3pm the Brigade Major talking on the telephone from Battalion HQ said the OC 6 Sherwoods wished to know whether he was to attack if there was no smoke. I replied, 'There is no question about the smoke. There will be smoke'.

By not answering the question asked Shipley had avoided giving Goodman either a direct order to attack regardless of the availability of smoke or the ability to say that he – Goodman – was ordered only to attack with smoke. Having spent the time interviewing the officers of 139 Brigade the Court restricted its conclusions to 137 Brigade. The Battalion diary of 1/6 Sherwoods makes no mention of any preparations for an attack at 3.30 p.m. or either Captain Wenger's visit or that of the Brigade-Major. It should be noted that the war diary of 1/6 Sherwoods can reasonably be described as generally terse.

On 3 July 1916, Goodman had sent a report to his brigadier on the operations on 1 July 1916. In that report Goodman did refer to the attack but he gives the times for the smoke as 3.25 p.m. He then gives a view that he did not proffer at the Inquiry:

> I was and am quite satisfied that there was no possible chance of reaching the objective and no result could have been achieved. As a matter of fact, owing to a mistake, a party of 20 did leave the trench, most of them were struck down at once.

Goodman had included the meeting with "a Staff officer" in his report and then referred to a small carrying party being organised and "bombers collected". Major Nielson's affirmation that Goodman's battalion was ready 'to advance' can now be squared with Second Lieutenant Lemon's alleged message that 1/6 Sherwoods were not preparing 'to attack'. For good measure Goodman sent his Brigadier a further report at 3.15 p.m. on the same day detailing all the problems with mud and smoke during the morning attack. Goodman had no desire to launch a fruitless assault and it is he who can claim the credit for sparing his men but with the Inquiry focusing on 137 Brigade, and the Court having accepted Cronk and Ball's inexperience, Goodman toned down his views from those he had previously expressed to his immediate superior. In the absence of a judgement by the Inquiry one is left with the impression that Brigadier General Shipley had knowingly given Goodman the leeway he needed to frustrate the orders received to attack in the afternoon.

Having made no comment on 139 Brigade the Inquiry apparently gratuitously decided to record that drunkenness had never been mentioned or implied by any witness. Was this to please Haig or just to add 56 words to what was otherwise a 170-word summary of three days of evidence? The manner in which the Inquiry was completed is therefore a further way in which it appears that once Montagu-Stuart-Wortley had gone the desire at the lower level, Brigade and below, to find those 'responsible' was limited. Where that evidence was uncovered it was ignored, or put down to great inexperience where possible.

The evidence produced at the Inquiry does prove that it was not Montagu-Stuart-Wortley who 'saved' his men. If anything he cost lives by failing to ensure the wire was properly reconnoitred prior to the night of Y/Y1 when it was probably too late to effect much change. If the Germans had worked hard on repairing the wire it must have been over more than two nights so the Corps orders for Y1/Y2 are flimsy in the extreme as an excuse for this having happened. It is fair to say that 46th Division was set an impossible task especially when they were expected to advertise their preparations. However, Montagu-Stuart-Wortley's reluctance to visit the forward troops and get close to the coal face of war clearly contributed to the failures on the day.

Montagu-Stuart-Wortley's successor was William Thwaites, a veteran of the South African War who had been in the 47th (London) Division since 1914, first as GSO1 and then as a brigadier. He had a reputation as a trainer and Haig clearly felt the 46th Division needed him. Thwaites was made a Temporary Major-General though not confirmed in that rank until 3 June 1918, shortly before his transfer to Director of Military Intelligence at the War Office.

Not everyone's reputation was tarnished by the affair. Brigadier General Williams (GOC 137 Brigade) was given command of 37th Division on 9 November 1916 and commanded it through to the Armistice. His pre-war career as a staff officer had been followed by two further wartime staff appointments.[66] His first field command was 137 Brigade. His failed attack earned him promotion and his superior the sack thus reinforcing the impression that it was essentially an issue of personalities that determined Montagu-Stuart-Wortley and the Division's reputation up to July 1916. Lieutenant Colonel Goodman was promoted to command 52 Brigade on 20 November 1916 with the temporary rank of Brigadier General. Captain Wenger MC had been the battalion Signals Officer at the Hohenzollern Redoubt, in July 1917 he was to receive the bar to his MC from Haig himself. Haig's comments on 13 October 1915 make the end of Wenger's citation on this occasion very relevant: "he rallied a company that had been held up, reorganised the attack... showing exceptional dash and a very fine offensive spirit". Wenger later won a second bar to his MC for rescuing an NCO in No Man's Land and for a week in October 1918 was acting commanding officer of 1/6 North Staffords.

Thwaites was the man charged with raising the performance of 46th Division, of which the opinions were generally so low. One immediate change of style is clear in that the Divisional Diary notes that on 15 July he visited the front line.[67] On the following day he was again in the front line – in this case that occupied by 1/5 Leicesters. The Brigadier, his Brigade-Major (Captain Godsal) as well as Lieutenant Colonel Thorpe (GSO1) accompanied Thwaites. The diary notes that "They realised

66   Thanks to Dr J.M. Bourne for providing information on Williams's subsequent military career.
67   TNA: WO95/2663, 46th Division War Diary, 15 July 1916.

the bad conditions of trenches due to frequent bombardments".[68] From this small beginning Thwaites was clearly attempting to break down the gulf that had existed under Montagu-Stuart-Wortley and of which Rawlinson and others had such a low opinion. In 1916, Montagu-Stuart-Wortley was 59 and on 2 July 1916 Snow wrote to Third Army that the Major-General:

> is not of an age, neither has he the constitution, to allow him to be as much among his men in the front lines as is necessary to imbue all ranks with confidence and spirit.

Thwaites's appointment provided fresh impetus to progress down the learning curve by adopting the aggressive attitude beloved by GHQ.

Three days later the Divisional Diary records that the Brigades were now "sending in proposals for raiding enemy trenches and keeping up constant patrolling".[69] Clearly, Thwaites had decided that there had not been an aggressive enough approach in the line and by 26 July the Brigades are described as "elaborating" upon their raiding schemes.

The first raid was carried out by 1/6 South Staffords, who captured four prisoners suffering only four casualties on the night of 1 August. During the preparations Thwaites had visited the men and the trenches from which the raid was to be launched. Thwaites recorded in the diary for 2 August: "It is highly gratifying that this success was obtained by the particular battalion and Brigade concerned".[70]

This comment on the Staffordshire Brigade can be better understood when set against the views of Brigadier General Williams expressed in his support for the death sentence being carried out on Lance Corporal Hawthorn:

> The general standard of efficiency of the non-commissioned officers of this battalion and of the Brigade as a whole is certainly – and I have no hesitation in saying so – very inferior and the losses on July 1st when we certainly lost a large number of the best NCOs did not help matters.

As if this was not scathing enough, Thwaites's counter argument too rested on the poor standards of the Staffords, when he then adds that executing Hawthorne would simply create "a sullen and dispirited attitude".[71]

Thwaites's reflections on the wider issues of 1 July 1916 were contained in a report to Lieutenant General Snow, entitled "Points of Interest", which he despatched on 13 July 1916 along with the Narrative of Operations for 1 July 1916. Whilst it cannot be

68   LRO: 22D63137, War Diary 1/5 Leicesters.
69   TNA: WO95/2663, 46th Division War Diary, 19 July 1916.
70   Ibid., 2 August 1916.
71   TNA: WO71/490:Courts Martial Proceedings.

said that Thwaites's report matches the formal 'after-action reports';[72] they do demonstrate that senior officers were applying their minds to the problems of operational strategy.[73]

Thwaites's first point is that reinforcements will only be able to get across if the German barrage is reduced by giving more attention to counter battery work. Thwaites was a gunner and this comment bears out Bidwell's point that British military thinking was held back by the "separate tables" approach which was overcome once gunners took command of infantry formations.[74] The increased effort given to this at Passchendaele, for example, suggests the British Army was belatedly learning that lesson. Thwaites then tries to draw a general lesson from the 46th Division and that of Fourth Army regarding German troops emerging from dugouts in the rear of leading waves. He proposes a solution would be for the "clearing parties" to be with the second or third waves rather than further back as was then usual.

So far this is a considered if unexceptional comment but then Thwaites says it would be best to limit the first objective "even more than is now usual" and then he makes a radical suggestion that "it will often be best to give the German first line trench as the first objective which must be definitely secured and consolidated before a further advance is made". Sensing, perhaps, the radical nature of his opinions he goes on to add this is only based on 46th Division experience and 'hearsay' from 'further-south'. Though not yet the finished idea it does contain the essence of what was to become the operational strategy of 1918 in so far as the 'leapfrog' system involved the leading wave securing the initial objective before other units passed through.

Thwaites then dealt with the issue of trench congestion. He wrote to Snow that one of the chief difficulties for the officers organising the afternoon attack was explaining to the men that "they were not now in their original formations, but that they had to begin afresh as something quite different – say '1st wave' instead of 'wire carrier in 6th wave'." He went on to add that when men did offload equipment to become assault troops that this caused obstacles in the trenches. Thwaites therefore proposed that no carrying parties should be loaded up before the assault. It is difficult to see how Thwaites could have foreseen implementing this without the need to dig extra communication trenches before an assault so that equipment could be stockpiled close enough to the start line that without incurring undue delay, if the assault went well, men could load up and follow the leading waves. By 1918, one could argue, the British Army solved this problem by making their counter-battery work so effective that both men and supplies could reach the objectives. The other way in which it was to be solved was by moving away from waves but that innovation was two years away.

72   See Rawling, *Surviving Trench Warfare*, passim.
73   Unless stated all the following references are to INA: WO95/2665, 46th Division War Diary, July 1916 – Points of Interest.
74   Bidwell & Graham, *Firepower* op.cit., Chapter 2.

Thwaites's opinions on smoke anticipate more closely the ultimate solution when he advocates smoke bombs thrown close to the German line since this would not prevent artillery from observing the infantry and would therefore free the latter from the thrall of a timetable. As we know this objection to smoke had been included in the CRA's report. Ultimately, Thwaites's idea was to be made more effective through smoke shells just as gas was to be made effective through the same delivery mechanism.

Thwaites also urged that Royal Engineers should be kept back from the line until it was secured as it was not practicable for them to work until then. Thwaites, a Royal Artilleryman himself, also pointed to the practical need to maintain stocks of buffer springs for the 18-pounders both at gun positions and in the Divisional Ammunition Column. This recommendation is taken from the CRA's report (and recommendations) that during operations for the week ending 1 July 1916, 151 pairs of buffer springs had had to be replaced, "but in each case the gun was out of action for not more than 2-3 hours". If we assume the average down time was 2.5 hours that gives a total downtime of 377 hours. There were 9 days of bombardment, equalling 216 hours so this downtime represents the equivalent of the Germans having knocked out 1.75 guns at the beginning of the week.

In his penultimate observation, Thwaites makes the point with which everyone subsequently has agreed; that is, that the British infantry men needed to go into battle as lightly equipped as possible. Again, future success in gaining artillery dominance of the assaulted sector would facilitate this since the heavier the destruction of the defences the less equipment the initial waves needed and the more easily further supplies could be brought up.

Thwaites's final point on the issue of surprise would be accepted generally even if we recognise that the plan for Gommecourt had knowingly deviated from the principle. Perhaps because of his artillery background, Thwaites also puts the emphasis on the infantry trusting to the artillery's accuracy:

> Infantry must be taught that they must take risks from their own artillery, and that any casualties that may occur will be far less than from hostile machine gun fire if the artillery lift too soon.

Hard as this might prove to be in practice Thwaites was correct and later successes were to prove the division capable of the challenge. Thwaites also put forward a view about timing that was to become the norm in subsequent British successes:

> The attack should be carried out as soon as there is light enough to see the gaps in the wire and find a way in the enemy's trenches.

This demonstrates that ideas contributing to the successful operational method of 1918 were already forming amongst officers. It is not possible to tell whether Thwaites's thinking reflects purely a response to 1 July or emerging views at 4th Division before his departure, probably both.

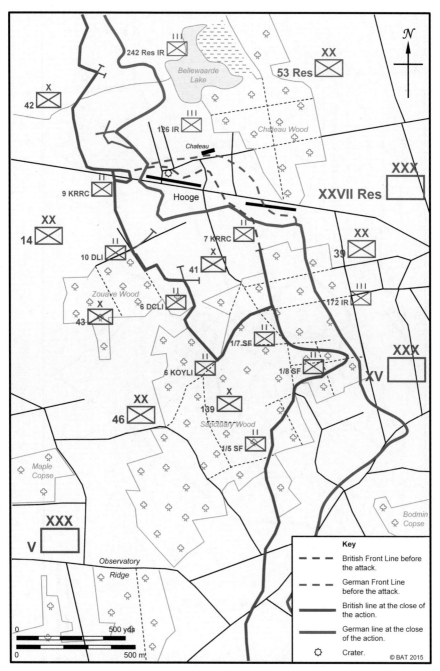

Map 1 Flammenwerfer Attack at Hooge, 30-31 July 1915

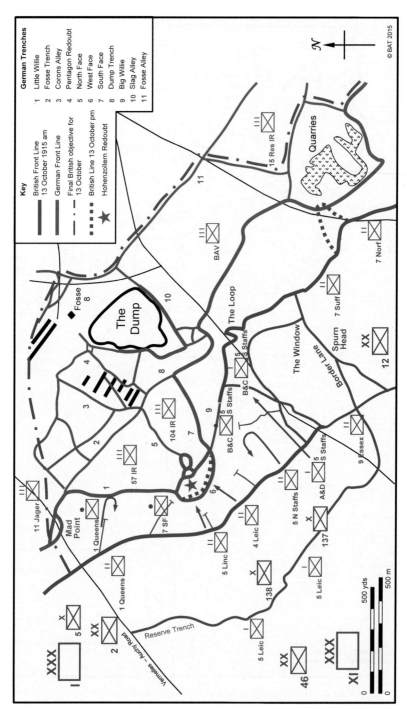

Map 2 Hohenzollern Redoubt, 13 October 1915

Key

Britsh Front Line
13 October 1915 am
German Front Line
Final British objective for
13 October
British Line 13 October pm
Hohenzollern Redoubt

German Trenches

1 Little Willie
2 Fosse Trench
3 Corons Alley
4 Pentagon Redoubt
5 North Face
6 West Face
7 South Face
8 Dump Trench
9 Big Willie
10 Slag Alley
11 Fosse Alley

© BAT 2015

Quarries

15 Res IR

BAV

7 Norf

Fosse
8

The Dump

10

The Loop

7 Suff

The Window

Spurn Head

XX
12

5 S Staffs

B&C

B&C 5 S Staffs

Border Lane

9 Essex

5 S Staffs

A&D

X
137

11 Jager

Mad Point

1 Queens

7 SF

57 IR

104 IR

5

6

9

7

8

3

2

1

4

1 Queens

1 Queens

5 Linc

4 Leic

5 N Staffs

5 Leic

5 Leic

X
138

XX
46

XXX
XI

Vermelles – Auchy Road

Reserve Trench

X
5

XX
2

XXX

500 yds

500 m

0

0

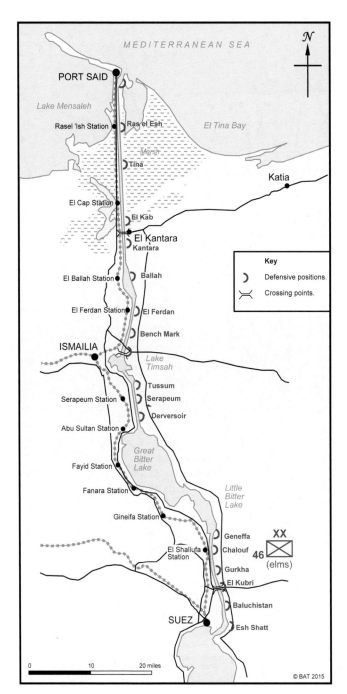

Map 3 Egyptian Interlude, winter 1915-16

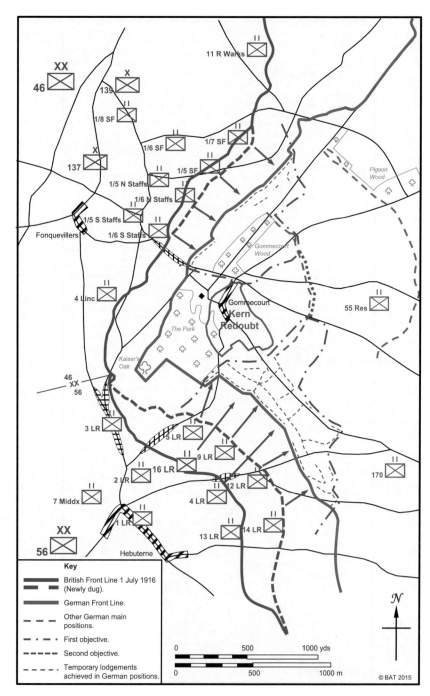

Map 4 Gommecourt Diversion, 1 July 1916

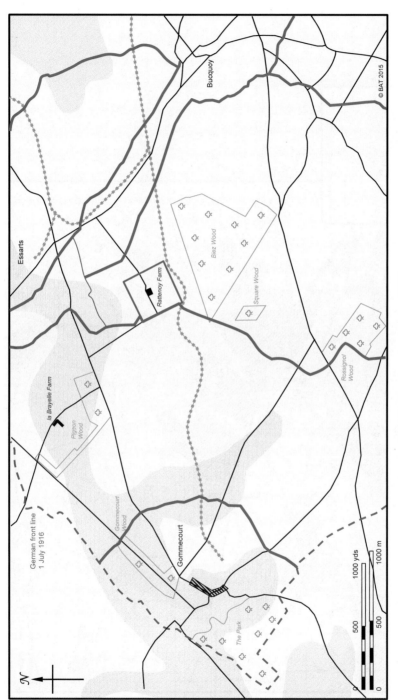

Map 5 Gommecourt, spring 1917

Key

- - - - British Line 20 April 1917
- · - · - Limit of British Occupation
——— British Line
——— German Line

Cité 2

Cité du Grand Condé

Fosse 2

Lens

Cité du Nord

Lens Canal

Fosse

Cité St Elizabeth

Cité St Antoine

Fosse 5

Fosse

Fosse St Louis

Eleu dit Leauvette

Avion

Cité St Theodore

Fosse 9

Hill 65

River Souchez

Cité du Bois de Liéven

Fosse 3

Cité St Pierre

Cité Jeanne d'Arc

Cité de Riaumont

Riaumont Wood

0   500   1000 yds

0   1000 m

© BAT 2015

Map 6   Lens: Urban Warfare summer 1917

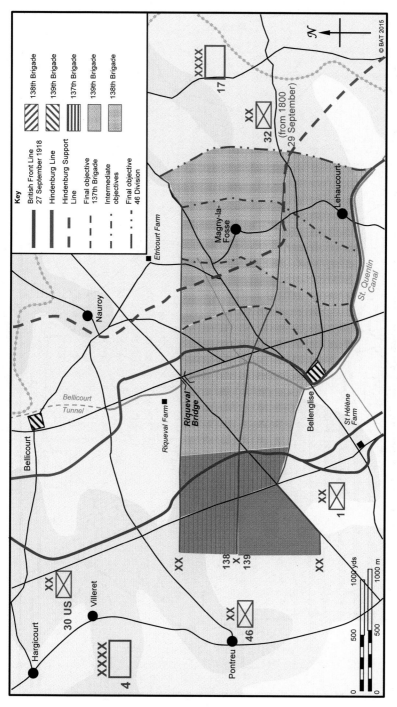

Map 7 Breaking the Hindenburg Line, 27 September 1918

Key

	British Front Line 27 September 1918
	Hindenburg Line
	Hindenburg Support Line
	Final objective 137th Brigade
	Intermediate objectives
	Final objective 46 Division

	138th Brigade
	139th Brigade
	137th Brigade
	139th Brigade
	138th Brigade

© BAT 2015

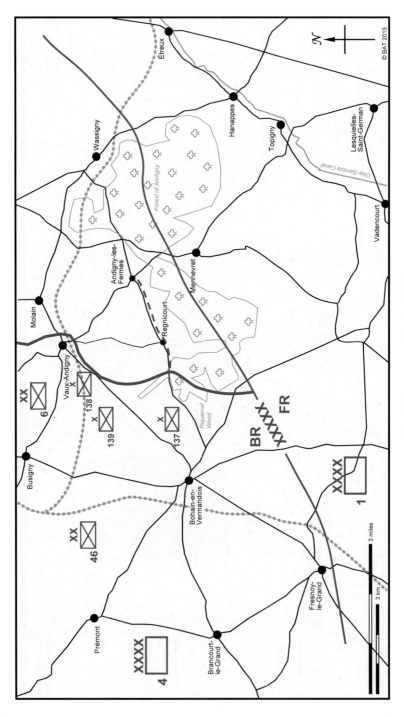

Map 8 Regnicourt, October 1918

However, it suggests that many ideas were emerging in 1916, which would bear fruit later as technological change and mass production provided the means of implementation such as the use of "BB" gas shells in the preliminary bombardment on the Hindenburg Line.

In the context of the views expressed about the Division at Gommecourt the fact that it was not required in the later stages of the Somme offensive will not come as a surprise. Raiding had become a standard activity and any German division who had been told that the 46th Division were a quiet lot to be opposite had to reappraise the situation.[75] Nonetheless, the Divisional Diary noted on 12 October 1916 that the Division was being used as a feeder for other divisions. On 15 November six subalterns were struck off 1/6 Sherwood's strength on their transfer to 11/Kings Royal Rifles. During this time men were on detachment to do work for Corps as well as Third Army and to dig trench mortar emplacements for 17th Division. Having been handicapped in their own offensive preparations by lack of help they were now being used as a reserve of manpower. Then, on 31 October 1916, Thwaites was able to hand over the Divisional sector to 30th Division and take the whole Division into training.

As well as all kinds of training such as musketry, drill and "elementary attack practice" there were to be football and boxing competitions with Divisional competitions to follow on from Brigade ones. The Divisional diary noted on 8 November that the GOC and his staff would visit training daily and three days later Corps advised them that they would probably get 4-5 weeks training time. A visit on 16 November by the Corps Commander included an afternoon football game in which the offices of 139 Brigade HQ beat those of Divisional HQ by three goals to nil. Included in the training programme for 1/8 Sherwoods was attacking in Open Warfare.[76] A more notable arrival on 17 November was the new commander of 137 Brigade, Brigadier General J.V. Campbell VC DSO, who was to command the brigade through to the last week of the war, when he was transferred to command a brigade of Guards.

The Division relieved the 49th Division on a front running from North of Monchy to the South of Fonquevilliers, noting that no work had been done around the latter since the 46th had left.[77] The Diary also notes that on 31 December 1916, Thwaites had organised an artillery test along the divisional front at midnight as a 'New Years' Greeting. The German retaliatory bombardment claimed ten casualties. The 46th Division was therefore ensconced opposite Gommecourt when news came on 25 February 1917 of the German army's retirement on Fifth Army's front.

In relation to the learning curve the point needs to be made that the continuity of officers, at divisional level, before July 1916 actually meant the 46th Division was on its own learning curve and contrasts sharply with Boyd's arrival as GOC in September 1918 and with Thwaite's arrival in 1916 which gave the 46th Division new impetus

75   See Ashworth, *Trench Warfare* regarding 'live and let live' in the front line.
76   WSF: War Diary 1/8 Sherwood Foresters, 6-21 November 1916.
77   Ibid., 7 December 1916.

and a fresh approach to new developments. Thwaites's report to Snow shows that the 46th Division had acquired a commander who was a practical thinker. The best way to picture the learning curve in late 1916 is to envisage a three lane motorway with most of the traffic in the slow lane and a few divisions, such as those in Maxse's Corps and the 36th Ulster Division, tentatively entering the middle lane whilst the 46th Division is re-entering the slow lane from the hard shoulder with a new driver. The replacement of Montague-Stuart-Wortley by Thwaites is indicative of Griffith's assertion that the high command was remorselessly asserting a firmer grip on the army leadership.[78]

78   P. Griffith, *Battle Tactics of the Western Front* (1994), p.13.

6

Shot at Dawn

On 31 July 1916, Lance-Corporal Hawthorne of 1/5th South Staffords was tried before a Field General Court Martial (FGCM) on a charge of:

> when on active service, misbehaving before the enemy in such a manner as to show cowardice.[1]

The essence of the charge was that Hawthorne was leading a group acting as cover for a wiring party and that when called, Hawthorne had said it was too light and therefore caused his men to initially refuse to obey the order. It was also alleged that once out of the dugout he didn't keep closed up and didn't follow the leading party out into No Man's Land.

Second-Lieutenant Arthur Speed told the Court of the accused's unwillingness to obey the order to leave the dugout but that he eventually did so. Speed also said that when 2nd Lieutenant Hattin joined him, he said to Hawthorne "Now, Corporal File Out" & that the accused had replied, "Its too light, its bloody murder."

Hawthorne had been serving with the Staffords since March 1915 having enlisted in September 1914. So here we have a veteran of the Hohenzollern and Gommecourt faced by his superior, in this case a 2nd Lieutenant who had joined the batttalion on 22 June 1916. The second officer, acting 2nd Lt. Hattin had joined the battalion on 14 May 1916 and was only confirmed in that rank on 16 October 1916.

Now it would clearly be completely wrong to question that the order was legitimately given or that Hawthorne was in the wrong to dissent but in reviewing the case Thwaites, the Divisional Commander wrote:

---

1   This and other references in this section are from TNA: WO 71/490, Courts Martial Proceedings.

> I am doubtful whether the officers, as a whole, inspire confidence and the new commanding officer, Major Llewellyn has not yet had time to make his influence felt.

and he noted that the officers involved were "only junior ones".

One of Hawthorne's problems in this case seems to be that he conducted his own defence which meant he had to cross-examine his officers which was never going to be easy in such circumstances. Hawthorne did not cross-examine the other ranks called as witnesses even though all of them effectively placed him as the guilty party.

Hawthorne's own attempt to give evidence 'not on oath' sought to make the grumbling a general one and his claims to have been held up by returning members of the wiring party were unsubstantiated by other witnesses. Hawthorne then called 2nd Lieutenant J Snape, who, in giving evidence as to character described Hawthorne as "quite an efficient non-commissioned officer".

Such a limited endorsement was hardly sufficient to convince Major Odling of the 4th Middlesex (then commanding the 6th North Stafford) or Captain Lister (5th South Staffords) and Lt. C.A. Ashford (6th South Staffords) to find him other than guilty. After the verdict the Adjutant, Lamond, was called as a witness to Hawthorne's service and having supplied the details added the hardly ringing endorsement:

> I have never found any fault with him as an NCO.

Hawthorne chose no to make any statement in mitigation – once again the absence of an officer to defend him appears to have been a handicap.

It was now necessary for the sentence to be confirmed and the accompanying correspondence provides an interesting insight into the views of senior officers about discipline and the Division.

Brigadier Williams immediately wrote a letter recommending the death sentence be confirmed and took great trouble to detail how he himself had been at the advanced Brigade HQ and knew that it was not too light.

Williams then commented on standards in the Brigade, beginning with the previous CO of the 1/5th South Staffords, Lt.Col. Raymer, "the best and most experienced of the commanding officers" so he had no cause to think standards in the battalion were below others but added that morale has been shaken by the heavy losses on 1 July.

This point might seem to be going to save Hawthorne but then Williams writes:

> The general standard of efficiency of the non-commissioned officers of this battalion and of the Brigade as a whole is certainly – and I have no hesitation in saying so – very inferior and the losses on July 1st when we certainly lost a large number of the best NCOs did not help matters.

As if this wasn't scathing enough he then adds "the chain of responsibility even for a territorial unit can hardly be said to exist", and he then states that it was entirely lacking in Hawthorne.

Given William's brief time in command this seems incredibly harsh and to raise the question that if Rayner was such a good CO why was the battalion so poor. Once again the prejudice against territorials seems very strong.

Hawthorne now appears to have no chance but the papers have to go to Thwaites who recommended that sentence be "commuted without suspension of sentence.". We have already seen that Thwaites felt the officers had not yet succeeded in gaining the respect of the men and he doubted that the operation had been very well organised which would have added to the men's concerns.

These points were Thwaites's last points, his first two deal with morale. In the first place he criticises the Staffordshire temperament:

> an extreme example may tend to produce a sullen and dispirited attitude.

Clearly his first impressions had not been good but he then argues for clemency in a way which seems almost guaranteed to ensure rejection by his superiors:

> The convicting evidence having been given by officers, and only junior ones, a very deep feeling amongst the officers as a whole may be engendered and the battalion will consequently become valueless.

The 1980s concept of encouraging people to have 'ownership' of decisions was not widely held in the British Army in 1916 as Lt.General Snow made clear when he in turn received the papers. In forwarding the papers to Allenby, Snow argued that he could not agree with Brigadier Thwaites. By referring to Thwaites's substantive rank Snow draws Thwaites down to William's level and therefore diminishes the weight of his opinion.

Snow argued that the case was clearly proved and that there were no mitigating circumstances. Snow then added:

> The effect of the sentence being carried out would be to bring home to the whole Battalion the enormity of such behaviour in the face of the enemy. An example is needed and I therefore recommend that the sentence is carried out.

Allenby as GOC Third Army simply recommended death and having passed through the hands of the Deputy Judge Advocate General the papers reached Douglas Haig who confirmed sentence on 7 August. Accordingly at 5.12 am on 11th August 1916, Hawthorne was shot by a firing squad under the supervision of the 46th Division's Provost Marshall, Major Newbold. As normal the paperwork confirming that sentence had been carried out made its way to Brigade then Division where Thwaites endorsed the papers:

I should like to place on record that Lance Corporal Hawthorne met his death like a man and a soldier.

One can only conclude that Thwaites still felt that the case need not have led to the soldier's death if handled differently on the night the disagreement occurred. Hawthorne was guilty as charged but his execution was as Voltaire said "pour encourage les autres" in the eyes of his superiors.

7

Lens: Urban Warfare 1917

The purpose of this chapter is to investigate whether the summer of 1917 was a pivotal period in the learning curve of 46th Division. As indicated at the end of chapter 4 it is possible that 46th Division was now being offered an opportunity to prove that it had made strides in efficiency since the Somme following its satisfactory performance in the spring of 1917. The attack to be mounted on 1 July 1917 then assumes a key role since it is this on which the Thwaites led division will be judged. In the longer term it is important to assess the extent to which the 46th Division did learn from its extended period at Lens and the contribution this makes to the Division's improved performance in September 1918.

On 27 March 1917 46th Division began to leave the Somme sector on its transfer to First Army.[1] Having initially been assigned to II Corps,[2] the division was transferred to I Corps on 17 April[3] to relieve 24th Division. If one is looking for evidence of an unofficial British policy of treating some divisions as "assault divisions" and others as "trench divisions", as Griffith suggests,[4] then the case of 24th and 46th Divisions is an interesting one.

46th Division was not deployed in the attack at Loos until 13 October 1915, whereas 24th Division was part of the infamous Reserve on 25 September 1915 whose handling was to lead to such controversy between Haig and French. According to Ray Westlake, 24th Division had completed its concentration in France between 28 August and 4 September 1915;[5] thus, it was deployed in the assault within three weeks of arriving even though 46th Division, with six months trench experience to its credit, was available.

---

1   TNA: WO95/2663, 46th Division War Diary, 27 March 1917.
2   Ibid., 30 March 1917.
3   Ibid., 17 April 1917. First Army was under the command of General Sir Henry Horne (1861-1929), a gunner like Thwaites.
4   Griffith, *Battle Tactics on the Western Front* op.cit., passim., see earlier references.
5   R. Westlake, *Kitchener's Army* (1989), p.98.

After its relief by 46th Division on 17 April 1917, 24th Division was deployed at both Messines and Third Ypres before ending the year facing the German counter attacks at Cambrai.[6] The decision to move 46th Division from the Somme, where, following the German retirement, there was clearly to be a period of calm, to Lens where no significant offensive action was envisaged appears to confirm the idea that 46th Division was not seen as an "assault" division.

The terrain facing the men of 137, 138 and 139 Brigades as they deployed opposite Lens was an industrial one, albeit one which had already become heavily scarred by war. For the many miners amongst the men, the rows of cottages grouped around pit heads would have been reminiscent of home. The French called these little communities "cite" and so names like Cite des Garennes and Cite St Theodore now appear in unit orders. On the southern Divisional boundary were the La Souchez river and a complex set of railways emanating from Lens, as well as a large electricity generating station. To the south of Lens, British forces continued their assaults, known as the Battle of Arras, into May but without significant territorial gains.

A little to the North of the La Souchez River, and therefore the commanding position opposite the right hand brigade, was Hill 65. When the Division was initially deployed this Hill was beyond the Cite de Riaumont. The elements of the Division were to find themselves taking part in a whole series of relatively small operations up to 2 July 1917, when the Division was to be relieved by 2nd Canadian Division following a major divisional assault on 1 July 1917. During the period of its deployment in this sector, 46th Division was to grind out an advance of approximately 1.5 miles on its southern wing decreasing to 200 yards on its northern boundary. In the North an advance of some 600 yards was achieved by breaking into Cite St Edouard. Unfortunately, this isolated success created an unhealthy minor salient.

If one is to assign a strategic value to 46th Division's operations at Lens it can only be in terms of pinning German forces down whilst Messines and Passchendaele were prepared and, in the case of the former, successfully executed. These operations also made a small contribution to preventing the Germans from exploiting the mutinies in the French army that followed the failure of the Nivelle Offensive.

The Division initially deployed all three Brigades in the front line but on 23 April 1917, 137 Brigade was withdrawn into Divisional Reserve,[7] Lieutenant Johnston's explanation being the need to provide 'training and rest'.[8] He goes on to note that it was decided to set a normal Brigade tour at twelve days in and six days out.[9] By the time it was decided to alter the Brigade deployment pattern the Division had already been in action.

6   Ibid., p.99.
7   TNA: WO95,/2663, 46th Division War Diary, 23 April 1917.
8   SRM: Lieutenant Johnston, *The 46th Division at Lens* pamphlet, p.9.
9   Ibid.

Lens from the air, showing Fosse 3 and Bois de Riaumont. (Hills)

Bois de Riaumont from the top of the slag heap with Boot Trench in the foreground. (Hills)

Red Mill, Lens, 1917. (Hills)

According to Johnston[10] the German withdrawal from the Bois de Riaumont had convinced "Higher Authorities" that the enemy was 'on the run' and that Hill 65 would be lightly held. In fact the British 1:10,000 map shows that although the Bois de Riaumont reaches a height of 75-80 metres the Cite de Caumont, in allied hands and rising over 70 metres, is only approximately 1800 yards away. Therefore, the Bois de Riaumont would have been a costly position for the Germans to hold and defend. The map also showed that the Germans retained part of the reverse slopes. This represented a tactical move by the Germans to conserve men. The Division was committed to the attack on the basis of faulty appreciation of the enemy's intentions; the error as usual tending to over-optimism.

The orders from I Corps were received on 20 April 1917 and the relevant instructions were then issued to the Brigades.[11] Meanwhile, 1/8 Sherwood Foresters reported that their patrols had a foothold in the houses on the Capper Road, which emerges from the centre of the wood opposite the Cite de Riaumont. The War Diary provides an account of the house-to-house fighting which stemmed from the patrols probing the German positions after the battalion relieved 1/7 Northants.[12] In these encounters the dominant weapons were the hand grenade and the Lewis gun.

The initial assault on 20 April 1917 was to be made by elements of 139 Brigade, in particular 1/8 Sherwood Foresters were to attack towards the Cite de Riaumont, whilst to their right 1/6 Sherwoods would assault towards Fosse 3. The two objectives were 1,000 yards apart, so the attacks were mutually supporting.

However, in attacking towards Fosse 3, 1/6 Sherwoods would find its left flank exposed if 1/8 Sherwoods were unsuccessful. Therefore, 1/6 Sherwoods were only to try to establish themselves in the two rows of houses to the south of the crossroads in the middle of the Cite de Riaumont if the 1/8 Sherwoods were successful.[13]

Each battalion was in effect moving the line forward to a point where a suitable jumping off point could be reached for a major attack on Hill 65. This concern for a straight jump off time reflects the problems encountered at the Hohenzollern Redoubt: many surviving officers would have been aware of this. On the night of 20 April 1917, the attack by 1/6 Sherwoods was carried out by 'A' and 'B' Companies. Both company commanders, Captain V.O. Robinson MC and Captain J. Tolson, had served with the battalion since it arrived in France. The battalion still had thirteen officers who had been present at the dinner given by the Sergeant's Mess to the Officers at Braintree in February 1915.[14]

Captain Robinson's report on the operations by 'A' Company throws some light on the level of development in infantry tactics at this time.[15] The actual attack was carried

---

10   Ibid., p.10.
11   TNA: WO95/2663, 46th Division War Diary, 23 April 1917.
12   WSF: War Diary 1/8 Sherwood Foresters, April 1917, Appendixes 1 and 2.
13   Ibid., Appendix 2.
14   Ibid., 3 April 1917 and Appendix 1.
15   WSF: War Diary 1/6 Sherwood Foresters, April 1917, Appendix 3.

out by three platoons with one held in reserve. This provided Captain Robinson with an uncommitted element that he was to use to good effect. Whilst the left platoon met with little opposition the centre platoon under Lieutenant Stubbs found itself halted by a German barricade. Captain Robinson then reports that the barricade:

> was rushed at the second attempt under cover of a barrage of rifle grenades from the platoon in the reserve.[16]

The successful use of the reserve platoon demonstrates that even before the '100 Days' of 1918, ordinary companies in average battalions were adapting their tactics to the growing arsenal of weapons available to them. In total 'A' Company lost one man killed and seven wounded in achieving its objectives. This tactical awareness would seem to have more to do with experience than stability of personnel since, although there was a core of long serving officers, such as Lieutenant-Colonel Johnson the commanding officer, there had been considerable turnover in the battalion's personnel during two years of active service.

It is pertinent to note that when Captain Robinson brought his reserve into action, he was supporting a platoon commander who was an ex-ranker. Captain Robinson says that this centre platoon was under the command of Lieutenant Stubbs. Second Lieutenant F.W.A. Stubbs had been promoted from Corporal on 4 January 1916 with seniority from 18 December 1915. In April 1916 Second Lieutenant Stubbs went to 46th Divisional School before going sick a week later. Having rejoined the battalion on 6 May 1916 he was wounded at Gommecourt and only returned to the battalion on 31 December 1916.[17] Stubbs's long period of convalescence probably cost him promotion since seven surviving Second Lieutenants in the battalion were made Temporary Lieutenants on 7 September 1916.[18] Even with the award of the Military Cross, there was no immediate 'fast track' and so he was still commanding a platoon when he was killed in action on 10 May 1917.[19] Clearly, this is only one case but the overall impression gained is that whilst winning the MC might enhance a junior officer's career it by no means guaranteed promotion.

It would require a more widespread survey to establish a fuller picture; but if 46th Division is not untypical, then senior officers may have distinguished between the qualities of courage and management. The qualities which enable an officer to conduct a successful one/two/three man patrol are not those which would ensure that all members of the platoon / company had protected their rifle bolts from rusting and their feet through the conscientious application of whale oil. Captain Robinson himself was subsequently posted to 1/5 Sherwoods on 14 July 1917 as Second in

16   Ibid.
17   WSF: War Diary 1/6 Sherwood Foresters, dates as quoted.
18   Ibid.
19   Ibid.

Command.[20] As mentioned in the last chapter, the Brigade seems to have found its officers from within; thus fresh ideas also had to come from within.

To the North of 1/6 Sherwoods at Lens, 1/5 South Staffords were training before entering the line on 23 April 1917. During the training the battalion received a visit from Major–General Thwaites, their divisional commander. On this occasion he presented the Military Cross to two officers, Captain Harrison (RAMC) and Second-Lieutenant G.E. Cronk,[21] the latter being the same officer who had appeared as the twenty-fifth witness at the Court of Inquiry into 137 Brigade at the Somme. Then only 18 and with four days of trench experience, the subsequent award of the MC vindicated Cronk and the Inquiry's benevolent judgement.

Johnston's account[22] links the activity on 28 April to the continuing operations at Arras and the possibility of general German retirement to the "East of Lens". Johnston therefore says that the "small raids" by 138 and 139 Brigades were designed to "secure identifications and inflict casualties".[23] In preparation for these "small raids" 1/4 Leicesters spent the whole of 27 and 28 April carrying gas for the Royal Engineers.[24] At 2.10 a.m. on 29 April this gas was fired at the Germans after Second Lieutenant G.E. Banwell and his party, of 'C' Company 1/5 Leicesters, had raided a German post which was found to be unoccupied. The same result had been achieved by Second Lieutenant B.J. Halliday's fighting patrol of 1/4 Lincolns.[25] In this case the same officer and four battalion scouts had previously reconnoitred the area raided and had only found three or four Germans patrolling it.[26] Thwaites congratulated Halliday on his patrol.[27] The raid by 1/5 Sherwoods resulted in eight casualties including two officers as German fire caught them at the second belt of wire.[28] As the casualties included four "missing", gas was not projected onto this area on 29 April but it was fired at Hill 65 a night later.[29]

The confused state of GHQ's thinking on tanks is revealed in the Divisional War Diary's record that 138 Brigade's task had been to make good the whole of Cite St Theodore "in case required as a jumping off point for tanks".[30] In fact, St Theodore was still occupied by the Germans on 2 July 1917, but even if secured earlier its suitability for tanks is superficial. Compared with assaults from other directions St Theodore was indeed the route to the main area of open country approaching Lens. However, two

20   Ibid., 14 July 1917.
21   SRM: War Diary 1/5 South Staffords, 15 April 1917.
22   Johnston, op.cit., p.12.
23   Ibid.
24   LRO: Diary 1/4 Leicesters, 26 April 1917.
25   MLL: War Diary 1/4 Lincolns, 28 April 1917.
26   Ibid., 27 April 1917.
27   Ibid., 30 April 1917.
28   TNA: WO95/2663, 46th Division War Diary, 28 April 1917.
29   Ibid., 29-30 April 1917.
30   Ibid., 28 April 1917, and Notes issued by Mackenzie are to be found with the related War Diary for April 1917.

major railway lines ran through this area forming a 'D' shape, with the back of the 'D' lying along the axis of any advance towards Lens.

The advance towards Lens would also have been vulnerable to German fire from the high ground provided by the railway embankments and two built up areas controlled by the Germans. German gunners, secure in their positions, would have picked off British tanks moving at one mile per hour with ease.

More relevant to the future of modern warfare were the notes issued by First Army on co-operation between trench mortars and machine guns. These notes accord with the development process now termed "disseminating / sharing best practice" and are therefore primary evidence of the learning curve reaching 46th Division.

Lieutenant Colonel Mackenzie, for the MGGS First Army, sent the notes to all the other four Corps, including the Canadian Corps. Mackenzie detailed how mortars and machine guns had been used in 6th Division, I Corps, on 21 and 23 April. 6th Division was one of the original regular divisions and on 21 April was operating in conjunction with 46th Division. Mackenzie's account of the fighting explained that troops of both Divisions were held up by a German strong point. Mackenzie then detailed how two machine guns had suppressed German rifle fire whilst two mortars were brought up to tackle the strong point. Mackenzie explains the prompt arrival of the mortars: "due to the Battalion Commander having sent early and accurate information back to the brigade". Unfortunately, we are not told how the information was conveyed, only the speed with which it was communicated. The second part of Mackenzie's analysis has a greater bearing on operational method:

> There was apparently no time for the Battalion Commander to give any compre-
> hensive orders for this co-operation, and it was chiefly due to the machine gun
> and mortar commanders playing into each other's hands and watching the situa-
> tion closely and intelligently and acting without definite orders.

This would seem to recognise that, once the battle has begun, tactical control inevitably devolves down to company/section level. This accords with the earlier account of the use of rifle grenades. In case this lesson was not clear, Mackenzie went on to write that the machine guns and mortars were placed under the orders of the battalion commander because the Brigadier favoured this system on most occasions. Mackenzie then quotes the Brigadier as going "as far as to say" he is prepared "at any time" to put machine guns or mortars under the orders of company commanders. Given the wide dissemination given to this advice it is reasonable to conclude that the devolution of tactical authority was becoming the dominant paradigm at First Army HQ. This is the osmosis to which Griffith alludes; by being placed in a dynamic corps the 46th Division were able to learn. No doubt, in part this reflects the enormous increase in the quantity of weapons available to the British Army by 1917.

It would have been difficult to discuss devolving machine guns to companies when a Battalion only had two. Therefore this is another occasion when we can identify the key role played by the expansion of industrial output in Britain's success on the

Western Front. By 1917, annual production of machine guns in Britain had risen to 79,700 (compared to 300 in 1914)[31]; and by July 1916 the annual output of mortars had risen to 4,279 from 312 in 1915.[32] As we saw with artillery, the expansion of weapons production was very important for territorial divisions who were relatively low in the pecking order.

Given the available material resources, First Army's endorsement of devolving tactical control accords with Paddy Griffith's views on the successive rise in the need for 'tactical initiators'.[33] Lieutenant Stubbs's presence only serves to underline Griffith's point, that due to the pressures of war the fact that an ex-ranker is in a key position emphasises the social upheaval. Why argue that a Lance Corporal cannot be entrusted with key decisions when his predecessor as section leader could now be his platoon commander?[34]

On 10 May 1917 the Divisional artillery and machine guns co-operated in supporting an attack by the Canadians. Otherwise, the Division spent the month carrying out raids and exchanging fire with the Germans. Apart from problems during raids the main black spot came on the 25 May when the Germans recaptured Nash Valley which the 46th Division had captured the previous evening.[35]

During June 1917, the focus of 46th Division's activity was the preparation for the assault on Hill 65. For example, on 19 June 138 Brigade captured German trenches west of Fosse 3 "to deny observation to the enemy and facilitate further operations against Hill 65".[36] The extent of future operations by I Corps had been passed on by Corps HQ on 13 June and the following day the Acting BGGS of I Corps had visited 46th Division. This meeting included information for 46th Division on the labour available for the preparations for the assault.

Those who had survived Gommecourt would have been conscious that this time they were not expected to do everything themselves. The Division was given the support of two sections of 3 Australian Tunnelling Company plus 253 Tunnelling Company and 2 Cavalry Brigade's Pioneer Battalion. As well as these specialists, 46th Division were also assigned the South Irish Horse and I Corps's own Cyclist Company. The only difficulty with being given the resources is that if things go wrong there are fewer places to hide.

Devotees of the Canadians will no doubt wish to emphasise their role in the operations against Hill 65. However, Army and Corps commanders met with Thwaites; and 46th Division had its own objectives, which it achieved on both 24 June and 28 June. On the former occasion 1/6 South Staffords captured 600 yards of trenches on the west side of Hill 65. Three days later the Divisional Artillery co-operated in the

31   N. Ferguson, *The Pity of War* (1998), p.260.
32   G.J. DeGroot, *Blighty* (1996), p.85.
33   Griffith, *Battle Tactics of the Western Front*, p.23.
34   Ibid.
35   TNA: WO95/2663, 46th Division War Diary, 24-25 April 1917.
36   Ibid., 19 April 1917.

Canadian assault that led to the capture of Elen. This Canadian advance was indeed vital, since the loss of the hamlet of Elen dit Leauvette, and the trench system just to the south east of it, effectively turned the flank of Hill 65.

However, the Germans did not immediately leave Hill 65, since the La Souchez river still provided them with a defensible barrier against the Canadians. The Germans were, however, forced to retreat when 46th Division assaulted Hill 65 on 28 June with elements of 137 and 138 Infantry Brigades. These gains were consolidated on 29 June before seizing 200 yards of trench in order to straighten out the line in readiness for further operations.[37]

Given that this was 46th Division's first successful assault it is important to identify any improvements which are evident. In contrast with the Hohenzollern Redoubt, where the battle had already become bogged down, and Gommecourt, which was essentially a diversion, 46th Division was given a clear and achievable task. In partnering the Canadians 46th Division could also rely upon first rate support. As outlined above, the Canadian success at Elen helped ensure the success of the second assault on 28 June.

Unless the Divisional Diary is a complete fabrication, a distinct change from 1916 was the personal involvement of the GOC at the front. On 26 June, Thwaites personally reconnoitred Hill 65 having previously spent 23 June at 137 Brigade HQ working out the details of the proposed operations.[38] Not only was wire cutting carried out on 27 June, but there were regular checks made on progress, especially by patrols from 137 Brigade. In fact, 138 Brigade only limited their patrols due to the artillery fire support being given to the Canadians assault on Elen.[39] Thwaites was a gunner by training, and so we can assume he brought expertise as well as energy to his role. Not only is there a contrast with the uncertainties, over the destruction of wire, on the Somme in 1916 but also with the failings in March 1917 by 137 Brigade, with whom Thwaites spent time planning this assault.

The artillery plan for 24 June included only a six minute field gun barrage on the German front line which would then advance 50 yards every 3 minutes.[40] Although Corps heavy artillery were to carry out a preliminary bombardment, the brevity of the local bombardment suggests that lessons were being learnt about the need to achieve tactical surprise at the point of attack. The comparison with raiding can be made by reference to the standing barrage. This was to fall 200 yards beyond Admiral Trench. The standing barrage is indicative of the limited scope of these operations but it also points the way to future, larger, "bite and hold" operations. Indeed, one can argue that in 1918 the methodology is essentially the same but is applied on a larger scale;

37   TNA: WO95/2663, 46th Division War Diary, June 1917.
38   Ibid.
39   Ibid.
40   SRM: War Diary 1/6 South Staffords, June 1917.

with a number of successive "bite and hold" operations (carried out by 'leapfrogging' battalions) joined together on the same day.

The pace of the advancing barrage may seem slow in comparison with those used in the "100 Days" but it has to be remembered that this was a much smaller operation and, more importantly, it was over an urban landscape which would afford greater potential cover for defenders. Evidence of the use of a variety of specialist weaponry can be found; the 2" mortars were to cut the wire in front of Ahead Trench whilst the much heavier 9.45" mortars were to bombard Agnes trench. The attack itself was to be supported by Stokes Mortars. The plan also included four machine guns barraging Hill 65. This feature of the plan was to be one of the elements for success at the Hindenburg Line.

Preparing for the attack on 28 June created a large amount of work for 178 Battalion MGC.[41] The machine guns had fired 98,000 rounds in support of the attack on 24 June and were to fire 16,000 rounds on 28 June. On 25 June they carried out 'heavy work' preparing their chosen gun positions. The pace of work was increased after 11a.m. 26 June when orders were received that Z day had been brought forward 24 hours, only to be told at 2.30 p.m. that Z day had been put back again to its original date. The British Army might have been getting better but some things do not change. During June the machine gunners had had to put a lot of work into getting new belt-feeding machines to work, since the prodigious amounts of ammunition being expended would otherwise have exhausted the labour available. Entries for June record 765,300 rounds being expended. This figure does not include any minor exercises or ranging fire. It also excludes the rounds fired in support of an SOS barrage at 7 p.m. on 29 June or in support of the assault on 1 July. The whole manner of the battalion's approach at this time imitates that of the artillery. The work needed to construct '[machine]gun positions' has already been noted. The problem of barrels becoming worn by heavy use is recorded as reducing accuracy in the operations by One and Three sections supporting the Canadians on 11 June.

It had been noted on 10 June that there was a shortage of barrels and therefore the available barrels had to be shared between sections. The OC 178 Battalion MGC also noted that he had to borrow Mark 1 barrels from DADOS as Mark 2 barrels were unavailable. Given the imminence of major operations at Messines and forthcoming events at Passchendaele, it is not perhaps surprising to find shortages of spare parts at Lens. Nonetheless, it demonstrates that, even with the enormous strides made in British production, the shoe still pinched occasionally in non-priority sectors.

The machine gunners were also developing the concept of indirect fire. For the raid on 8 June they fired at a range of 1700 yards, at an average elevation of six per cent. On this occasion it was not possible to observe the fire directly but on 11 June their fire was observed by the OC 138 MGCoy. Whilst there is no reference to the heavy machine guns as a kind of tactical artillery it was noted that on 19 June there

41   TNA: WO95/2679, War Diary 178 MGC, June 1917.

was an MG barrage without an artillery one. The attack was successful and three German counter attacks were also driven off. This suggests that the role of the heavy machine gun was undergoing a reappraisal even in the military "backwaters" of the 46th Division.

This reappraisal naturally follows from the decision to create battalions of heavy machine guns. The evolution of their operational strategy can also be linked, in this case, to a period of continuous operations during which the lessons learnt from one day can be rapidly tested in a succeeding operation. It could, therefore, be argued that informally labelling a division as a "trench holding" one becomes self-fulfilling. The 46th Division was ill prepared for offensive operations, in March 1917, after a period of static defence, but was capable of improvement given a series of more limited tasks. Having a GOC, in Thwaites, who was persona grata with his superiors was also a novelty.

The recognition of the changing operational perception of the machine gun can also be found in the convening of a machine gun conference on 2 May 1917. This conference involved not only the CO 178 Battalion MGC but also all the OC's 137/138/139 MG Coys. The GSO2 46th Division and the Corps Machine Gun Officer were also present. The reason given for convening the conference was to "arrange defensive barrage and prepare for an offensive barrage".[42] This conference came a week after Major Ellwood, OC 178 Battalion MGC, had toured the Divisional Line with the CRE and Corps MGO. On their tour they selected thirteen of the fifteen gun positions required.[43] Thereafter, Major Ellwood and three of his section commanders toured the selected positions in company with the CRE and the OC 466 Field Company Royal Engineers and agreed upon fields of fire.[44]

The work to emplace the machine guns was then carried out. On 31 May 1917, the Corps MGO, Major Basden MC, inspected the guns in their emplacements. During his tour, if not before, he would have been informed of the trials carried out with armour piercing SAA. It had been found that on three-eighths of an inch loophole plate the maximum penetration was three-sixteenths of an inch at a range of 15-50 yards and that this penetration diminished when the range was increased to 100-200 yards.[45]

During May 1917, Major Ellwood made several visits to each of the Brigade Machine Gun Companies; and, his comments suggest he put forward a large number of ideas for improvements.[46] In the case of 46th Division it would therefore seem to be appropriate to suggest that the operational use of machine guns was evolving through the cascade process. Specialists, such as Major Basden MC and Major Ellwood

---

42 Ibid., 2 May1917.
43 Ibid., 24 April 1917.
44 Ibid., 25 April 1917.
45 Ibid., 13/14/31 May 1917.
46 Ibid., May 1917.

himself, were instrumental in spreading 'best practice' down to the lower echelons. It seems to be instructive that, between the original tours to select positions and the inspection by Major Basden MC, it was Major Johnson, GSO2 46th Division, who carried out an interim check on progress. Given that it is usually the senior person who carries out the final inspection this would suggest 46th Division were keen to be thought well of at Corps level and that Thwaites was keeping a close eye on progress.

Major Ellwood's view on this occasion was that most of the emplacements were too high and consequently conspicuous and that several had been misplaced.[47] If Major Johnson shared these views then no doubt the OC 466 Field Company Royal Engineers would have come to share them too! One of the advantages enjoyed by the 178 Battalion MGC was that they suffered relatively few casualties so therefore there was less difficulty in maintaining continuity of knowledge. The war diary records one officer and thirteen other ranks becoming casualties in June. The 178 Battalion MGC received twenty other ranks as reinforcements in this period as well as four officers.

The officers joining the battalion included Second Lieutenants Driscoll (South Wales Borderers) and Wilson (Royal Scots) who had come from the MGC base. Driscoll was subsequently posted to 137 MG Coy. Two other officers were returning to the battalion; whilst Lieutenant Noall came back from MGC Base, Lieutenant Cashin was rejoining from hospital. Lieutenant Cashin was immediately given command of No. 2 Section whose previous OC, Second Lieutenant Wilson, was transferred to HQ company under Lieutenant Carmichael. Lieutenant Noall was given command of No. 3 Section with Second Lieutenant Highwood as his second in command. Highwood had had a spell in charge of No. 2 Section when Lieutenant Bryce had reported sick in May. Ellwood appears to show good management skills in moving Highwood to No. 3 Section instead of simply putting a more senior officer in charge and reducing him to second in command.

It would therefore seem reasonable to conclude that 46th Division was about to enter the operations of 1 July 1917 with an experienced heavy machine gun element, which was, under the keen eye of Corps, seeking to raise the standard and effectiveness of machine gunnery within the Division by sharing best practice. Specialists in machine gunnery were evolving new ways in which their weapons could be used and this was feeding into the operational method of the Division in the execution of brigade level assaults.

As part of its continuing operations against the German positions, 46th Division was ordered to attack the line represented by the German trenches named Aconite and Aloof on British maps. The flank of the assault would therefore lie along the railway line running into the centre of Lens from an approximately north-westerly direction. Even with the capture of parts of Adjacent, Ague and Adroit trenches on 28 June the Division faced the problem that the start line was not parallel with their objectives. The Division had already experienced the painful consequences of this at

---

47   Ibid., 9 May 1917.

the Hohenzollern Redoubt. It was therefore decided to launch a preliminary assault with the axis provided by the Lens–Lieven Road. The capture of the German position known as Alarm Trench would provide a starting line parallel to Aconite trench.

Thus the thinking behind the planning was broadly sound. However, the strategic reasons for the assault are less clear. By capturing Hill 65, 46th Division had, with the gains made by the Canadians to the south, opened the way for an assault on Lens itself. The distance separating 46th Division's forward units from the centre of Lens was only about 1km. An advance towards the centre, however, would create a salient. It is surprising that the Corps should wish 46th Division to advance, since in earlier operations the successful formula had been for the Canadians to push forward in less heavily built up areas and outflank the Germans, before 46th Division were launched against the core defences.

The orders for the main assault were received at 2 p.m. on 29 June, almost exactly 36 hours ahead of the planned assault at 2.47 a.m. on 1 July.[48] The preliminary attack was set for 2.34 a.m. on 29 June, i.e. only twelve hours after Corps' orders were received. This first assault was to be a joint operation by 1/6 North Stafford and 1/7 Sherwoods, of 137 and 139 Brigades respectively. Thwaites reported that he had to use troops used in the assault on 28 June because there was insufficient time for fresh units to reconnoitre the ground.[49]

At 7.10 p.m. on 27 June, 1/6 North Staffords had advanced to capture Abode and Adult trenches. The operation had been successful despite a 5.9inch battery opening fire. The battalion described the British barrage as effective and accurate, and it was noted that two Stokes mortars and two Brigade machine guns had gone forward with the assaulting troops. A subsequent German bombing attack was repulsed.[50]

Lieutenant Colonel Stoney decided to attack with all four companies in line because of their numerical weakness. To assist his men, 'A' Company 1/6 South Staffords acted as the carrying party. Given that all four companies were in line, Stoney arranged for the second wave to close to ten paces from the first wave so that they could mop up. Stoney is very complimentary about the quality of the British barrage and the timing, noting that casualties were only caused when men did not recognise the battered German positions and strayed too far forward.

Stoney reported that the Stokes mortars and machine guns were valuable in neutralising the enfilade fire suffered the day after the assault. Snipers in nearby buildings posed the main problem. Despite the apparent ease of the operation, the battalion lost thirty killed and 100 wounded. To those nurtured on Martin Middlebrook's analysis of 1 July 1916 these casualties could seem light. However, the war diary gives the battalion's strength on 28 June as 28 officers and 696 other ranks, of which eight officers and 222 men were on detached duty. Out of a field service strength of twenty

48   TNA: WO95/2664, 46th Division War Diary, Thwaites' Report to Corps, 3 July 1917.
49   Ibid.
50   SRM: War Diary 1/6 North Staffords, 28-29 June 1917.

officers and 474 men the battalion suffered approximately 24 per cent casualties. The low number of men in the battalion is another indicator that 46th Division was not in a priority sector. Therefore, when Thwaites uses the battalion again against Ague trench he knows it is weak.

Stoney's account of the attack on Ague begins by emphasising that there was no time to put the men in the right place or explain the operation to them. He puts the initial failure of the attack, "across the open", down to wire and machine gun fire as well as lack of time to organise.[51] Stoney concludes by saying that his officers then led the men from each end of the trench and established a series of posts by the afternoon. He also noted that elements of the trench mortar battery, supporting his battalion, were more effective in suppressing enemy machine gun fire than in dislodging snipers.[52] Meanwhile, 1/7 Sherwoods, whom Thwaites described as "well led", seized their objectives without significant incident. Thus, with some difficulty, tired troops were able to set the stage for the assault on 1 July 1917, exactly a year after the fateful assault on Gommecourt. As at Gommecourt, the Sherwood Foresters seemed to be marginally outperforming the Staffords.

Unlike at Gommecourt, all three brigades were to take part in the assault. On the northern wing, 139 Brigade had 2 Sherwood Foresters, of 6th Division, attached. Even though its 'regular' character would have been diluted by July 1917; the inclusion of a regular battalion of their own regiment must have been intended to stiffen 139 Brigade's resolve. In the centre of the assault were 1/5 North Staffords, of 137 Brigade, attacking along the corridor created by the Lens-Lieven and Lens-Riaumont roads. On the Southern flank were 138 Brigade, 1/4 and 1/5 Lincolns being the assaulting battalions.

Once again, 1 July did not prove to be an auspicious day for 46th Division. In his covering letter to I Corps, dated 3 July 1917, Thwaites stressed that the assault was against the "main line of resistance" and that the Germans only recaptured the ground taken by use of superior force. Thwaites adduced the capture of a member of the 5th Guard Grenadiers to add weight to this point. Thwaites also stresses the short time available to prepare the assault; and, concludes by saying that the attack will continue to influence the Germans against withdrawing men from this sector. Thwaites may well have been unwise to write on 3 July, as he had not yet had reports from the Brigades and "cannot therefore be certain of all the facts". On 8 July Thwaites sent a further report to I Corps; enclosing the relevant lower echelon reports. Thwaites asked for these reports to be returned to him suggesting the evidence had been hastily assembled and copies had not therefore been made. Since there were three separate brigade level assaults it is best to analyse the problems separately, as some caused more controversy than others.

---

51   TNA: WO95/2664, 46th Division War Diary, Report dated 6 July 1917.
52   Ibid.

Working from South to North, it is appropriate to begin with 1/4 and 1/5 Lincolns who were assaulting the Cité du Moulin. Thwaites reported that as many as 6 machine guns per company front were found. The heavily built up area provided numerous obstacles to the advance. As so often was the case in the Great War, a lot depended upon where one happened to be put. Whilst 1/5 Lincolns were suffering in the Moulin, 1/4 Lincolns were able to reach their objectives with "few casualties and little opposition."[53] However, having gained contact with the Canadians south of the Souchez River 1/4 Lincolns withdrew their left flank to conform to the lack of progress by 1/5 Lincolns. Once again, this begs the question why this assault, by 1/4 Lincolns, was not carried out before the main Divisional attack so that they could have joined the assault on the Cité du Moulin from the South and helped the 1/5 Lincolns, entering from the West. The haste with which preparations were made seems to have precluded such a preparatory assault. However, General Sir Henry Horne, commanding First Army, was subsequently to conclude that 138 Brigade 'fought hard' and so this aspect of the operations was not controversial.[54]

The controversy surrounded 137 and 139 Brigades, as it had done a year earlier. Moving to the centre of the assault the spotlight falls on 1/5 North Staffords, the only assault battalion drawn from 137 Brigade. The Staffords were effectively the pivot between the assaults by the other two brigades. Although the distance to be covered was estimated at approximately 500 yards, there were three streets running parallel to the start line. These streets would have to be crossed before Aconite trench was reached. Lieutenant Colonel Fawcus therefore made careful preparations for his battalion's assault. Under "very difficult" conditions the start line was taped out by Lieutenant Thompson of 466 Field Company RE. Fawcus was trying to learn from events on 28 June, when the German barrage had come down on the British line "within 10 seconds", by having the tape laid 40 yards west of Ague so that the men would be "well clear" before the German shells fell.[55]

Fawcus's deployment partly anticipates that used at the Hindenburg Line; and it is also interesting because he seems to have taken account of the issue of Germans emerging behind the assaulting troops as mentioned by Thwaites in his report on the earlier operations. Fawcus divided each of his four companies into two waves. The first wave advanced in line of sections in columns. Each company's first wave was followed by half a platoon of "moppers up", found by 1/6 South Staffs. The distance between the first wave and the "moppers up" was 40 yards. At the same distance behind the "moppers up", came the second wave organised in line of half platoons in column. The carrying parties, also found by 1/6 South Staffs, were to follow 100 yards to the rear of the second wave. Fawcus praised Captain the Honourable W.B. Wrottesley, commanding the carrying company, for pushing on to the start line even when his

53   MLL: War Diary 1/4 Lincolns, 1 July 1917.
54   TNA: WO95/2663, 46th Division War Diary, Horne to Thwaites, 13 July 1917.
55   SRM: War Diary 1/5 North Staffords, 1 July 1917, report undated.

guides missed the rendezvous. Fawcus emphasised that this formation was adopted not only to be able to clear the expected German barrage but also due to a lack of reconnaissance; there had not been time to send out reconnaissance patrols.

Under the creeping barrage, each of the first waves of Fawcus's two right companies' reached their objectives. Unfortunately, the second waves were held up by severe house to house fighting. Fawcus attributed this to the moppers up losing their officers and senior NCO's and therefore going forward with the attacking wave. Fawcus may have been thinking of the contrast between the "moppers up" and Lance Corporal Wain who was awarded the Military Medal for collecting a group of stragglers and clearing a row of cellars and houses.

On the left progress took much longer as this was where the uncaptured part of Ague trench lay. Aconite was captured at 3.15 a.m., signalled by golden rockets, i.e. 28 minutes after the assault began. The situation was confirmed by a wounded man at 4.45 a.m. when he brought a message from the two company commanders. Only at about 7 a.m. did Fawcus learn that the attack on each flank had failed. He says he responded by telephoning Brigade to offer to support renewed attacks with the support companies. Then Fawcus received news of the problems of his own left companies. The news he received was that only one officer remained unwounded. Fawcus therefore sent Captain Wenger forward from the Report Centre to take command of the left; whilst Major Graham went forward to the Report Centre. Captain Wenger's citation for the Bar to his Military Cross commended his conspicuous gallantry in rallying the troops and pushing them forward in bitter house to house fighting which led to the capture of several Germans and their machine guns. Wenger was wounded and had to leave, delegating command to Lieutenant Jones of 1/6 South Staffords, before reporting to Fawcus on the way to the dressing station. Once again, a junior officer becomes a key person in a difficult situation.

Fawcus then deployed two platoons, from the support companies, one on each flank, at about 8.15 a.m. Subsequently, the Germans counter-attacked the battalion's front and isolated the forward elements in Aconite trench. On his own initiative, Major Graham went forward to organise a counter–attack and lost contact with Fawcus; he was subsequently killed in action. The courage and commitment of the Staffords seems fully evident, though it will be challenged. Fawcus's battalion was then relieved by the 1/5 South Staffords.

In a statement, which must sum up the feelings of many officers in the Great War, Fawcus wrote:

> Information took a considerable time to come through and by the time it reached the report centre the situation had changed.[56]

---

56 Ibid.

The perennial problem of command and control was to lead to greater tactical delegation of authority by the end of the war.

According to the longer of his two reports, written on 3 July 1917, Lieutenant Colonel Lamond, commanding 1/5 South Staffords, framed orders for an attack at midnight on 1 July. Despite the orders having been issued at 22.05 it was not until 23.10 that Captain Ivatt commanding the right company received them. Captain Wathall, who was commanding the left company, did not receive his until 00.15, i.e. a quarter of an hour after the attack was supposed to have begun. Due to a mistake by the guide, Walthall's men had only reached their positions at 00.05. At 00.20, Walthall and Ivatt conferred and decided that given that there was no sign of an attack in progress they too would not attack.

For those familiar with the Inquiry into Gommecourt, Walthall and Ivatt's decision would have a sense of déjà vu. In essence they were correct in realising that they were on their own but for a Division whose reputation had always been shaky their decision was to prove embarrassing. Lamond sought to excuse his battalion partly by blaming the non-appearance of 4th Dragoon Guards. By 3 July 1/5 South Staffords had arrived at the Divisional rest billets at Burbure. Lamond was not therefore filing a brief report in action followed by a longer report at rest. One could also reasonably argue that as a former Adjutant Lamond was good at paperwork. One possible hypothesis is that he began a full report on 3 July and dashed off a short report in response to an urgent Brigade request on 4 July before completing the original report. Either way, given the social cachet of the Dragoon Guards it was probably impolitic to blame them. The story about meeting an officer has the weakness of being checkable, and who would doubt the word of an officer of the Dragoon Guards (shades of the Hohenzollern)! So Lamond settles for the lame but incontrovertible excuse that he could not find them in the dark of a confused battlefield.[57]

Thwaites did his best to extricate Lamond by both criticising him and then praising his good work to date. Thwaites told Corps that Lamond should have taken control of the situation more quickly and firmly when he realised things were going wrong but Thwaites spread the blame to Brigade, too, for not sending a staff officer forward. Thwaites said that he believed Lamond was correct when he said that 1/5 South Staffords would have done their best if the attack had been carried out. However, in praising Lamond, Thwaites paid a back handed compliment to the battalion when he said that Lamond has "done a very great deal to raise the spirit of his men during the two months he has been in command".[58] General Horne's response was uncompromising.

---

57   SRM: War Diary 1/5 South Staffords, July 1917, Appendix.
58   TNA: WO95/2663, 46th Division War Diary, Thwaites' Report to Corps, 3 July 1917.

He did not accept that 1/5 South Staffords could justify abandoning the attack. Horne also said that since communication was possible between battalion and brigade HQ's, Lamond could have attacked had he "taken more active steps."[59]

Horne's greatest criticism was reserved for 1/5 North Staffords, whom he held to have surrendered too easily in Aconite Trench. Horne accepted that they were in a difficult position owing to the failures on their flanks but believed they could have held out until mid-day on 1 July if they had fought harder. The battalion's own records show eight officer casualties and eight missing with the equivalent figures for other ranks being 58 and 116.[60] This would represent a relatively high proportion of people missing. The most interesting aspect of the correspondence is that Thwaites did not seek to rebut the charge against 1/5 North Staffords and even includes in his preliminary report a reference to approximately twenty men being rounded up and marched to the rear. To make such an observation in a report to Corps with the obvious possibility of it reaching the Army GOC was tantamount to an accusation.[61]

Nevertheless, for those like Captain Wenger and Private Worthington (whose bravery was recognised) there was to be a presentation, by Field Marshal Haig himself, on 16 July 1917. Only the day before, General Horne had distributed medals to other members of the battalion of whom collectively he had been so critical.[62] This combination of public applause and private judgement reflects the need to maintain morale whilst making sensible judgements about battle worthiness. However, such private judgements can simply reflect prejudice; either in the narrow sense, e.g. about Territorials, or in the wider sense of this is not a good battalion/brigade in a poorly reputed division so expectations are low, and were not exceeded.

In this context, the performance of 139 Brigade can be assessed. Brigadier General G.G.S. Carey produced an impressively comprehensive report detailing what happened to each battalion. Carey was careful to include notable acts of leadership by individual officers to balance more problematic points. This enabled Thwaites to highlight such points as Captain Roberts, 'D' Company 2 Sherwoods, killing fifteen Germans; and thus making some amends for the company attacking prematurely and being caught by the British barrage.[63] One of Carey's conclusions was heavily scored in the margin, and was included in Horne's remarks as a lesson. They both stress that to attack in the dark across a complicated urban landscape was a mistake and that zero hour should have been later.[64] This is clear evidence of analysis and dissemination in practice.

Carey also pointed to the lack of depth of the attacking troops and that therefore there were insufficient men for mopping up and for use as reserves. In the margin

59   Ibid., Horne to Thwaites, 17 July 1917.
60   SRM: War Diary 1/5 North Staffords, July 1917.
61   TNA: WO95/2663, 46th Division War Diary, Thwaites' Report to Corps, 3 July 1917.
62   SRM: War Diary 1/5 North Staffords, 15-16 July and 6 July 1917.
63   TNA: WO95/2663, 46th Division War Diary, Carey's report to Thwaites dated 7 July 1917.
64   Ibid., Horne, op.cit.

his superior, presumably Horne, noted that 9 Norfolks, who had been allocated as divisional reserve, were not used. Unless Thwaites was deliberately trying to undermine Carey, it is not likely that he would have written on a copy of the report being sent to Horne. This is especially true since he highlights points in his covering letter and refers to them as being marked by a letter.[65] So the marginalia reflect Horne's view that Thwaites had not made use of all the resources allocated to 46th Division.

The battalion history of 1/5 Sherwoods gives their effective strength as eight officers and 270 men. The battalion historian puts the attack frontage at approximately 550 yards. According to this battalion, they only received the change from 2.45 a.m. to 2.47 a.m. "almost immediately before zero hour".[66] According to 1/5 Sherwoods their jumping off line was also altered at the last minute causing confusion.[67] Carey simply said that the tape had to be laid amongst houses.[68] The two accounts might be made to agree if one accepts Carey's as stating the original intention. Carey's problem was that every time he drew attention to good performance his superiors cross-referenced it to weaker units. For example, Carey's report on 'A' Company of 1/5 Sherwoods detailed how they repulsed a German bombing attack, launched in three waves, at 2 p.m. on 1 July. Horne treble scored the margin beside the report on 1/5 Sherwoods and added the comment "This shows what can be done". The rest of 1/5 Sherwoods came in for more critical comment. Horne was pleased to read that 'C' Company overran a trench mortar emplacement, but queried the retreat of a party when "the supply of grenades were exhausted". Horne annotated this "Rifles?"

Horne goes on to mention this specifically in his final remarks, on 17 July, when he writes that 139 Brigade "do not appear to have made much use of their rifles".[69] Horne also took exception to a report of 30 men of 1/5 Sherwoods retreating to Cavalry Trench – he obviously felt 30 men was a group which should have stood and fought. Some of Horne's other comments are less contentious. For example, in Carey's report on 1/6 Sherwoods there is reference to a large party of Germans advancing "over the top" along the railway cutting. Horne's marginal comment on this is "a Lewis gun would have closed in cutting". Tactically, this is correct but it ignores the fact that the British party concerned had been reduced to one NCO and four men.

Studies of 1914 make reference to the influence of the *Boys Own Paper*.[70] Some of Horne's comments seem to betray a sense of frustration that lone Lewis Gunners do not automatically set themselves up to hold back waves of German soldiers. The men's section officer, Second Lieutenant Dolley, had advanced down College Trench

65   Ibid., Thwaites, op.cit.
66   de Grave, *The War History of the Fifth Battalion The Sherwood Foresters*, p.119.
67   Ibid.
68   TNA: WO95/2663, 46th Division War Diary, Carey, ibid.
69   Ibid., Horne, Remarks 17 July 1917.
70   P. Parker, *The Old Lie: The Great War and the Public School Ethos* (1987).

and was believed by the men to have been killed or captured. One of the difficulties of this sort of fighting is that small groups of men rapidly become isolated from their colleagues. The urban landscape creates natural 'posts' in which a Lewis gun or bombing squad could be stationed. However, in the dark, or when movement is very restricted by enemy fire, during daylight these posts come to rely heavily on the natural leadership skills of perhaps one or two men. The rationale for retreat is constantly expressed in the exhaustion of particular weapons, e.g. grenades, or being outflanked i.e. "we did our best but someone / something else let us down".

This throws into question the training given to young officers and NCOs. Due to the psychological pressures of "going over the top" it was vital that subalterns led by example, however much they shared their men's fear. The difficulty arises, though, in fighting such as this at Lens, where junior officers are lost early in an action and are not available to stiffen resolve later. The myth of the German infantry as supermen was partly based on the psychological pressures faced by small groups of men left apparently isolated in hostile territory. This pressure bore on the British, as they were the attackers, more than on the Germans. The quality of Territorial NCOs is a theme that recurs throughout this work.

No men ever reported retreating from a less numerous enemy. We get into the Great War's version of Vietnam syndrome. For psychological reasons, the US Army had to say that Viet Cong dead were a multiple of US casualties. Similarly, every group withdrawing in the Great War sincerely believed that it was outnumbered or outflanked/surrounded. Apart from the elements of the 46th Division, 2 Sherwoods had to face these testing conditions. Everyone agrees that 2 Sherwoods lost direction and therefore crossed with the advance by 1/5 Sherwoods. Apart from noting the change in zero hour and Captain Robert's leadership, Horne's comment was that the junction with 1/5 Staffords should have been firmly established. This is, of course, correct but many senior commanders were also keen that battalions pushed forward to their objectives since care for one's flanks often proved self-defeating.

Horne was not prepared to accept that 2 Sherwoods affected the outcome since he argued that 139 Brigade still reached its objectives. Therefore, Horne focused on 46th Division and what he called its "want of determination and tenacity" from which, as we have seen, he saw 138 Brigade as an exception. Horne argued that the four-hour delay before the German counter-attack was ample time to prepare the captured trenches for defence; and that the absence of an artillery barrage, or evidence of stout resistance, reflects poorly upon 139 Brigade.

Horne was similarly scathing about large numbers of 1/5 North Staffords allowing themselves to be captured. His comments on Lamond have already been dealt with. Horne, himself a gunner, added that failure to know Aconite Trench was no longer in British hands hampered subsequent operations since it was believed an artillery barrage could not be used. Horne also asked Thwaites to give particular emphasis to his remarks on rifles, quoted above, and the "want of initiative and absence of push" amongst junior officers that he felt to be evident. It is interesting that Horne focused on officers rather than NCOs. Horne is surely correct in emphasising that once an attack was launched higher command temporarily lost control of the situation and that four hours should have been adequate time to prepare for a counter-attack.

In his written remarks to Thwaites, Horne acknowledged that 46th Division was 'very much' below establishment and fatigued but countered this by saying that the troops should have been buoyed up by the success of recent operations against the Germans. Horne's next three points on individual units have been included in the analysis given above. Horne then went on to deal with Thwaites' argument that the attack was too hurried. Here, Horne adopted classic rhetoric about the German withdrawal and the likelihood, given prompt follow up that the Germans would retreat to the Drocourt–Queant Line. Clearly, Horne had imbibed the official intelligence appraisal. That he applied it by pushing against the enemy's central defences in a major town rather than seeking to outflank it, says more about Horne than it does about the perennially over-optimistic intelligence summaries.

Unlike Montagu-Stuart–Wortley a year earlier, the final remarks revealed that Thwaites at least had a sympathetic superior in not taking things further. Horne went on to state that "I recognise that the division has made great progress under the command of Major General Thwaites". Given Horne's general criticisms this was hardly a ringing endorsement but it at least partially exonerated Thwaites. Thwaites would not be de-gummed but his replacement prior to the Hindenburg Line assault is foreshadowed in the remainder of Horne's judgement. This read:

> and have perfect confidence that both he and the infantry brigade commanders are doing their best to develop the fighting spirit amongst all ranks, and I look forward with confidence to the future.

Apart from the obligatory final phrase, the modern spin doctor would immediately recognise this as code for "they're not up to it". Thwaites's future lay elsewhere than in an operational command in the field, but unlike his predecessor he was not being pursued by Haig in a personal vendetta.

It has been remarked before in this study that the history of the Division reveals an official policy of assault/trench divisions. Given Horne's views, as expressed above, it should come as no surprise that they are not used for another major assault until September 1918, a period of 14 months in which new second–line territorial divisions would be blooded. The poor showing, in official eyes, of 137 Brigade leaves Brigadier General Campbell VC in command of it until 10 November 1918 after the triumph at the Hindenburg Line, when he received command of a Guards brigade. As a Guards officer, VC, and given the turnover of men ahead of him he might well have been promoted earlier but for the criticisms made of him by Horne.

Despite the more positive comments about his brigade, Brigadier General Rowley remained as commander of 138 Brigade for the duration of the war, though as he had only arrived on 16 June 1917 his total tenure was seventeen months. Thwaites's own field command career seems to have come to a standstill, and the energy and involvement he showed in his first year of command were not evident in the following year, if the war diary is a reliable guide.

Ironically, as with Brigadier General H.B. Williams at the Somme, it was Brigadier General Carey at the centre of controversy who was subsequently to achieve promotion. Having only been appointed to 139 Brigade on 27 May 1917, he could reasonably argue he was new and unlike Campbell he was not singled out for criticism. Unlike Campbell, Carey did benefit from the turmoil of March 1918 being appointed to command 14th (Light) Division in April 1918. Ironically, he was succeeded by Brigadier General P.R. Wood whose own tenure as a Major General had been brief and unsuccessful.

After months of hard fighting High Command's perceptions of the division crystallised around one dark morning. For 46th Division, 1 July was not a 'lucky' day, the entrails had been examined and the judges had found what they expected. The judgement by men safe from enemy fire must always seem harsh to those who had to fight in cellars and ruined houses. One might wonder why Thwaites or Carey did not put up a more stubborn defence of the latter's brigade. The answer may lie in a paragraph in Lieutenant Colonel Fawcus's report. Fawcus describes British troops falling back from Cornwall trench across "the racecourse" with "no artillery bombardment" and with only "desultory rifle fire". Thwaites may have forwarded Lamond's report on 1/5 South Staffords, rather than Fawcus's, since Lamond's actions were those under greater scrutiny, but he may also have wished to avoid giving Horne more ammunition than was necessary.

However, Thwaites did his best to defend Lamond whereas he accepted Horne's criticism of those who surrendered in Aconite Trench. To have forwarded Fawcus's report could have led to a full blown inquiry into the conduct of 1/6 Sherwoods, whom Carey reported as having established posts in Cornwall Trench. Given that the actions of 1/6 Sherwoods had been questioned at Gommecourt, Thwaites would hardly have wished to draw attention to them again. Like a modern day criminal barrister, Thwaites chose to argue only where his client's past record need not be discussed. His predecessor had been de-gummed at an Inquiry and although Thwaites' position was by no means so insecure his senior officers would have recognised that a full inquiry would leave none of them untarnished.

During the period covered by Horne's correspondence with Thwaites, 46th Division had an opportunity to reflect upon the experience it had gained at Lens. For a brief period of three weeks from 4 to 25 July, 46th Division was relieved from its role in the line. It is therefore important to see what 46th Division did to take advantage of this opportunity. Having been relieved by 2nd Canadian Division, 46th Division concentrated near Bruay and immediately re-organisation began. This process reflected the need to catch up with events since the last reorganisation. Battalions would take the opportunity to balance new men with older hands; and, Company commanders would review the roles of NCOs.

Following a period of sustained fighting, 46th Division had a number of gaps to fill. For example, 1/6 North Staffords increased from 562 to 608 Other Ranks during

July, helped by sustaining no casualties in July. The Adjutant of 1/5 Leicesters was very pleased with the 167 men received on 13 and 17 July describing them as "good lots" and noting many had previously served with other Leicester battalions.[71]

These new arrivals were probably amongst those inspected by Major General Thwaites on 11 July when he reviewed men arriving from the Divisional Depot. Accompanied by the GOC First Army, General Sir Henry Horne, Thwaites inspected 138 and 139 Brigades. Thwaites had inspected the men of 1/4 Lincolns and the rest of 138 Brigade the previous day. In line with the official policy of treating criticism confidentially, the 1/4 Lincolns record that Horne expressed pleasure at their recent performance and his confidence in the future.[72]

On 18 July, 1/4 Lincolns returned to the more serious task of completing the Divisional Musketry Test,[73] as did 1/8 Sherwoods, who gave special attention to musketry.[74] Whilst extra training was given to indifferent shots in 1/6 North Staffords on 23 July, there were extra incentives for men in 1/5 Leicesters.[75] When 1/5 Leicesters took their Divisional Musketry Course on 9 July there were twenty Francs on offer to the NCO or man who had the highest score over two courses. There was also a prize of fifty Francs for the ten men in any company with the highest combination score.[76] One can almost hear brigadiers being reminded to 'drop into conversations' with Horne, during inspections, the progress being made on musketry.

To help to give all this effort a focus Thwaites organised a Divisional Rifle Meeting for 19 and 20 July. This was also a high profile way of showing Horne that heed had been taken of his strictures. 1/5 Leicesters duly recorded their triumph in winning the GOC's Cup by a margin of 60 points. As well as gaining a large number of second and third places they could boast the winners of the Officers Revolver (Team) Competition, and in Corporal F. Spencer they had the Individual Aggregate Champion as well as the runner up, RSM Small.[77]

Second in the GOC's Cup were 1/8 Sherwoods, 139 Brigade, who came six points ahead of 1/6 South Staffords. This was largely due to the efforts of 'B' Company who won the Lewis Gun competition, as well as the Inter-Company snap-shooting and rapid-firing competitions. Additional points were won by the Officers team that won the knockout competition. The team consisted of the CO, Lieutenant Colonel Blackwell, as well as Captain Bedford and Second Lieutenants Martelli and Tomlinson. This team beat seventeen others whilst two men of the battalion, Corporal Hall and Private Colton, won the Individual Assault Pool.

71   References are to the battalion war diaries on dates indicated.
72   MLL: War Diary 1/4 Lincolns, 17 July 1917.
73   Ibid., 18 July 1917.
74   WSF: War Diary 1/8 Sherwood Foresters 23 July 1917.
75   SRM: War Diary 1/6 North Staffords, July 1917.
76   LRO: War Diary 1/5 Leicesters, 9 July 1917.
77   Ibid., 9 July 1917.

One would imagine there may have been some satisfaction for a lot of the men when Sergeant Clements, 137 Brigade HQ, scored 39 out of 42 to win the revolver pool by one point from three officers; Major Cooper DSO RA, Second Lieutenant Newbold, 137 Brigade HQ, and Lieutenant Colonel Fawcus MC, 1/5 North Staffords, were those who tied for second place. The Judging Distance competition was won by Brigadier General Wingfield-Stratford, the CRE, demonstrating that senior officers were involved. Two Staffords dominated the sniping competition with Corporal Hinsul of 1/6 South Staffords coming second to Private Newbold of 1/6 North Staffords. At the battalion level, musketry competitions offered prize money and it would appear this precluded officer participation. Typical prizes offered at the 1/5 North Stafford rifle meeting were five Francs for first place, three for second and two for third.

To aid physical fitness, Lieutenant Colonel Fawcus also organised an Athletics programme for 14 July. This featured such events as a wheelbarrow race, for warrant officers and sergeants, as well as an Inter-Company Pillow Fight. Presumably aware of his own relative age the Officers race was a "100 Yards Handicap". The prizes offered for the athletics events were the same as for musketry but there was no prize for the officers race. One could imagine that a certain amount of side-betting might have taken place.

1/4 Leicesters had held their athletics day on 11 July, after rifle practice in the morning. Much of the 'rest' period was spent by the Leicesters doing drill, including ceremonial drill ready for General Horne's inspection. This cannot be seen as directly contributing to enhanced combat performance. However, their sister battalion had a two day visit from the Divisional Gas Officer who went through respirator training.

Major Fielding-Johnson conducted the training for 1/4 Lincolns; Lieutenant-Colonel Yool was on leave. He emphasised musketry and smartness, holding several inspections. On 14 July Brigadier General Rowley inspected the battalion and was recorded as being "well pleased" with their bearing and appearance. The War Diary also recorded that the companies were "normally organised and not sized or equal-ized". Major Fielding-Johnson clearly impressed his superiors; he was made CO of 1/4 Leicesters a fortnight later.

1/6 Sherwoods did not record their training programme; except that they held their sports day in conjunction with the brigade machine gunners and trench mortar battery. The battalion's Adjutant focused on the many changes amongst the officers. With only one company participating in the most recent attack their only officer casu-alties were one Lieutenant and two subalterns. One officer returning to the battalion was Second Lieutenant K.H. Bond MC, who had been wounded (remaining on duty) on 23 April before being transferred to England on 7 June. When Captain Telson went on a month's leave, on 6 July, Bond was authorised to wear the badges of a Captain. Subsequently, on 24 August, he was promoted along with two Lieutenants.

Tolson's departure followed the return of Captain V.O. Robinson MC and Bar, who was initially given command of 'A' Company before being posted as second-in-command to 1/5 Sherwoods, at which point Bond took over 'A' Company.

The available evidence therefore suggests there was no rigid programme of training laid down even at Brigade level. However, Thwaites's decision to hold a Divisional Rifle Meeting guaranteed that all the battalions would focus a lot of time on musketry. Therefore we can conclude that there was a broad overall theme which related well to recent criticisms. General Horne always confined himself to praising the men for their efforts, indeed singling out 1/4 Lincolns for praise when he reviewed 138 Brigade. The several inspections held by Horne and Thwaites also guaranteed that a lot of time would be given over to traditional "spit and polish". Given the predominant view that Territorials in general, and especially 46th Division, were inferior this was no doubt viewed as time well spent. Nevertheless, it is difficult to see any evidence that this period of training contributed directly to the improved performance in September 1918.

However, in August 1917, the 46th Division was involved in supporting the Canadians in their assault on Hill 70. This involved Thwaites in meeting the Canadians to discuss combined machine gun shooting and subsequently, on 18 August, Thwaites attended a demonstration on machine gun barrages. Thus a key element of success in the "Hundred Days" was entering the learning curve.

During the operations in Lens the 46th Division had made some progress along the technical learning curve of the British Army. Through combat experience, and under encouragement from Army and Corps, the 46th Division was beginning to integrate a variety of weapons into its operational method. It had benefited from being connected to the learning curve of I Corps. Indeed the evidence here would suggest that I Corps should be seen as an innovative formation which was actively seeking to implement new ideas in the light of operational experience. However, the 46th Division was not seen to have enough "push" and therefore it was not to be placed in offensive sectors again until the autumn of 1918; it would remain in the middle lane of the learning curve.

8

Breaking the Hindenburg Line

The publication of the Imperial War Museum volume on 1918, complete with jacket cover depicting 137 Brigade on the banks of the St Quentin Canal, has firmly placed in the reading public's mind 46th Division's breaking of the Hindenburg Line as the epitome of the revival of British arms at the end of the war.[1] It also provides a central plank in the revisionist arguments in favour of a "learning curve". As Brian Bond argued, the "learning curve" has become an orthodoxy for military historians whilst public perceptions remain fixed on the Somme.[2] The breaking of the Hindenburg Line is important to revisionists because, unlike at Amiens, the key breakthrough was achieved by an ordinary English "county" division not one of the elite formations, such as the Canadian Corps, that had spearheaded the assault on 8 August.[3]

For the revisionists, the success of 46th Division is doubly important because it was the first time that any of their major operations had gone well. It is as though Port Vale had been drawn away to Manchester United in the FA Cup and had beaten United's first choice team by four goals to nil. Indeed, one of the reasons for selecting 46th Division for study in the first place was that the Hindenburg Line provided a clear contrast with earlier failures. The humiliating process of being subjected to a Board of Inquiry in July 1916 had marked 46th Division as a weak formation.

According to the SHLM Research Group, 46th Division could be ranked at 65th out of 66 in an order of merit of British divisions with only the 31st Division ("Thirty-worst") below them. The criteria for judging Divisions are inevitably arbitrary and struggle to take account of the varying tasks to which they were assigned. The tasks assigned to 46th Division in 1915 and 1916 were difficult and thankless, and make performance very difficult to assess. In March 1917, they performed more effectively

1   M. Brown, *The Imperial War Museum Book of 1918 – Year of Victory* (1998), dustcover.
2   B. Bond & N. Cave (eds), *Haig: A Reappraisal 70 Years On* (1999), p.xiv.
3   Unfortunately, Gordon Corrigan's focus on Patton means the 46th Division is not mentioned in *Mud, Blood and Poppycock*, (2003) p.394 and the date given is 27 September.

during the German retreat to the Hindenburg Line and were then given the opportunity of serving in I Corps in operations at Lens. Whilst their technical proficiency improved at Lens their "want of push" in the eyes of General Horne led to them being returned to the "slow lane" of the learning curve occupied by trench-holding divisions. Even so, the 46th Division noted the benefits of the leapfrogging system in a raid on 31 October 1917 and Thwaites also noted the benefits of counter-battery fire and the close support of the units of the RFC assigned to assist the 1/6 North Staffords.[4] Therefore the learning process was continuing whilst in the First Army sector but they were not specifically involved in offensive operations which form the central focus of the learning curve.

On 21 January 1918, the 46th Division, having been relieved by the 11th Division, prepared for a long period of training. Having undergone the general re-organisation of January 1918, the 46th Division returned to I Corps in early March and returned to the line by taking over the Cambrin sector. They remained there until 12 April when they were relieved by Canadians and became part of First Army reserve. They were then used to relieve 3rd Division in the Gore and Essars sector near Bethune, after the latter had stopped German attacks. The 46th Division remained in this sector until it was transferred to Fourth Army in September 1918.

On 5 September 1918 General Sir Henry Rawlinson (GOC Fourth Army) was concerned that he needed to rest the Australians and so he requested fresh troops to be released by GHQ. Rawlinson then noted that his chief anxiety was to get the railways "through on time".[5] Although Rawlinson commented on 8 September that he had "got nothing out of him", Haig had told Rawlinson that IX Corps would be found about 12 September with Lieutenant General Sir Walter Braithwaite to command it.[6] Two days later Rawlinson expressed his frustration that he could not "remain one and a quarter-hours by motor from my Corps Commanders" but that his new headquarters should be ready by the end of that week.

Meanwhile 46th Division was fighting alongside 55th Division on their old battle-grounds of November 1915. On 4 September 1/5 Leicesters followed up an attack by 55th Division on the previous day that had secured the flank for this assault. The barrage was set for 100 yards every two minutes, which was faster than we have seen or will see on other occasions, but the "Men kept very close and advanced in excellent order".[7] The battalion diary also noted that there was no German counter attack but that the Germans had left a note in many of the captured positions. This note is an interesting one in the light of the eventual German defeat. It read:

---

4   TNA: WO95/2664, War Diary 46th Division, November 1917, appendix.
5   CCC: War Journal of General Sir Henry Rawlinson.
6   Ibid
7   LRO: War Diary of 1/5 Leicesters, 4 September 1918.

Dear Tommy, You are welcome to all that we are leaving. When we stop, we
shall stop, and stop you in a manner you won't appreciate.
Fritz.[8]

Much of the sentiment is very similar to that expressed by Herbert Sulzbach in
his memoirs, *Four Years with the German Guns*, although he was normally facing the
French. Although Sulzbach was a Jew who later fled from the Nazis he was keen to
express his belief that the German Army was not defeated in 1918.

The reason for selecting the evidence that the 46th Division was fighting effectively
on 4 September is that this was two days after Major General William Thwaites's term
as GOC ended. 46th Division, in concert with 55th (West Lancashire) Division [TF]
and 19th (Western) Division [New Army] was performing creditably as part of First
Army. It would seem that Thwaites's reputation as a trainer was vindicated, but that
as demonstrated in the spring and summer of 1917 the process had been a slow one.
It is important to recognise that the improved performance at the Hindenburg Line
did not come out of the blue. This puts the arrival of the new GOC, Major General
Gerald Boyd, into context.

Until the day before, Boyd had been the Temporary Brigadier General commanding
170 Brigade, which formed part of 57th Division. Having served both in the ranks
and as an officer in South Africa, Boyd has some claim to be a ranker General. Boyd
had ended the South African campaign with both the DCM and the DSO, so his
personal bravery is not in doubt.[9] John Terraine notes that Boyd had failed to gain
entrance to the RMA Woolwich.[10] At the outbreak of the war, Boyd was serving as
Brigade Major of 11 Brigade and remained in that capacity under Brigadier General
A.G. Hunter-Weston until 23 February 1915. He then spent two months as GS02
to Major General R.C.B. Haking, GOC 1st Division. Boyd's steady promotion
continued when he left Haking to be GSO1 to Major General Charles Ross, GOC
6th Division. Boyd was to hold this position until 19 June 1916. Thus far Boyd had
served in increasingly important staff positions with three Regular divisions. Given
his combat record it is a little surprising that he did not receive an executive posting,
like Brigadier General H.B. Williams in 1916, to a frontline formation, but his being
wounded would probably account for this.

On 18 March 1915 Boyd was gazetted as a Major in the Royal Irish Regiment,
having previously been a Captain in the Leinster Regiment since 19 March 1904.
Even when he was given command of 46th Division his substantive rank was still that
of Major. An important aspect of the Great War that has not yet been analysed is the
policy of delaying substantive promotions even when the officer was acting two steps

8   LRO: War Diary of 1/5 Leicesters, 4 September 1918.
9   I am indebted to John Bourne for the details of Boyd's career, any opinions expressed are
     my own.
10   J. Terraine, *To Win A War* (1986), p.165.

Major-General G. Boyd, 46th Division commander from early September 1918. (Author's collection)

up. It would be interesting to know if it was a Treasury policy to reduce pension costs or a War ministry policy. If the latter, it was presumably to restrict claims on post-war ranks to Regular soldiers.

It is also surprising that as a Regular staff officer Boyd was not posted to one of the New Army divisions, which were often seeded with Regulars in staff positions. The only reasonable conclusion is that Boyd was not at this stage seen as a future divisional commander. As we saw, his contemporary, Brigadier General Williams, was given command of 137 Brigade before being moved on to command a Division. Boyd was to follow the same pattern in 1918. In 1916 Boyd was posted as BGGS on the staff of V Corps.

Derek Boyd's article in the Army Quarterly in 1976 quotes from the confidential assessment of Boyd at the end of the war: "[Boyd] can and does, breathe his own indomitable spirit into his men."[11] This is an interesting judgement as Boyd only held two combat commands, the longer of which only lasted ten weeks. Almost certainly

---

11   D. Boyd, *Army Quarterly* (October, 1976), p.447.

this report was influenced by the events at the Hindenburg Line. Otherwise, it is hard to understand why he was not promoted before, except for his being wounded.

Although Boyd's arrival came before 46th Division entrained on 12 September the orders for the divisional relief were received by the battalions on the same day.[12] The selection of the division for inclusion in IX Corps is interesting. If we just consider the events of 1918 then we need to review the employment of the other 68 divisions, excluding the Guards. For the purposes of this analysis the Dominion divisions are also excluded because they were subject to special political considerations and the Canadians had already been used at Amiens and it was the need to rest the Australians that had led to Rawlinson's request.

The 12th, 18th and 58th divisions had been employed at Amiens. Excluding Fifth Army, whose divisions had been badly mauled, a further ten divisions had been caught up in the March Offensive. Since 59th Division, amongst others, had been in both actions, this leaves 56 divisions. Excluding the divisions released to Fifth Army on 21 March 1918, leaves 42 divisions that had not been involved in any of the above operations. A further eight divisions had been used in blocking the German offensive by 26 March, leaving 34 "unused" Divisions. The 1st, 32nd and 46th Divisions that were assigned to IX Corps had in common that they had not been used in the above actions. The release of the Regular 1st and US 27th Divisions to Rawlinson, who already had the Australians and American units, probably meant that Haig selected the 46th Division from the remaining pool of nine New Army and nine first-line Territorial formations. The choice would have been further restricted by the imminent offensive by Second Army. Plumer's preparations were so far advanced that presumably it would have been inappropriate to withdraw units from Second Army.

Whilst it may be unjust, as the SHLM group suggested, to rank the 46th as 65th on the GHQ "rankings" it is clear that they were in the lowest quartile. On 19 September 1918, two weeks after Rawlinson's request, and Boyd's appointment as GOC, 46th Division was released to IX Corps from GHQ Reserve. It has been noted, in Chapter Four, that prior to the Somme there were a number of staff changes. Before Haig released 46th Division, Boyd lost his AA & QMG Brevet Lieutenant Colonel W.H.M. Freestun DSO (Somerset Light Infantry), who had been posted as Assistant Adjutant General Third Army. Freestun had served in that post since 17 July 1916 and therefore his tour with the Division almost exactly matched that of Thwaites. Freestun was replaced by Major R. Duckworth DSO (South Staffords). However, on 20 September, after 46th Division was released to IX Corps, Major S. Hays' sideways posting as GSO2 to 15th Division was cancelled. Perhaps Boyd had had time to intervene.

As CRA, Boyd inherited Brigadier General Sir S.H. Child Bt. DSO, who had replaced Brigadier General H.M. Campbell on 13 March 1918, when Campbell was wounded. Child had landed with 46th Division in France in 1915 as a Lieutenant

---

12   LRO: War Diary of 1/5 Leicesters,12 September 1918.

Colonel in command of 2nd North Midland Brigade, RFA. Child had been 46th Division's representative on the 1916 Inquiry. Child also deputised for Thwaites as GOC when Thwaites was on leave during the latter's final months in command. Boyd himself was not the only decorated ex-ranker on the staff of 46th Division. At this time the Deputy Assistant Adjutant General was Major H.N. Forbes MC DCM.

Therefore Boyd faced his task with a largely settled team and brigades whose unit composition, subject only to the January 1918 reduction to three battalions per brigade, had remained constant since their arrival in France three and a half years earlier.

On 22 September 1918, Rawlinson met his Corps commanders and noted in his diary that he had "finally settled" the "objectives and dispositions" of the Australian and American divisions.[13] The debate had centred on Lieutenant General Sir John Monash's [GOC Australian Corps] proposals regarding the best means of attacking the "tunnel" area.[14] Prior and Wilson explain in detail Rawlinson's disagreement with Monash regarding the possibility of a direct assault upon the canal.[15] From Rawlinson's journal it would appear that the success of the preliminary attacks on 18 September left him "satisfied that we can attack the main Hindenburg Line with success later on".[16]

All the available evidence confirms that Prior and Wilson are correct in asserting that on 29 September 1918 46th Division was to receive the heaviest level of artillery support of any British division in the Great War.[17] However, before the Division was to experience its greatest day the approaches had to be secured. On 27 September 1918 Rawlinson noted that:

> The 46th Division jumped their advance line overlooking the canal at Izel Eglise which makes their task much easier.[18]

Three days earlier, 138 Brigade had begun offensive operations centred on the village of Pontruet. The action at Pontruet is best known for the assault on Fagan Trench in which Lieutenant John Barrett of 1/5 Leicesters won the Victoria Cross. As his citation stated, he and his men had lost their way owing to the combination of darkness and a smoke barrage. Nonetheless, he led his men forward together with others he had collected, and despite being repeatedly wounded he co-ordinated his troops following the assault on the German machine guns. Although this initial attack on Pontruet was not successful, Lieutenant Barrett's gallantry ensured that all three brigades in 46th Division had a VC winner by the armistice.

13 CCC: War Journal of General Sir Henry Rawlinson.
14 Prior & Wilson, *Command on the Western Front*, pp.358 ff.
15 Ibid., p.366.
16 CCC: War Journal of General Sir Henry Rawlinson, 18 September 1918.
17 Prior & Wilson, *Command on the Western Front*, p.366.
18 CCC: War Journal of General Sir Henry Rawlinson, 27 September 1918.

Lieutenant J.C. Barrett VC. (Hills)

Even a short visit to Pontruet, today, reveals the difficulty of attacking at night. The village slopes down with intersecting streets often at right angles to the slope. It was difficult to keep a formed body of men together in any Great War assault especially at night. Given the inconsistent slopes and irregular breaks provided by the village, momentum could easily be achieved but only at the cost of cohesion. The Division was given little notice and officers of 1/5 Leicesters attended a conference at Brigade HQ at 4.00 p.m. on 22 September 1918. Since 138 Brigade had only relieved 45th and 14th Battalions AIF on 21 September, in trenches that the Australians themselves had only recently taken, knowledge about the topography of Pontruet was very limited.

Whilst the Brigade conference was being held, the Adjutant was proceeding on leave only to be recalled. It has been noted above that Boyd had been able to delay certain staff changes. It is perhaps reflective of a new style of leadership that 1/5 Leicesters did not go into the attack without the benefit of their Adjutant. As Priestley's account makes clear, the assault went well at first but eventually 1/5 Leicesters and supporting elements from 1/4 Leicesters were forced out of the village by the heavy weight of German reinforcements that fought their way into the village.[19] Nonetheless, the capture of one German officer and 136 other ranks puts this failure into context

19 R.E. Priestley MC, *Breaking the Hindenburg Line* (1919), pp.27-29.

compared with previous battles in which 46th Division had made no progress at all. Twelve of these prisoners fell to the two officers and forty men of 1/4 Leicesters who were engaged.

For those, including most officers, with memories of doing Latin "unseens" the Adjutant's battle report would have made stirring reading:

> the dead of the 5th Leicestershire Regt. Were lying with their rifles and bayonets still with them and with all wounds in front.[20]

The report also stated that Second Lieutenants Quint and Asher had penetrated to the farthest end of the village before being killed. On a small scale, therefore, the action shows that the front line can usually be overrun but that in this case the Germans responded in pre-Autumn 1916 manner by immediately launching a counter-attack. Priestley offers evidence from German prisoners that an attack was expected and that therefore strong reserves were at hand.[21] It should also be added that the darkness, both natural and contrived, which had hampered the Leicesters in keeping direction had also served to hide the deployment of German reserves from British artillery observers.

The plan to use two Stokes mortars in the assault is further evidence that by late 1918 the British army was integrating tactical supporting firepower even into small-scale assaults. Nevertheless, it is also true that Pontruet suggests that the German units at the Hindenburg Line were not a spent force prior to the assault. It might, of course, be argued that the troops selected for the counter-attack were chosen because they were the best available.

With regard to the tactical evolution of the British Army it is interesting to note that ten days earlier 1/5 Leicesters had been practising "field firing" and "fire and movement".[22] The latter represents a major step towards delegating the initiative to individuals in a tactical situation. It would also have been particularly appropriate to the assault on Pontruet where the ground was largely unreconnoitred. Putting the emphasis on fire and movement also assumes that morale is good. The improvement in the Division is also shown in that they had only practised the "blob" formation for the first time on 10 September 1918.[23] Interestingly, it was described as requiring "eight paces between men in both directions" and that this was as "introduced by GOC". Boyd himself was therefore part of the learning curve as we have seen with Thwaites. Improved tactics and morale may both be linked to the GOC; the GOC had visited

20   LRO: War Diary of 1/5 Leicesters, September 1918.
21   Priestley, *Breaking the Hindenburg Line*, pp.27-29.
22   LRO: War Diary of 1/5 Leicesters, September 1918.
23   Ibid., 10 September 1918.

1/5 Leicesters on 7 September and the war diary recorded that before addressing all the officers Boyd was introduced to them.[24]

The detailed battle report submitted by 1/5 Leicesters is largely a narrative of the action. In most cases the number of enemy machine guns is cited to explain the level of casualties and therefore the inability to hold the ground gained. In addition, there is a regular refrain that ammunition frequently ran out. By 9.00 a.m. movement was too visible to be practicable and therefore requests for further supplies of bullets and grenades went unanswered. Nonetheless, in a concluding paragraph, the report offers two possible ways in which success might have been achieved. Having noted that the parties could not keep in touch at night in a rambling 700 yard long village, the report goes on to say that they would have concentrated on the rest of the village had they known the eastern end was empty. Hindsight is of course infallible but this problem highlights the costs of such rapidly arranged assaults.

The second suggestion is that success might have come through the Sherwood Foresters, on the battalion's right, being swung round to conform. The report states that a party of the Sherwoods had advanced into the East of Pontruet but had been unable to contact "C" Company of 1/5 Leicesters. As a result the officer in charge of the Sherwoods had withdrawn his party to their original positions.[25] The war diary of 1/6 Sherwoods conflicts with this. It states that "B" Company, which was assisting in the occupation of Pontruet, was withdrawn under orders from Division. This view cannot be substantiated by reference to divisional records.[26]

The report of 1/5 Leicesters also mentions that the troops engaged were able to attract the attentions of a tank operating with 1st Division, but that it was soon knocked out. This is further evidence that lone tanks in close order fighting were not a decisive weapon.

The renewed focus on 1918 in Great War scholarship has drawn attention to the considerable casualties incurred in 1918. The report by 1/5 Leicesters gives their casualties, after subsequent inspection of Pontruet, as 166 including four missing. The price of leadership is evident in that four officers were killed and eight wounded, including six Second Lieutenants (three killed and three wounded). Amongst the 31 other ranks killed, two sergeants are named. With 114 men wounded, the dead amount to approximately 20 per cent of the casualties amongst the other ranks. Although the ratio at Gommecourt had been over 50 per cent, Pontruet helps to explain the heavy cost of 1918 since during the "100 days" small actions like this were being mounted almost every day.[27]

---

24   LRO: War Diary of 1/5 Leicesters, 7 September 1918.
25   Ibid., appendix for September 1918: Report on Operations Round Pontruet, 24 September, 1918.
26   WSF: War Diary of 1/6 Sherwood Foresters, 24 September 1918.
27   Heavy casualties were sustained during the various German offensives earlier in the year.

On 25 September 1918 1/4 Leicesters recorded approximately 1,000 artillery rounds of mixed calibre falling on their positions. This early morning "hate" was responded to in kind when the British artillery harassed the Germans with a mixture of gas and high explosive at 5.00 a.m. on 26 September. The divisional war diary noted that a mustard gas attack would be delivered between 10.00 p.m. on 26 September and 6.00 a.m. on 27 September "subject to wind".[28] The ready availability of large stocks of weapons was increasing the lethality of warfare and is further evidence of the significance of economic mobilisation in Britain, and of the importance of the naval blockade of Germany. British ammunition production could be achieved without diverting significant levels of nitrates from agriculture.

Meanwhile, on 25 September a Divisional conference was held at Boyd's Headquarters. The outcome was issued, classified as "Very Secret", on 26 September 1918 as "46th Division G114/4, Operation C".[29] One interesting aspect of these orders is that they contain handwritten amendments and are described at the top as "(Based on notes of a conference held at Divisional Headquarters, 25 Sept: 1918)". This and their description as "Instructions No. 2" suggests Boyd incorporated amendments proposed at the meeting. This also ties in with Priestley's oblique reference to "the first Divisional Order" being issued on 25 September.[30] It would be to Boyd's credit that he listened to the views of his experienced formation commanders. The original document stated that on the night prior to the assault 138 and 139 Brigades would be in the line with 137 Brigade in the rear. The plan then assumed that on the night of the assault 137 Brigade, on a three battalion front, would move through the Brigades in the line, and would form up on the jump off line ready to follow the barrage. In proposing a plan similar to that used by the Fourth Army at Amiens, Boyd appears to be trying to copy success. However, this proposal was not adopted.

Since this was Boyd's first assault as a divisional commander he would naturally look to implement trusted methods. He had already introduced 46th Division to the "blob"[31] formation, now he was outlining how success had been achieved at Amiens. Since they were part of Fourth Army he was unlikely to be criticised for following Rawlinson's approach. Nevertheless, he appears to have altered his plans following consultation with his brigade commanders. The amended instructions make it clear

---

28   TNA: WO95 2666, War Diary 46th Division, September 1918, Appendix 47.
29   Ibid., September 1918, Appendix 46.
30   Priestley, *Breaking the Hindenburg Line*, p.30.
31   Although there is no simple definition of a "blob", the best way to describe it is as a company advancing in a dispersed formation of platoons with each platoon dispersed in sections in a diamond formation. Each platoon's advance would be led by a rifle section with a rifle grenadier and machine gun section to either flank and slightly behind. The rear of the diamond would be the command section. Upon encountering resistance the rifle section would attempt to pin down the enemy whilst the rifle grenadiers and machine gunners sought to move to the flanks and suppress and destroy the point of resistance.

that 137 Brigade was to be in the line prior to the assault. Presumably, it was felt that 137 Brigade's presence would not betray their intentions, in the way that the Canadians would have done, even though the Staffords had taken a lead part in every divisional assault. Therefore, little surprise would have been gained at the expense of considerable difficulty and risk. As a Guards officer, and a VC, Brigadier General J.V. Campbell would have been a difficult man to gainsay, especially as Boyd's own tenure as a brigade commander had been so short.

The original instructions specified that 138 and 139 Brigades would each have a one battalion frontage. Thus 137 Brigade would have had to pass through three fairly closely packed formations before reaching the jump off line. The amended instructions, however, did retain the plan for each of the supporting brigades to advance on a one-battalion frontage. Given the introduction of the "blob" formation, and the perennial difficulties in retaining cohesion during an assault, it was probably thought to be easier to allow each of the supporting brigades to follow through behind each other. With the reduction of infantry brigades from four battalions to three, assaulting on a two battalion frontage became problematic as the brigade had only one battalion left, which it had either to spread thinly or to have one assaulting battalion unsupported. As the attack on the Hindenburg Line was against well-prepared positions, it was logical to use the whole of the assaulting brigade in the initial assault and to concentrate rather than diffuse the thrust of the following formations.

We have already noted that Rawlinson wanted to be close to his immediate subordinates. Boyd, too, said that he wanted all three Brigade Headquarters to "be together". However, this bears a hand-written amendment "if suitable accommodation can be found". There was little time to establish new Brigade HQ's and it may have been felt that the disruption would outweigh any improvement in communications. Since the orders for 138 and 139 Brigades to advance were to be given directly by the GOC it can be seen that Boyd was trying to be in a good position to co-ordinate the three brigades. The uncertainty about the outcome, against such apparently strong prepared positions, is also evident in Appendix 50 to the Divisional Diary for September 1918, which refers to responsibilities for reinforcement.

The instructions state that if 137 Brigade "having crossed the Canal, are being outfought through lack of support" [emphasis in original] then the lead battalions of the supporting brigades were to advance to reinforce 137 Brigade, "on their own initiative and without waiting for orders". 46th Division and its commander appear to be under no illusions that they have been assigned to kick in the front door. Boyd's instructions are clear that he retained the authority to commit 138 and 139 Brigades unless 137 Brigade were successful in crossing the canal. This additional instruction reflects a clear appreciation that if the brigade commanders were in contact with him (i.e. at the rear of their formations) then tactical control would inevitably devolve upon the officer commanding the lead battalion in each supporting brigade. This order therefore has a Nelsonian element, under which any officer leading his men forward can say that he conformed to his general's instructions whilst anyone holding back may be concerned that he will be judged to lack initiative. By providing a presumption in favour of attack Boyd was taking account of the all too frequent breakdowns in communications and the 46th Division's reputation as a 'dud'.[32]

Since the Staffords, in this scenario, would be across the canal the likely position of the lead support battalions would be the old German trenches to the west of the canal. If the German defensive barrage came down it would be on this line and therefore 46th Division would face the same problem it had so cruelly faced at Gommecourt. This time it was planned to give the Division massive artillery support, so hopefully at least some reinforcement of the Staffords would be possible as long as there was no hesitancy –hence the relevance of Boyd's orders.

The need to achieve the rapid establishment of a bridgehead is also evident in Appendix 56, where it is laid down that for the first one hour and forty minutes that the barrage will go forward at 100 yards every two minutes. This rapid pace was to be balanced by the weight of the barrage. Boyd's Instructions No. 2 stated that there would be one field gun for every 25 yards and "considerable depth of barrage during the earlier stages."[33] Ironically, Prior and Wilson do not quote this figure in comparison with their earlier calculations for Rawlinson's battles. Their calculation for Neuve Chapelle is one gun for every six yards, which they compare favourably with Loos.[34] Prior and Wilson also quote a figure of 300 lbs per yard of trench for the original plan for the Somme, which matches that for Neuve Chapelle.[35] By way of comparison they rely on Priestley in suggesting that 126 field gun shells were landing per minute on every 500 yards of trench. They also assert that this intensity was sustained for the entire eight hours of the attack.[36]

Whilst it might be tempting to rely upon Priestley, it has to be recognised that he is treating all shells as the same. The records of 46th Division's A & Q Branches detail the ammunition expended by the Division on 29 September 1918.[37] Clearly, these figures do not include the ammunition used by the Corps Heavy Artillery or the brigades of Royal Field Artillery detailed to support the attack. The records of 46th Division show that the amount of shrapnel fired exceeded that for high explosive, if we look at field guns only. The standard 18-pounders fired 27,148 shrapnel shells to 22,873 high explosive ones. In addition, some 13-pounders guns were brought into action to deliver 2,549 shrapnel and 2,182 high explosive shells. Thus the total was 29,697 shrapnel and 23,055 high explosive shells. Shrapnel accounted for approximately 58 per cent of field gun fire, excluding smoke. The 18-pounder guns also expended 8,126 smoke shells, which means that shrapnel represented under half the total shellfire.

---

32 Griffith, *Battle Tactics of the Western Front*, p.80.
33 TNA: WO95 2666, War Diary 46th Division, September 1918, Appendix 56.
34 Prior & Wilson, *Command on the Western Front*, p.113.
35 Ibid., p.113.
36 Ibid., p.374.
37 TNA: WO95/2666, War Diary 46th Division, September 1918.

Given the strength of the Hindenburg Line defences this can be explained by the focus being upon suppressing the defenders rather than attempting to destroy the extremely strong emplacements. The Corps artillery support, utilising 60-pounders, would have provided the main battering ram and therefore the balance of high explosive shell. Evidence of this can be found in the destruction of the wall on the inner bank.[38] Secondly, the Divisional assault had the support of trench mortars. To support and secure his flanks Boyd planned to send trench mortars forward. He allocated two to 1/6 North Staffords on the left and four to 1/6 South Staffords on the right. Although Boyd had the Regular 1st Division on his right flank the South Staffords had to deal with Bellenglise. Whilst these light mortars would accompany the infantry the heavy mortars were to be part of the bombardment. Both elements are developments of the approach used at Gommecourt. The 6" trench mortars fired 520 bombs but we lack evidence on their use. Such heavy mortars were normally targeted on strongpoints. The allies had captured plans of the defences so it would have been possible to use the mortars to good effect. The breakdown of ammunition expended by the 4.5" trench mortars is more revealing. In total, 9,721 4.5" mortar bombs were fired, of which 8,080, over 80 per cent, were high explosive. Given that 46th Division had captured a commanding line and that plans of the defences were available such a volume of fire would have had a devastating impact. The 4.5" mortars were also able to target the Germans with 516 gas bombs. This is further evidence of the British Army applying the lessons learned from previous battles. The mortar batteries also fired 1,125 smoke bombs. Combined with the 8,126 fired by the 18-pounders this gives a total of 9,251. This represents approximately one-eighth of the shells and bombs expended by the Divisional artillery. Individual accounts give mixed responses to the use of smoke, leading to its efficacy being questioned.

Some caution therefore needs to be applied to Prior and Wilson's figures, which quote Priestley.[39] Their figure is 50,000 shells for every 500 yards of front to the depth of the Divisional objectives. As one-eighth of the shells were smoke it would be appropriate to reduce this figure to 43,750. This is, however, a massive level of support. For possibly the first time in its career, 46th division was being given appropriate, if not generous, support. Lieutenant General Braithwaite had given 46th Division the task least likely to bring glory but he had given them enough support for it to be feasible.

After 46th Division stormed the canal, 137 Brigade posed with lifebelts and this was the image reproduced in the newspapers, thereby focusing attention on the infantry. In emphasising the role of the Fourth Army Major General Sir Archibald Montgomery stressed the artillery support given to 46th Division.[40] Montgomery specifically refers to the use of the first consignment of "BB" gas shells, 30,000, being concentrated

38   Prior & Wilson, *Command on the Western Front*, p.373.
39   Ibid., p.374.
40   Major General Sir Archibald Montgomery, *The Story of the Fourth Army in the Hundred Days* (1920), p.153.

upon German HQs.[41] It is fair to comment that literature on "the 100 days" still puts much more emphasis upon technique than upon the massive amounts of gas used. For example, Harris emphasises "fog" and "morale".[42] In reality, Montgomery was applying the lessons of the German use of gas in March 1918. Further evidence of the 'learning curve' can be seen in Montgomery's reference to 'normal artillery preparation'[43] from 6.00 a.m. on 27 September, consisting of counter-battery, harassing and wire cutting. Whilst the latter would have been included in 1916 the former reflects the application of lessons learnt in 1917.

Priestley's map[44] indicates an assault frontage of approximately 2000 yards and Montgomery states[45] that 46th Division had the support of 1,044 field guns and howitzers plus 593 heavy guns, including four long range siege batteries, or 1,637 guns in total. Therefore there were approximately four guns per five yards to be assaulted. However, if we consider the level of fortifications involved then in terms of yards of trench the figures would have to be reduced significantly. The map used by Fourth Army, and reproduced, in part, in *Topography of Armageddon*, shows how complicated the defence systems were.[46] Chasseaud also reproduces the artillery plan for the 46th Division assault for the six Field Artillery Brigades providing the infantry barrage. As the canal's course arced it was reached during the 10th, 11th and 12th 'lifts', which underscores the need for further supporting fire to ensure the German defences were suppressed whilst all the troops reach the canal. For a more sophisticated solution to such problems see the account of Audigny in October 1918.

In total, the artillery plan laid down 40 lifts punctuated by four protective barrages as well as a fifth protective barrage to support 46th Division once they had reached their final Green Line. Each of the lifts was a constant 100 yards, but the pace of 100 yards every two minutes to the canal was reduced to 100 yards every four minutes, once 137 Brigade moved beyond its initial objectives. This reflects Boyd's concern, discussed above, to ensure that 137 Brigade were reinforced if they found themselves heavily engaged once they were beyond the canal. The standard pace of four minutes per 100 yards was then applied to the assaults by 138 and 139 Brigades, once they had leapfrogged 137 Brigade. These details should be used to evaluate those given by Griffith since they make the entry on the 46th Division look less anomalous as the speed in phase 3 would be more in line with general practice.[47]

Given the weight and precision of the artillery effort involved in the assault on the Hindenburg line it is natural that it has drawn a lot of attention. This is especially true for Prior and Wilson whose central thesis is based around the correct application of

41   Ibid., p.153
42   J.P.Harris, *Amiens to the Armistice* (1998).
43   Ibid.
44   Priestley, *Breaking the Hindenburg Line*, endpapers
45   Montgomery, *The Story of the Fourth Army in the Hundred Days*, p.153
46   P. Chasseaud, *Topography of Armageddon* (1991), p.197.
47   Griffith, *Battle Tactics on the Western Front* op.cit., Table 9 on p.146.

overwhelming artillery superiority. If a criticism of their approach to the Hindenburg line can be made it is that since it fits so neatly into their thesis (which they regard Amiens as demonstrating) they have not shaded the picture to set the artillery in context. Harris points to not only the fog which helped to shroud the advance of 137 Brigade, but the rain on the preceding days, which prevented the German air force from identifying and disrupting the assault. Better weather would undoubtedly have benefited the Germans more than the British, given that the British had the plans of the German defences, whereas the Germans needed to monitor the British. However, given the opening of the artillery offensive on the night of 26 September the Germans had ample warning of the assault. Since this was not a Bruchmüller-style hurricane bombardment, the German batteries should have been able to begin identifying British batteries in advance of 29 September. Indeed, in 1916 such notice had been used against the British to notable effect at the Somme.

A key to the way in which the British dominated the German artillery was the use of a night gas bombardment on 26-27 September. This move to disable the German guns before opening a 36-hour artillery assault can be likened to the modern priority given to destroying enemy tracking stations before opening an air assault.

The use of a longer period of artillery preparation is also noteworthy because it emphasises the extent to which the British were not slavishly following the Bruchmüller model. It would seem that the British recognised that there was no real benefit here regarding surprise. The Fourth Army had advanced since Amiens and now faced the last serious set of entrenched positions between it and the Franco-German border. Unless the British were to accept that the war could not be won in 1918 they were bound to attack. Loos in 1915 had extended into October, whilst the battle of the Somme (1916) and First and Third Ypres had dragged on into November, which was the same month as the Cambrai Offensive.

In this context the surprise element was 137 Brigade's use of lifebelts etc. to launch themselves across the canal. A classic solution to the problems faced by Fourth Army at the Hindenburg Line would have been to outflank and simply use 46th Division to pin the enemy to his front. The provision of massive artillery support made it possible that, not only would the Germans be outflanked, but also that the front door might be kicked in. The Germans might therefore have expected the 46th Division simply to seize the West bank of the canal whilst other divisions sought to outflank the Hindenburg line as a whole. At Gommecourt 46th Division's flanks had been open on one side, whilst on the other the 56th Division had been partially successful. Placed in the centre of Braithwaite's assault, the 46th Division not only had the Americans to its left but also the Regular 1st Division to its right. The latter achieved all of its objectives and thus secured 46th Division's flank, especially at Bellenglise.

One of the other key factors in the assault upon the Hindenburg Line is the use made of machine guns. As will be shown later in regard to other battles the use of machine guns as short range "artillery" was becoming an integral part of offensive operations. As well as its own machine gun battalion the Division was to have the assistance of 6 Battalion MGC and 100 Battalion MGC. Their work was to be arranged by IX

The canal at St Quentin near Bellenglise. (Milne)

Corps with the objective that they should barrage the canal bank.[48] In the event the support came from the 100 Battalion MGC and 2 Battalion (Life Guards) of the Guards Machine Gun Regiment. The Life Guards mounted two groups totalling seven batteries of machine guns.

For the first thirteen to fifteen minutes the Life Guards were to maintain a steady rate of fire of 250 rounds per minute. This period would cover 137 Brigade from when it left the trenches to when the flank elements of 1/6 North Staffords and 1/6 South Staffords reached the canal banks on the left and right respectively. The fact that the troops were attacking into a salient would leave 1/5 South Staffords short of the canal at this point. However, the problems associated with not assaulting in a straight line would be evident to those who remembered the Hohenzollern Redoubt. The integration of the machine guns is also evident in that they moved from their first task to their second task after between five and eight minutes, that is when the flanking infantry were scheduled to be about half way to the canal.

Meanwhile, 100 Battalion MGC were disposed in three groups and given the job of laying down variable rates of fire. Group No. I was assigned two tasks – one of which required firing 250 rounds per minute for five minutes alternating with 150 rounds per minute for ten minutes. It was charged with maintaining this effort for five and a half-hours. This coincides with the ending of Protective Barrage B, that is the

48   TNA: WO95/2666, 46th Division War Diary, 23 September 1918.

start of the assaults by 138 and 139 Brigades. Thus this barrage is designed to limit the ability of the Germans to reinforce their forces west of the canal or counter-attack the hoped-for bridgehead on the eastern side. Group No. I's other task is to maintain a low rate of fire (twenty rounds per minute) on selected points.

Group No II of 100 Battalion MGC's work was, initially, like the Life Guards, to support the assaulting troops with a 250 round per minute curtain. It was then tasked to move to Protective Line A, thirteen minutes ahead of the guns, presumably again with the intention of interdicting reinforcements. For this curtain it was to fire 250 rounds per minute for two minutes, which would have a devastating impact on any German units moving forward to counter-attack. Their fire was then to reduce to 150 rounds per minute for the next ten minutes before dropping to fifty rounds a minute for the subsequent half-hour. This then left 43 minutes of firing at twenty rounds per minute. This latter rate of fire would therefore be from $Z + 57$ minutes, by which time it was planned that 137 Brigade would have had 29 minutes to consolidate along its initial objective line with the added benefit of Protective Barrage A. No. III group of 100 Battalion MGC was to open fire at $Z + 30$ i.e. two minutes after 137 Brigade were due to begin consolidating their initial objectives. Its task was to aid consolidation by laying down a curtain of fire of five minutes at 250 rounds per minute and ten minutes at 150 rounds per minute. This was to be followed by 30 minutes at fifty rounds per minute and a further 25 minutes at twenty rounds per minute. This level of planning can reasonably be deduced to demonstrate that by late 1918 the integration of heavy machine guns into assaults was very advanced.

The substitution of Lewis guns for Vickers within battalions gave the British army greater mobility. It has also provided students with a headline figure of only two machine guns in 1914 compared to 32 per battalion in 1918 with which to measure the British Army's advance, and the impact of economic mobilisation. The use made of the Heavy Machine Guns at the Hindenburg Line demonstrates that the headline figure conceals a major difference between 1914 and 1918. IX Corps' plan integrated lessons learnt elsewhere and this included the protection afforded to the infantry by brigaded heavy machine guns.

The fact that Boyd's orders explicitly refer to Corps organisation provides a clear instance of the learning curve in practice. As has been seen above, Thwaites had raised the general performance of 46th Division by the time of his departure. Boyd brought in new formations for the infantry to advance in, and the Corps created a more successful environment in which to implement Boyd's plans. Terraine describes the detailed planning of the attack as a model for 1944.[49]

This planning extended to Boyd's own machine gun battalion. Boyd's aim can be summarised in his own words:

---

49   J. Terraine, *White Heat* (1982), p.323.

The 46th Bn., M.G. Corps, will closely support the infantry, working in two Groups, and moving from one fire position to another, so that at least one Group is always in action supporting the advance.[50]

Boyd also ordered that one company be in close support of the infantry when the final objective was reached. He added that the rest of the companies would be disposed back to Knobkerry Ridge, which lay beyond 137 Brigade's objectives, so they would be within 2,000 yards of the Line to be reached by the Division. The commanding officer of 46 Battalion MGC was to have his headquarters[51] at the advanced Divisional Headquarters. Boyd's decision to have his brigade commanders close at hand has already been noted. Lieutenant Colonel B.H.H. Mathew-Lannowe DSO, commanding 46 Battalion MGC, had arranged for two supply tanks to advance bringing supplies of small arms ammunition, water, picks and shovels as well as 30 spare barrels as Boyd had ordered that dumps must be created as soon as possible to avoid drawing upon supplies carried across by the gunners themselves. Presumably, Boyd was trying to ensure that momentum was maintained. As in later engagements, Mathew-Lannowe's orders stressed the need for assigned units from the Life Guards and 100 Battalion MGC to protect the flanks of the assault and engage any forces threatening the infantry's advance.

The supporting barrages were to be fired by the attached units because 46 Battalion MGC were to advance to assigned points to support the infantry. Mathew-Lannowe's orders stressed the need to ensure that the infantry were sufficiently clear before opening fire on specified lines. This makes it clear that the machine gunners were to be firing obliquely i.e. at unseen targets. It is also clear from the orders that the other units were subordinated to 46 Battalion MGC, thus ensuring greater operational cohesion. Reflecting why he held the DSO, and definitely in the GHQ spirit, Mathew-Lannowe instructed his men:

The task of the sections which advance will be to consolidate the territory captured, to assist the infantry in their advance, and to seize every opportunity of inflicting loss on the enemy.

As if this was not clear enough he went on to add that they were to "handle their sections with the greatest boldness and determination". He then went on to stress that the plan indicated good positions but that "the actual placing of the guns will be left entirely to the 'officers' on the spot" and that they should "dispose them according to the tactical situation and the needs of the infantry".

It is therefore clear that he is encouraging the use of initiative – a tone that has already been noted in Boyd's orders. By putting the term officers in inverted commas

50   TNA: WO95/2666, 46th Division War Diary, 26 September 1918.
51   TNA: WO95/2679, 46 Battalion MGC, 28 September 1918.

he is also making it clear that authority is being delegated, in effect, to whoever is in charge of the gun. Given the inevitable problems of command and control he is trying to establish that "every opportunity of inflicting loss" on the enemy in support of the infantry is the over-arching consideration. It is also interesting to see machine gunners refer to infantry battalions as 'the infantry'. The awareness of being in a separate Corps is clearly present. Boyd also said that he would get a tot of rum per man across as soon as possible. Given the early start and cold water this would no doubt be appreciated and reflects Terraine's view on the depth of planning, cited above.

Another order may have played a role in the prompt discovery of the intact Riqueval Bridge as Boyd instructed them that "The positions of existing bridges and dams are probably the most suitable places to cross".[52] Whilst this could not prevent the Germans blowing the bridge it helped ensure that 137 Brigade would pay it an early visit. None of the surviving material indicates whose idea it was to use lifebelts. The A & Q Branch records are silent on the matter even though they would presumably have had to arrange the requisitions.

The planning had been done with great thoroughness and now it was time to test it in battle. As the men of 1/5 Sherwoods advanced under cover of darkness to their starting positions they encountered artillery, cavalry, tanks and infantrymen of British, American and Australian units. Nevertheless, by 4.00 a.m. they were able to inform Brigade HQ that they were in position.[53] For the men of 1/5 Leicesters 28 September had not been a good day. At 6.00 a.m. the Germans had hit the battalion area with mustard gas. Although 'C' under "Banwell" moved out promptly 'B' company was not convinced of the problem and only departed two hours later by which time over 30 cases had been sent to hospital and by the morning of 29 September 'B' company's ranks had become severely depleted.[54] Therefore, it was decided to make 'B' company the support unit for the battalion's operations on 29 September.[55]

In Appendix V, where Priestley gives the order of battle for 46th Division on 29 September 1918, he lists the Company Commanders as including Lieutenant A.E. Broadribb MC.[56] According to the battalion diary, however, Broadribb had gone to the QM Stores ' for a rest'.[57] In fact Broadribb's departure to the transport lines was part of a major reorganisation of the battalion on 25 September following the action at Pontruet, and the subsequent relief of 1/5 Leicesters by 1/8 Sherwoods at 2.30 a.m. that morning. According to the diary, Lieutenant A.E. Hawley, whose company were to suffer from the gas, had only commanded 'B' since 25 September. Priestley lists Hawley as a Captain, which anticipates his subsequent promotion.[58] Priestley

52   TNA: WO95/2666, 46th Divisional Orders.
53   de Grave, *The War History of the Fifth Battalion The Sherwood Foresters*, p.176.
54   LRO: 1/5 Leicesters War.Diary, 28 September 1918.
55   Ibid., 28 September 1918.
56   Priestley, *Breaking the Hindenburg Line*, p.189.
57   LRO: 1/5 Leicesters War Diary, September 1918.
58   Ibid., 25 September 1918.

makes no mention of Captain Petch, who was placed in charge of 'A', nor Lieutenant S. Corah, who took over command of 'D' Company. Petch's appointment reflects the fortunes of war, since he had been left with the battle detail prior to the action.[59] Priestley also lists Captain J.W. Thomson, even though he had been killed on 24 September leading 'B' Company HQ in charging three German machine guns at Pontruet. Although they overcame two of the guns the third one remained. The official report on the battalion's operations said that Captain Thomson was shot through the head whilst attending to the Signal Corporal who had been hit previously. Since only two of this group were able to return to the British lines, this offers some explanation for the slow response of 'B' on 28 September as its "management team" was very new.

The fourth company commander listed by Priestley is Captain Brooke MC, who had been wounded twice on 24 September. Brooke had been leading the attack on a German machine gun position on the Saint Helene-Bellenglise road at the time. The battalion report notes that he was "carried out" after being wounded a second time. His name heads the list of wounded in the battalion diary. Elements of Brooke's 'D' Company were criticised by the battalion diarist for not getting on top of the ground but preferring to work up the trenches. However, the same report says the stiff resistance from four German machine guns, supported by grenades and a trench mortar was "unexpected". Brooke became a casualty after his two junior officers, Lieutenant Sloper and Second Lieutenant Buckley, were wounded. The enemy post was eventually rushed by 'D' Company under the command of Acting Company Sergeant Major Marston. The resilience of the company in surviving this high loss of officers reflects the changing calibre of 46th Division by 1918. The contrast with the alleged "lack of push" in 1916 is marked.

Recent research on 1918 has emphasised that British losses in 1918 were heavy. The research has not impacted on public perceptions like the battles of the Somme or Passchendaele. The attack by 'D' Company draws parallels with the 1944-45 campaign, in that advances are made but casualties are constant. The battalion lost 35 killed, but as the prelude to a great victory it was hardly going to lead to a Court of Inquiry. For those who are looking for indications of the state of the German army in late 1918 then the evidence is mixed. It is facile to say it all relied upon machine gunners. 'D' Company were eventually able to overrun the machine gun post but not the supporting trenches. Defensive firepower was still in the ascendant in small actions and some German defenders could be resolute. Major actions in which artillery was effectively deployed shifted the balance away from the defenders.

The resilience of 1/5 Leicesters as they approached 29 September was not based on a naïve 1914 enthusiasm but on the determination bred by a combination of discipline and experience. The diarist records that fog reduced visibility for 1/5 Leicesters to five yards and says that Lieutenant Colonel Griffiths overcame this by closing the

---

59   Ibid., 22 September 1918.

battalion up and leading them by compass. Even the Adjutant was temporarily lost, rejoining the battalion at 10.15 a.m., 65 minutes prior to the jump off.

Ahead of them 1/5 South Staffords had to modify their operational orders for 29 September due to losses sustained in confused fighting, with Germans occupying trenches not cleared by 138 Brigade.[60] During 27-28 September they lost one officer and two men killed. In addition, eleven men were wounded and two were reported missing; the Germans had actually penetrated the British trenches at one point. These spoiling attacks certainly suggest some German units were not entirely passive. Meanwhile, 1/1 Monmouths had continued their labours; twenty men of 'B' Company had spent 26 September working on the Advanced Divisional Headquarters whilst the rest had worked on the roads. Subsequently, the whole battalion had spent the night of 27 September carrying the ammunition needed by the trench mortars. Using this ammunition 46th Division Trench Mortar Battery was able to direct four of its tubes against selected targets on 28 September.

Lieutenant-Colonel White of 1/5 South Staffords reported in his "Narrative of Operations" that they moved off "under a magnificent barrage" but that although the light was good "at once fog and smoke made it impossible to see".[61] The decision to incorporate smoke into the barrage was probably more of a hindrance than a help but, of course, no one had, or could have, planned for fog. Half of 'B' Company on the right of the battalion found the bridge intact and used it to cross whilst the rest were able to use the canal. This report by White contradicts Priestley, who specifically says that as no "no bridges [were] found intact" 1/5 South Staffords had to cross the canal.[62] Priestley would also appear to be wrong in detail where he correctly says the fighting on 28 September had forced 1/5 South Staffords to reorganise. However, Priestley then says "the third and fourth companies being combined into one supporting company",[63] but White's report makes it clear that he combined 'C' and 'D' as the left assault battalion and retained 'A' Company in support.

If we assume that Colonel White wrote his Narrative of Operations having checked the details with his company commanders then this suggests two 'bridges' were found. The Riqueval Bridge was on the left of the front of 1/6 North Staffords, who were themselves on the left of 1/5 South Staffords, 'B' Company were on the right flank of 1/5 South Staffords i.e. furthest away from 1/6 North Staffords. White specifically says it was his right company that used the 'bridge'. Since so much attention has focused on the drama surrounding the Riqueval Bridge one can only assume White is referring to a minor structure, such as a maintenance platform, which only afforded limited access to the far side of the canal

60   SRM: War Diary 1/5 South Staffords, September 1918, Appendix XXII.
61   Ibid.
62   Priestley, *Breaking the Hindenburg Line*, p.55.
63   Ibid., p.54.

The advance was not unopposed. White records that the German barrage came down behind the old British support line. This error by the Germans was subsequently corrected to bring fire down between the Support and Front lines. This initial failure by the German artillery is reflected in White's report that most of the casualties on "this side of the canal" were due to machine gun fire. The difficulties of the German artillery can be used to support Harris's view that the preceding period of poor weather had denied the Germans the ability to carry out aerial reconnaissance. However, 1/5 South Staffords were also in close proximity to German positions, and so the German artillery may have initially sought to fire beyond their own men, and only subsequently amended this when, perhaps, reports of ground having been lost became overwhelming.

To the right of 1/5 South Staffords were 1/6 South Staffords. Reflecting their 400 yard frontage, the battalion was formed up in company strength waves 100 yards behind the other. Each company had four platoons in two lines with 30 yards between them. Priestley records that the canal here was largely empty of water and that the barrage suppressed the Germans long enough to enable the Staffords to reach them.[64]

The War History of the 1/6 South Staffords disagrees regarding the water, which it cites as between twelve and fifteen feet. The attack is described as being led up the ladders by the officers who then waited until "all were out". The subsequent advance is recorded as being at "the pace of a slow walk" with three yards between each man and therefore took about "5 minutes per 100 yards".[65] This account also records the machine gun barrage as passing about a "yard or two overhead" whilst visibility was four yards.

If the battalion history is to be believed, therefore, this battalion advanced in a manner akin to that on 1 July 1916, but this time they had the benefit of overwhelming artillery support, fog and an earlier start time of 5.50 a.m. rather than 7.30 a.m. According to the battalion history the German barrage only began when they were halfway to the canal. The historian also adds that the German trenches on the near side of the canal were only sparsely held and that once across the canal the battalion advanced across unoccupied trenches before assaulting the main fortified line. According to this account the Germans who surrendered did so with the explanation that the artillery had cut off all support for the past 24 hours.[66]

There has been a penchant in British history to assume that the Germans are brilliant soldiers and that the British only win by dogged determination due to the German army being reduced to the boys and the unwilling. It might therefore be argued, as Travers does, that the German defeat in 1918 was due to the exhaustion of the German army. The surrender of large bodies of men could be adduced to support

---

64   Priestley, *Breaking the Hindenburg Line*, pp.51-52.
65   Anon., *War History of the Sixth Battalion the South Staffordshire Regiment (T.F.)* (1924), p.216.
66   Ibid., p.217.

Men of the Staffordshire Brigade at the St Quentin Canal. (6th South Staffs)

this argument. As Colonel White reported, "cases of parties of 11, 20 and 30 strong surrendering to individuals was common". However, a parallel should be drawn with 21 March 1918 when considerable bodies of British troops surrendered having been overrun in fog under devastating artillery fire with communications systems deluged with gas. Given that their own fire support had been neutralised and that the British had made it across to their positions the Germans followed a logical approach and surrendered.

A Social Darwinian belief in racial struggle may necessitate a view that British virtues of bulldog determination explain why having lost the opening battles, Britain was able to win through. In reaching this view positive comparisons can then be drawn with the French, who mutinied, and the Americans who arrived too late. The reality is that when a German conscript army in 1914 defeated a British professional army it had a massive numerical advantage. When however, two conscript armies fought each other in 1918 the British, enjoying enormous material superiority, were the victors, hence the significance of economic mobilisation. A German infantryman surrendering on 29 September to the Staffords had been under artillery fire since 10.30pm on 26 September, starting with "BB" mustard gas shells followed by high explosive shells using 106 fuses so they were more effective than at the Somme, and had then been subject to heavy artillery, a field gun barrage and a machine gun barrage by the time British troops reached him armed with Lewis guns, rifle grenades and other personal weapons supported by trench mortars and heavy machine guns in close support.

Having addressed the issues raised by the success of 1/6 South Staffords it is necessary to look at the well documented attack of 1/6 North Staffords on the left of 137 Brigade's assault. As mentioned above, the action here revolved around the dramatic seizure of the Riqueval Bridge. Priestley's dramatic account of Captain Charlton's men stopping the Germans destroying the bridge certainly reflects Parker's references to the *Boys Own Paper*.[67] Interestingly, Priestley follows the original version of the Brigade War Diary in saying that there were four Germans on the bridge whereas the amended version states that there were only two.[68] The diary says that 1/6 North Staffords found "several foot-bridges". This helps to support Colonel White's contention that his men too found "a bridge". Priestley makes it clear that the seizure of several bridges was critical in enabling the battalion to cross quickly and in sufficient strength.[69] Immediately behind the assaulting infantry of 1/6 South Staffords were four guns of 137 Light Trench Mortar Battery but only one section came into action "owing to the speed of the advance" and therefore the personnel were deployed as rifle sections.[70] Meanwhile, Major Boughey MC, led 'C' Company of 46 Battalion MGC across the canal in the rear of the infantry to stiffen the defensive firepower available to 137 Brigade on their Brown Line.[71] The prompt and flexible support is a measure of how far 46th Division's operational method had improved by 1918, as well as of the efficacy of the artillery umbrella.

Major Fordham led 466 Field Company RE in helping the men across the canal and, vitally, the prompt repair of the Riqueval Bridge.[72] The seizure of the canal is, of course, the greatest single achievement by 46th Division in the Great War but what made 29 September so special was that the leapfrogging brigades were successful too.

67   Parker, *The Old Lie*, passim.
68   TNA: W095/2684 137 Brigade War Diary.
69   Priestley, *Breaking the Hindenburg Line*, p.59.
70   TNA: W095/2684 137Brigade War Diary, 1 October 1918.
71   Ibid., 1 October 1918.
72   Ibid., 1 October 1918.

Crossing of the St Quentin Canal at Bellenglise by the 46th Division, September 1918.
Drawing by J.P. Beadle. (Milne)

In his report, Colonel White wrote that parties of the Leicesters were passing his forward report centre by 10.05 a.m. Twenty-five minutes later he noted his headquarters were shelled by the Germans with the result that some captured Germans were killed. Thus it would appear that the German artillery were still able to respond if only after some delay to the continuing advance.

By 11.20 a.m. 1/4 Leicesters had occupied their assigned positions in the Brown Line, despite the loss of both their CO, Lieutenant Colonel F.W. Foster, and their Adjutant, Captain Howarth, during the approach. Major Beckett MC was in the rear with the battle details, and only assumed command of the battalion when he arrived at 8.00 p.m. Captain Lea led the battalion in the assault before handing over command to Captain Ledward. Since the operations orders specified that the battalion would advance in "lines" this suggests old techniques were retained. However, at position 'B', i.e. its position at zero hour, it was to form up in "new artillery formation". However, the orders still referred to lines with all four companies in line, each with two platoons forward. Each company was to occupy a frontage of 440 yards. It would appear therefore that they advanced in "lines of blobs". 1/4 Leicesters reported that they were able to reach their objectives and that they encountered only limited resistance. By assigning these companies a frontage only a little larger than that of an assault battalion, 46th Division appears to have been applying a basic rule about how to achieve a successful assault by speed and concentrated effort.

That your fate in battle can be determined by where you happen to be, is illustrated by 1/5 Leicesters, also part of 138 Brigade's assault. They had assembled despite the difficulties caused by the fog. At 11.20 a.m. 1/5 Leicesters advanced to the canal in artillery formation before crossing over using two dams. Having crossed, they formed up in "lines of sections in 'blob' formation". By noon the battalion was in position just west of the crest of Knobkerry ridge, whilst 1/4 Leicesters were consolidating and 1/5 Lincolns advanced to their objective. The battalion was able to identify Australian and American units to the left, but could not identify any Sherwoods on the right flank. At 12.35 p.m. 1/5 Leicesters advanced to where they could leapfrog the Lincolns. Tanks now, belatedly, appeared on their right flank having been delayed by fog. The immediate result of the tank's arrival was heavy shelling which forced 'A' Company under Captain Petch to seek cover in some old trenches. In the words of the Adjutant, Captain J.D. Hills, the advance met with "considerable inconvenience" when at 2.30 p.m. the barrage ceased and German batteries in Levergies and Le Tronquoy opened fire. At this time the battalion's left flank was in the air due to the American Corps not having reached their final objective.[73] Despite this, elements of 'C' Company had captured the guns of a German battery near the Old Mill at Merville. The men had rushed through their own barrage to prevent the Germans limbering up. In total the battalion captured five 77-mm guns, two 4.2" long guns and a 5.9" howitzer.

Captain Hills also noted that the Germans knocked out ten tanks by shellfire. This is another example of how on the battlefield tanks were often ineffective in 1918, especially when dispersed to support infantry formations. One might also consider the influence this would have had upon future German commanders. Within the blitzkrieg methodology was an operational strategy to rupture weak flanks and encircle the main body of the opponent's forces. This avoided tanks making direct assaults upon established enemy positions. German commanders had seen how well their own artillery could destroy enemy tanks.

At 5.30 p.m., 32nd Division passed through the Leicesters with the objective of capturing Jouecourt and Levergies. 32nd Division failed in its attack due to the German batteries in those villages. This is an object lesson in the application of 'bite and hold' – without a further advance by the supporting artillery, determined German resistance could continue to cause heavy casualties. Plumer at Passchendaele and the '100 Days' proved that proper preparation was essential to maximise the material advantages of the BEF.

Whilst 138 Brigade passed through 137 Brigade from Billiard Copse southwards, to approximately 150 yards north of Bullet Copse, it was 139 Brigade's objective to push through Bellenglise before capturing Lehaucourt and Echades Trench. The first stage of 139 Brigade's assault was to be carried out by 1/8 Sherwoods. Second Lieutenant Davis, with ten men, was detailed to keep touch with the rear of 137 Brigade, whilst Second Lieutenant Winter liaised with 1/6 Sherwoods who were to follow. Two officers were also assigned to liaise with 137 and 138 Brigade HQs. Even when things were going well the fog of war intervened. At 8.30 a.m. when 139 Brigade HQ (upon hearing the Staffords were across) wanted to order its battalions

73   LRO: War Diary of 1/5 Leicesters, ibid.

forward it had to use runners, as the phone lines had been broken by shellfire. The runners reached 1/8 Sherwoods at 9.37 a.m.[74]

1/8 Sherwoods crossed the canal on plank bridges. 'A' Company found considerable opposition in clearing up Bellenglise and had to be reinforced by 'C' company. The battalion history credits the bravery of Second Lieutenants Bradwell and Shackleton. In aiding the left of 'A' Company, 'C' lost its commander, Lieutenant Cairns MC. The position was eventually rushed and all the defenders bayoneted. Meanwhile, elements of 'B' Company had strayed into the area allocated to 138 Brigade. In this fighting the Germans not only badly wounded Second Lieutenant Bloor, 'B's CO, but also mortally wounded Company Sergeant Major Rawding. Rawding had served with the battalion since mobilisation, rising from the rank of private.

Having fallen ten minutes behind the barrage, the battalion had the added problem that the planned tank support had failed to arrive. Fortunately, they encountered little opposition beyond Bellenglise and moving in extended order they reached their objective by 12.15 p.m.[75] The tanks now arrived in time to assist 1/6 Sherwoods. The major problem for 1/8 and 1/6 Sherwoods was, once Bellenglise had been cleared, 1st Division had not made headway south of Bellenglise where the canal bends to run westwards. Although 1/8 Sherwoods' history credits 1st Division with preventing a German counter-attack, the advancing battalions would be subject to enfilade fire.[76] According to the war diary of 1/6 Sherwoods they aided 1/8 Sherwoods in clearing Bellenglise. Most of the German trenches were close to the canal and therefore facing 1/6 Sherwoods' right companies. 1/6 Sherwoods war diary records that the seizure of Hill G35 on the left forced the Germans to surrender in large groups. Although seizing this ground technically out flanked the Germans, it does provide evidence that some men were less willing to fight on than others were, since the German positions by the canal had the support of their colleagues, south of the canal, whose fire troubled the British advance.

A German battery south of the canal in Elbe Valley accounted for five tanks. According to 1/6 Sherwoods the Germans also attempted two 'feeble' counter attacks from south of the canal but were driven off by Lewis gun fire. By 1.30 p.m., six platoons of 1/6 Sherwoods had established posts in Lehaucourt, which was technically within 1/5 Sherwoods' objectives. However, for 1/6 Sherwoods to continue taking the fight to the enemy under the combative leadership of Lieutenant Colonel Bernard Vann was unsurprising. In total they had captured eight field guns as well as 400 prisoners and ten to fifteen machine guns. The battalion had sustained seven killed (including two officers) and 44 wounded, (including two officers) as well as eight men missing. The following day the awards of the DCM to Sergeant Lievesley and Lance Corporal E. Smith were confirmed.

74   *War History 1/8 Sherwood Foresters*, p.267.
75   Ibid., pp.268-69.
76   de Grave, *The War History of the Fifth Battalion The Sherwood Foresters*, p.178.

Having already advanced twice, in accordance with orders, 1/5 Sherwoods were in the old British front line at 10.50 a. m. when ordered to advance to their objectives. The battalion history notes that they would receive no more orders from Brigade.[77] This latter point seems to reflect Boyd's policies of making information available and then encouraging people to get on with their role, and of encouraging initiative. Advancing well after the assault began, 1/5 Sherwoods were glad of the fog as cover. They noted field artillery crossing a bridge over the canal as well as the advancing tanks as the sun began to break through. The battalion historian records that German 77-mm guns, from south of the canal, soon knocked out the tanks. 'B' Company advanced along the canal bank mopping up and "making use of the bayonet in cases where there was a disinclination to surrender".[78]

The Germans in Lehaucourt put up only limited resistance and, once the village was cleared, at about 4.00 p.m., 1/5 Sherwoods began to prepare to assault their final objective – Escades Trench. Despite heavy machine gun fire this trench was in the Sherwoods hands by 5.00 p.m. Due to the darkness and destruction, as well as the problem of getting across trenches, the men's rations did not reach them until dawn on 30 September. In order that the limbers could be got away quickly, prisoners were used to carry the rations to the line. On his way back to the rear the Quartermaster, Lieutenant Mackenzie and his runner, Private Hitchcock, crossed the canal too soon and met a German patrol. Mackenzie was killed in the ensuing melee. However, the captured Hitchcock was released by a picket of 1st Division attracted by the noise. The picket released Private Hitchcock and "meted out justice".[79] Overall, the battalion lost one officer and five men killed and two officers and 26 men wounded with two officers and two men missing.

By the evening of 29 September 1918, 46th Division sat astride its final objectives and the congratulatory messages flowed in. Boyd's own message to the Division congratulated all sections on their contribution to the success. A congratulatory telegram from 1st Division was definitely an honour for a Territorial division. General Braithwaite, GOC IX Corps, sent this message to Boyd: "To you personally very hearty and sincere congratulations on your complete preparations and fine leadership".[80] Rawlinson, as Army Commander, added his congratulations, making especial mention of 137 Brigade.[81]

The war diaries of the units involved do not contradict the received wisdom that the overwhelming artillery support, combined with the benefits of the fog, were key factors in the success of 46th Division. However, the detailed planning including the application of advanced artillery tactics and use of the most modern ideas on

---

77   Ibid., p.180.
78   Ibid., p.182.
79   Ibid.
80   SRM: 1/5 South Staffords War Diary, September 1918, Appendix XVIII.
81   Ibid., Appendix XX.

deploying heavy machine guns proved vital in enabling the men to reach their objectives. Tanks proved only to be magnets for German artillery and were not involved in 137 Brigade's assault. It would, therefore, be easy to conclude that apart from Captain Charlton's exploits at the Riqueval Bridge and the clever idea to issue lifebelts 46th Division contributed little.

However, whilst Pétain is hardly a fashionable source of military wisdom he did argue that one would always require the infantry to occupy the ground which the artillery could deny to the enemy. For a unit with its history, 46th Division was hardly guaranteed to succeed even with the support available. Having surveyed its history there does seem to be a tangible difference in the spirit of the Division on this occasion. For example, Lieutenant Colonel White was expecting the support of one company from 1/5 Sherwoods given the casualties sustained by 1/5 South Staffords prior to the battle. Despite the non-arrival of 1/5 Sherwoods, 1/5 South Staffords moved away on time.

Major Griffiths closing his battalion up to enable it to reach the jump off in time and men advancing through their own barrage to cut off a German battery; these are the actions of men who are on top of their roles and want to succeed. Thwaites had trained

Across the St Quentin Canal! (Meakin)

St Quentin Canal - the famous slopes without the troops. (Milne)

them well and Boyd brought them up to date with developments, such as "the blob". Critically, too, the assertive leadership of Vann in taking 1/6 Sherwoods forward even though their flank was in the air; insecure flanks had been a reason given by many units in the war for awaiting others. This time 1/6 Sherwoods, who had used that argument at the Somme, advanced and beat off counter attacks. Given the success of the Staffords, clearing Bellenglise was a minimum objective for 139 Brigade, but it would have been easy to argue that they had to conform to 1st Division and sit tight, thus encouraging 138 Brigade, too, to consider its flanks. Clearly, Boyd helped to bring enthusiasm and the new 'blob' formation suggested to the men that greater consideration was being given to their survival. Boyd also insisted upon tight planning which Montagu-Stuart-Wortley had not done, and Thwaites had tried but not succeeded totally in doing except in the smaller scale enterprises which characterised the fighting being undertaken by 46th Division towards the end of his time in command.

Long term members of the division have been noted but it must be remembered that many of these men had not been there in 1915 or 1916, and so were not carrying the burden of those earlier defeats. Given its casualties at the Hohenzollern Redoubt, the Somme and Lens, the Territorial character of the Division had been diluted. It would by 1917 have more nearly resembled the average New Army division. Having passed this test it was in a much better position to face those that were to follow, even when circumstances were to be less favourable.

Major-General Boyd (left), Brigadier-General J.V. Campbell (right) and others inspect the temporary memorial to the Division's fallen near Bellenglise. (Milne)

It has also been noted that officers were being encouraged to think for themselves and take responsibility for tactical decision; for example, the tactical deployment of the machine guns. It is also important to consider the context of the assault. Since 8 August the British Army had been advancing. 46th Division was now part of a "can do" culture and given its history to date, this must have helped to overcome the feeling that it was somehow unable to do what it was asked to do. 46th Division had demonstrated just how far it had progressed along its own learning curve. It had joined the "fast-lane" Fourth Army and it was able to sustain the pace.

9

Beyond the St Quentin Canal: The Final Battles

Having seen that the 46th Division reflected the British Army's progress along the learning curve in the development of a successful operational method in the assault on the Hindenburg Line the later battles are analysed here to see if this was a "one-off" or whether by November 1918 the 46th Division was in the forefront of the British Army's developments. The actions at Sequehart-Ramicourt and Andigny also throw light on the pressures on Rawlinson to maintain pressure on Germany and therefore to try to short-cut the new operational methodology.

Sequehart-Ramicourt

46th Division was to launch an assault on a two brigade front; forming the left flank of IX Corps' assault using 137 and 139 Brigades.

For 137 Brigade the orders followed hard upon the celebrations of victory on 29 September. At 7.00 p.m. the entire Brigade had been assembled on the banks of the canal for the now famous photograph. By 9.00 p.m. the battalion commanders in the Brigade were meeting Brigadier General Campbell to receive their orders for the assault eight hours later.[1] The Adjutant of 1/6 Sherwoods simply records that the orders were received late at night on 2 October.[2] The diary of 1/8 Sherwoods reveals that on 2 October they were preparing to form a defensive flank for 32nd Division, but that this was then cancelled, and at 11.30 p.m. they left to take part in the proposed assault.[3]

The reason for the sudden rush may be in General Sir Henry Rawlinson's decision to bring 2nd Australian Division up for the assault, and the fact that on 30 September 1918 he had anticipated the assault by 46th and 32nd Divisions being made on

---

1   SRM: War Diary 1/5 South Staffords, 2 October 1918.
2   WSF: War Diary 1/6 Sherwood Foresters, 2 October 1918.
3   WSF: War Diary 1/8 Sherwood Foresters, 2 October 1918.

1 October 1918.[4] That the events of previous years had not yet entirely changed the ideas of the High Command is clear from Rawlinson's additional comment, that once the Beaurevoir line was captured "the cavalry corps are ready to pass through".[5] Having achieved a brilliant breakthrough at the Hindenburg Line, through careful planning and massive artillery support, IX Corps was about to throw 46th Division forward at six hours notice. That the enemy was fighting hard was reflected in Rawlinson's diary for 2 October 1918, which notes the inability of the French to advance to Sequehart and the success of German counter-attacks.[6]

Although 46th Division was summoned at short notice to carry it out, the plan itself bears further examination. Rawlinson's diary gives the total frontage to be attacked as 10,000 yards.[7] The history of 1/8 Sherwood Foresters indicates that 137 Brigade was to attack on a frontage of approximately 900 yards, whilst 139 Brigade had a frontage of some 1300 yards.[8] Thus 46th Division only accounted for around twenty per cent of the frontage to be assaulted. The initial objectives for 139 Brigade were set approximately 2,300 yards distant, in a straight line almost parallel to their start line and placing them on the crest of the hill to the north-east of Ramicourt, astride the Ramicourt-Montbrehain railway. During the attack problems were to be encountered in keeping battalions on the correct line of attack. Even for 139 Brigade, whose objectives (to the Red Line) appear as a rectangle, the task of alignment was complicated by their frontage at the Red Line being 200 yards wider than at the jumping off point. Therefore some spreading out had to occur, whereas bunching was the normal result of encountering resistance.

The Red Line objectives for 137 Brigade reflected the problems encountered by 1st Division around Sequehart. The left assault battalion, 1/6 North Staffords, were simply assigned objectives in parallel to those given to 139 Brigade, but those facing 1/6 South Staffords effectively formed a refused flank. On its left this battalion was to advance 2,300 yards but on its right it had only to advance 1,500 yards. The problems for companies in maintaining their axis of advance are evident from this alone. However, if one visits this quiet part of rural France today a further problem is immediately evident. The countryside is one of rolling hills that fold into each other, and therefore the view is frequently obscured by the rising ground. It would therefore be difficult, especially in battle, to maintain contact with neighbouring units. A piece of higher ground, running for some 500 yards, set approximately one-third of the way to the Red Line and astride the inter-Brigade boundary, would have further interrupted visual contact.

4   CCC: Rawlinson War Diary, 30 September 1918.
5   Ibid.
6   Ibid., 2 October 1918.
7   Ibid., 3 October 1918.
8   Weetman, *The 1/8 Battalion Sherwood Foresters in the Great War 1914-1919*, facing p.288.

Having defined the initial objectives of 137 and 139 Brigades it is important to look at the second objectives and line of exploitation. The Blue Line (Second Objective) for 139 Brigade was approximately 1,000 yards further on except on their boundary with the Australians, where they are only expected to advance approximately 200 yards beyond the Red Line. Whilst no extension of a battalion's objectives is simple, at least this largely required only continued forward movement from the Red Line. For 137 Brigade the plan was more complicated and, arguably, flawed. The Left battalion was to advance to a Blue Line which would form an extension to the refused flank created by the right battalion on their Red Line (see above). If successful this would result in the left battalion of 137 Brigade linking the right battalion of 137 Brigade to 139 Brigade.

Thus far the plan is sensible in that it would see the capture of Ramicourt and Montbrehain and 137 Brigade would effectively outflank Sequehart, thus alleviating the problems faced by 1st Division. The flaw would appear to lie in indicating a line of exploitation into the open country between Montbrehain and Fresnoy-le-Grand, approximately 2,000 yards to the South-East, and Brancourt-le-Grand, approximately 1,100 yards to the North-East. The line of exploitation would take the troops into open country. It would also follow, in the case of 137 Brigade, the general shape of the refused flank. Individual companies would have to be tightly controlled to ensure that, having advanced varying distances, they would be correctly echeloned at the end. It is always important for the military historian to avoid allowing hindsight to blur the analysis of plans. However, in this case the plan contains a clear contradiction. As the plan was based upon a bite and hold strategy, and therefore assigned 137 Brigade the role of supporting the flank (by occupying the unpopulated area to the right of the main assault) there was no need to extend the line of the refused flank towards Fresnoy-le-Grand since this was clearly judged to be beyond the scope of this operation. Therefore, this is a case of the same confusion which had bedevilled planning at the Somme two years earlier between "bite and hold" and breakthrough.

Those who remain unconvinced about the degree to which the senior officers of the British Army had learnt anything since 1914 might now refer back to Rawlinson's note on 30 September 1918, that the Cavalry Corps was ready to exploit a breakthrough.[9] Given the country immediately ahead, it might have been tempting to imagine cavalry racing ahead to seize Fresnoy-le-Grand or Brancourt-le-Grand, but it would have shown little recognition of the destructive firepower of even a few well sited machine guns or a single German battery. To those who feel this is twenty-twenty hindsight, it could be said that the actions of Alvesleben's Corps at Mars-la-Tour (in 1870) during the initial encounter phase offer sufficient precedents that would have been available to Rawlinson, not to mention the fate of the cavalry attempting to occupy High Wood in 1916. Given the short notice at which the assault was to be undertaken, such an ambitious concept as a breakthrough would seem even less likely to be achieved.

9   See Chapter 7.

One of the battalions, which had to make its own plans on how to carry out the attack, was the 1/5 South Staffords, the support battalion of 137 Brigade. It was to advance 600 yards behind the other battalions. For this assault the battalion effectively formed around a 200-yard square. The leading Companies, 'A' and 'D', were 200 yards apart and 200 yards ahead of C and B, respectively. Within each company the four platoons adopted a similar formation with two platoons forward and two in support. The gap between them and the support platoons was 100 yards.[10] Why the battalion adopted this approach may be explained by the compiler of the War Diary of 1/5 Leicesters who wrote on 10 September 1918 that they practised battalion attack formation using flags to represent tanks and continued:

> Laid down that Btn. Will always attack with 2 Comps. in the line, 2 Comps. in support. Comps. always with 2 Platoons up and 2 back.[11]

This shows that there was now a general operational formation for battalions to confirm to and that they were doing so. No army, however, seems to persuade everyone to conform at the same time and in the neighbouring 139 Brigade 1/8 Sherwoods record that they advanced with "leading companies extended in two lines. Rear comps in lines of Platoons in sections in file".[12] If "sections in file" approximates to the injunction that platoons advance in line with sections in 'blobs' then it would appear that at least at the back 1/8 Sherwoods were following the GOC's orders.[13] To have the leading companies in "extended lines" could mean eight paces between the men, but it sounds suspiciously like retention of the earlier 'wave' formation.

1/8 Sherwoods also record another interesting refinement, in that once the barrage began it "opened 500 yards in front of assembly positions, remaining stationery for 10 minutes, to enable infantry to get close to the protective screen".[14]

Sir Archibald Montgomery says that 46th Division had to form up behind the line to facilitate a straight line barrage because, many of the batteries were not in position until after dark.[15] It may also explain why 1/8 Sherwoods rather than the Australians took Wiancourt, even though the village was assigned to the Australians. The option to fire a static barrage for 10 minutes is further evidence of the extent to which the British Army in the "100 Days" benefited from the enormous output of munitions at home.

It is appropriate to begin the account of the assault with 1/8 Sherwoods since they were the left-hand battalion of 46th Division. Their War Diary records that the barrage advanced 100 yards every four minutes, but declares this "was found to be

---

10   SRM: War Diary 1/5 South Staffords, October 1918, Appendix 5.
11   LRO: War Diary 1/5 Leicesters, 10 September 1918.
12   WSF: War Diary 1/8 Sherwoods, October 1918, Appendix 1.
13   See Chapter 7.
14   WSF: War Diary 1/8 Sherwoods, October 1918, Appendix 1.
15   Montgomery, *The Story of the Fourth Army in the Hundred Days*, p.321.

rather slow".[16] The battalion was nonetheless very successful in dealing with a machine gun and trench which formed the defences to the southeast of Wiancourt but which could therefore have taken the battalion in the flank as it advanced. The War Diary then records that the battalion attacked and cleared Wiancourt, since the Australians could not advance.[17] Such an event will of course provide a real shock for those who are paid-up members of the "it was the Colonials that won it" fraternity, but it is a salutary reminder of the limitations of mono-causal explanations, as well as indicating the extent to which 46th Division now had "the push" it was seen to lack in 1917. Some criticism may be made here of the plan, since the resistance at Wiancourt could have thrown the whole attack into disarray. However, as long as 139 Brigade achieved its objectives they would have made Wiancourt untenable. Thus, the success of 1/8 Sherwoods ensured that they would benefit from the Australian's subsequent advance on the left flank of Ramicourt. Having resumed their advance the battalion encountered stiff resistance from German machine gunners in Ramicourt. This is further evidence that the German army was not crumbling in 1918, especially when it was well entrenched. That the British were developing appropriate tactics is clear from the fact that the German machine guns "were eventually overcome mostly by outflanking and rushing the posts".[18] This shows that platoon level flexibility was being achieved, presumably using the diamond / blobs learnt in September, and therefore reflecting the diagrammatic exposition found in Griffith.[19]

However, the British were not having it all their own way. Possibly because of the haste in which the attack had been put together, and therefore the lack of preparatory counter-battery fire, German guns beyond Montbrehain were able to fire over open sites and to cause many casualties. These guns also accounted for most of the armoured support available for the assault.[20] It is interesting to speculate whether the British Army's experience of gun-tank encounters in the "100 Days", with the former usually triumphing, influenced the decisions of those who, in the 1930s, questioned Liddell Hart's belief in armour as the ultimate weapon.[21] Apart from the guns on the hills, the battalion also met stiff resistance from the garrison of the house at the crossroads west of the cemetery. Despite what had been learnt, a frontal assault was attempted. The house was subsequently captured by a party from the right support company outflanking the house. When the house's garrison surrendered it was found to consist of 60 men and ten machine guns.[22]

Such resistance poses interesting questions for those trying to assess the fighting qualities of the German army in October 1918. That the house had been fortified

---

16   WSF: War Diary 1/8 Sherwoods, October 1918, Appendix 1.
17   Ibid.
18   Ibid.
19   Griffith, *Battle Tactics on the Western Front* op.cit., Figure 6, p.97.
20   WSF: War Diary 1/8 Sherwoods, October 1918, Appendix 1.
21   See Harris *Men, Ideas and Tanks* (1995), passim regarding these developments.
22   WSF: War Diary 1/8 Sherwoods, October 1918, Appendix 1.

clearly suggests that field skills were still present, but it does seem that the Germans concentrated on establishing fixed defensive points, which would inevitably be outflanked given the mobility of the front.[23] In contrast with the fighting retreat by the British in March-April 1918 the Germans seemed to be operating an extended version of defence in depth, as their army pulled back from the front to the German border now that the Hindenburg Line had been breached. Given that the Germans were retreating it is natural that their, often inexperienced, soldiers were grouped around strong points with the security of machine guns. Judging by the problems encountered by the Sherwoods at least adequate stocks of small arms ammunition must be available to German soldiers in this period. The Germans would, however, have suffered by the constant loss of war material as these defensive strong points were captured. If one is seeking an explanation for the insistence by Haig on the surrender of machine guns under the terms of the Armistice, then the key role these weapons played in German resistance during the "100 Days" provides it.

1/6 Sherwoods followed up behind 1/8 Sherwoods and passed through them to carry the assault on to Ramicourt and Montbrehain. During this assault 1/6 Sherwoods had the support of the only tank to survive the earlier fire of the German 77mm guns.[24] This tank succeeded in clearing a nest of sixteen machine guns before it too was knocked out.[25] Although initially successful, 1/6 Sherwoods were forced to give up Montbrehain by German counter attacks. At the time of these counter attacks the battalion was vulnerable due to the flanking units having been held up. Nevertheless, the battalion captured field guns and machine guns as well as 1,500 prisoners at a cost of 133 other ranks, of whom 25 were killed and two were posted as missing. 1/6 Sherwoods also lost seven officers of whom four were killed. The most notable loss was their commander Lieutenant Colonel Bernard Vann MC, who was to be awarded the Victoria Cross posthumously. Vann had been transferred from 1/8 Sherwoods to command 1/6 battalion and had personally led the assault on a German battery. On 4 October the battalion was withdrawn to Lehaucourt to reorganise.

On the right of 139 Brigade's assault were 1/5 Sherwoods, who had approached the jump off point from the Joncourt-Sequehart road, which ran parallel with the German lines. By 3.00 a.m. Lieutenant Colonel Hacking was informed that all companies were in position with 'D' on the left and 'B' on the right to lead off with 'C' and 'A', respectively, in support. From this limited evidence it would appear that divisional operational procedures were being observed. Presumably, the plan that Battalion headquarters should remain in the sunken road until the first objective was reached derived from the same source.

23   Ibid.
24   Ibid.
25   de Grave, *The War History of the Fifth Battalion The Sherwood Foresters Notts and Derby Regiment*, p.190.

Lt. Col. (acting) Bernard Vann
VC. (Author's collection)

The assault by 1/5 Sherwoods began with a barrage at 6.10 a.m., which was stationary for six minutes, another example of using methods which had proved successful before. Owing to the thick mist, which descended after deployment, the companies had to advance on compass bearings, further evidence of "push". A brief clearing of the mist showed Lieutenant Colonel Hacking that 'B' company was losing direction so he left his HQ to correct the problem. Despite Hacking being wounded and the Adjutant killed, with command devolving temporarily upon Captain Littleboy MC the 1/5 Sherwoods did not lose its cohesion.[26]

From a technical point of view the opening barrage is interesting for two reasons. First, the standing barrage is only for six minutes compared with the ten minutes employed at Bucquoy Graben, which had been noted to be too long; a clear instance of the learning curve in practice. The second aspect is the use of heavy machine guns to supplement the barrage, as at the Hindenburg Line. The 2nd Life Guards, as well as 46th Division's own Machine Gun Battalion, provided support. Given the absence of a preliminary bombardment, as the guns were not in position soon enough, and the speed with which the assault had been ordered, it is arguable that the storming of the Fonsomme Line by 1/5 Sherwoods is indicative of the growing capacity of the British

26   Ibid., p.190.

Sergeant W.H. Johnson VC.
(Author's collection)

Army to capture tactical objectives even when it did not prepare carefully and that 46th Division could match the highest standards in the British Army of late 1918.

The history of 1/5 Sherwoods says that the majority of the German machine gunners were bayoneted at their guns. If this was entirely true then students of tactics must attribute 46th Division's success not to declining German morale but to the skilful integration of all arms by the platoons. The outstanding example set by Sergeant W.H. Johnson that day was to be recognised by the award of the Victoria Cross. Johnson was serving in 'D' Company, on the left of the assault, when, although he was severely wounded by a hand grenade, he rushed two successive machine gun nests, which had pinned down his platoon.

Having gained the Fonsomme Line the men of 1/5 Sherwoods faced continued fighting along the sunken roads, which lay in the 2,000 yards between them and Ramicourt. In order to meet the enfilade fire coming from the south of Ramicourt, 1/5 Sherwoods veered to the right. The resulting gap between 1/5 and 1/8 Sherwoods was filled by 1/6 Sherwoods whom Vann led into Ramicourt.[27] The capture of Ramicourt yielded some 400 prisoners before the advance continued, despite the machine gun fire from Manequin Hill and artillery fire from the cemetery, which lies just behind the crest of the hill, where the Germans had sited some 77mm guns.

27   Ibid., p.190.

Owing to delays in the Australian advance before Wiancourt, 1/8 Sherwoods were deployed to cover the flank whilst 1/6 Sherwoods, and 'A' and 'D' companies of 1/5 Sherwoods, advanced to capture Montbrehain. Lieutenant Potter, 1/5 Sherwoods, managed to take his platoon to the edge of the cemetery, which enabled them to remove the gunners though not to destroy the guns. By noon 1,000 prisoners had been sent to the rear, but the number of casualties and the gap, which had opened up between 139 and 137 Brigades, made the situation tenuous. 1/5 Sherwoods estimated that this gap amounted to half a mile. The main body of the cavalry was still on the Western side of the canal so it was unable to reinforce the Sherwoods or exploit their success. It was only after 4.30 p.m. and the German recapture of Montbrehain that several troops of cavalry arrived only to be dispersed immediately by machine gunfire. Once again the cavalry had proved to be ineffective.

A week later Rawlinson wrote in his diary "I have pulled out the Cavalry Corps as they are blocking the roads and doing no good".[28] The logistical requirements of the cavalry for fodder meant that even their presence was a hindrance to Fourth Army operations. Rawlinson's diary for 3 October 1918 recorded that the Germans had eventually retaken Montbrehain. The History of the 5th Sherwoods records that the German reinforcements could be seen detraining at Fresnoy-le-Grand, but that delays in getting messages through prevented the artillery from being able to capitalise upon this opportunity. The history notes that Lieutenant Edson brought a captured trench mortar into action, but in the absence of artillery support Montbrehain was lost. Despite the eventual outcome 1/6 Sherwoods' efforts were rewarded with the award of fifteen Military Medals, five more than were awarded for Bellenglise. To the right of the successful 139 Brigade was 137 Brigade.

Immediately on 139 Brigade's right was 1/6 North Staffords, with 1/6 South Staffords to their right. 1/5 South Staffords, in support, recorded that they formed up on high ground owing to German gas shelling.[29] 1/6 North Staffords were able to capture the Fonsomme Line with the aid of tanks and were able to send back 2,000 prisoners as well as capturing 'numerous' machine guns. However, after the battalion reached Mannequin Hill it was counter-attacked and, lacking artillery support, was driven back by the Germans. During this period Lieutenant-Colonel Evans was killed and Major Dowding DSO MC, who was attached to 1/5 South Staffords, replaced him. Dowding's presence seems to indicate that the practice of using outsiders to fill vacancies had not entirely ceased. Dowding was an officer of the Kings Own (Royal Lancaster) Regiment, whilst Evans himself had been a Royal Welsh Fusilier. It is notable that 137 Brigade went into this action with no battalion commanded by a Stafford. Apart from Evans, the commanding officers, Lister (1/6 South) and White (1/5 South), had been commissioned into the Northamptonshire and East Surrey Regiments respectively.

---

28   CCC: War Diary of General Sir Henry Rawlinson, 3 October 1918.
29   SRM: War Diaries of cited battalions, October 1918.

The most famous individual to take part in this action was Lance Corporal Coltman who, as a medical orderly, saved three men under fire having administered first aid. For his "conspicuous bravery" Coltman received the Victoria Cross. In some ways what is more remarkable is that he already held the DCM and Bar and the MM and Bar. In his report on the fighting, Brigadier General Campbell wrote that 1/6 South Staffords encountered little resistance until they reached the high ground where they overcame considerable opposition. Moving forward, the troops encountered concrete emplacements, which were silenced by bayonet charge.[30] Campbell further explained that, as 1/6 North Staffords moved further to the right than planned, he inserted 'C' Company of 1/5 South Staffords into the gap, another example of tactical command and flexibility which contrasts sharply with the inertia facing officers reorganizing rear waves on 1 July 1916, and that they went on to help take the Fonsomme Line. He states that the gap between 1/6 North Staffords and 139 Brigade reached about 1,000 yards, which agrees with 1/5 Sherwoods' view quoted above.

Campbell explained that the Brigade drifted to the right because of the uncertain position regarding Sequehart. He stated that his right battalion, 1/6 South Staffords, dropped companies to their right to cover their flank as they pushed forward. It would seem that the result was that their left company edged to the right so as not to lose touch with the rest of the battalion and that 1/6 North Staffords conformed to this movement. It is a very interesting observation, as earlier in the First World War one might have expected forward momentum to be lost. Instead it was maintained albeit at the expense of the axis of advance. Having explained his use of 'C' Company, Campbell reported that he had sent one platoon to maintain contact with 139 Brigade and another to mop up Chataignies Wood. This latter action would have helped to maintain the advance, but demonstrates the relative paucity of resources where a Brigadier General is doling out (nominal) packets of 60 men.

Campbell then says that as the gap widened he had to use the rest of the reserve battalion to fill it, and therefore he had no reserves until 1/5 Leicesters arrived. He goes on to explain that touch was finally lost with 139 Brigade when 1/6 North Staffords encountered two field guns firing over open sites until Lewis guns could be worked round the flank and accounted for the gunners. This type of vignette offers contradictory evidence about the state of the German army in 1918. Certainly, it helps to explain the high losses suffered by the British Army. However, the emphasis is on machine gunners, and gunners rather than infantry may suggest that the morale of the newly arrived conscript riflemen was waning. Campbell's report also describes the British barrage as "excellent" and that sticking close to it saved many lives and enabled the infantry to "surprise garrisons of enemy positions". Campbell puts great emphasis on the morale of the troops following the Hindenburg Line and adduces as evidence of their fighting spirit "25% of the men actually used their bayonets".[31]

30   TNA: WO95/2684 137 Brigade War Diary, 21 October 1918.
31   Ibid.

Brigadier General J. Harington DSO (GOC 139 Brigade), put rather less emphasis on bayonets and noted that the British barrage, although thick, included more short shooting 'than usual'. Given that the batteries were late getting into position this judgement could be more accurate. It is also more consistent with 46th Division A&Q's records of ammunition expenditure.[32] Whilst it is important to remember that Divisional Artillery was not tied to the operations of its own parent unit, it is interesting that the 4.5" howitzers fired only 1,044 shells on 3 October compared to 1,260 on the following day and 2,516 the day before. Similarly, the field guns fired a total of 3,763 18-pounder shells on 3 October compared to 12,559 the day before and 13,133 on 4 October. The difference helps to explain the delays encountered by the Sherwoods, and the proportion of "shorts" in obtaining artillery support from guns in the process of repositioning, and the wear on barrels used extensively only two days earlier. Harington was more positive in stating that the tanks affected enemy morale and were invaluable where machine guns nests were encountered. However, he also noted that they fell behind his infantry initially, but that they caught up at Ramicourt. Again, however, his report details that nearly all the tanks which reached Ramicourt were knocked out. Once again this demonstrates the vulnerability of the tanks and their inability to win the war on their own.

Campbell reported that each of his two assaulting battalions was accompanied by a section of a Light Trench Mortar Battery. Lieutenant Gregory commanded the four "guns" attached to 137 Brigade and the two guns assigned to 1/6 South Staffords on the right flank were used to guard its flank. When the battalion fell back they were placed on the flank once again. Similarly, 1/6 North Staffords used theirs to cover a flank. It has been noted above that in 1917 there was a growing tendency to deploy 'heavy weapons', to use the modern idiom, on the flanks. It would seem that this practice was developing in 1918, using the growing variety of weapons available. It is an interesting development, because in 1916 there was a great problem in getting infantry waves forward if their flanks were threatened, or if neighbouring units were not making as much progress. It would therefore seem that part of the reason for more successful assaults was the maintenance of momentum through the deployment of machine guns and mortars on the flanks. Each brigade had a company of 46 Battalion MGC attached to it, which is reflected in the Life Guards providing support and thereby replacing the elements which had been attached to the infantry.

Brigadier-General Campbell's final remarks, after referring to the stubborn resistance encountered and the accuracy of the German artillery, related to airpower. He complained that the RAF left the German airforce undisturbed whilst the British infantry were harassed by German planes. However, he also refers to heavy fog, which would have limited any air activity during the early part of the attack. It is also probably true that with the end of trench warfare the infantry would only have time to notice those German aircraft that attacked them rather than any dogfights above

---

32   TNA: WO95/2666, War Diary 46th Division, October 1918.

them. For those historians looking for the existence of After Action Reports, these reports by Brigadier-Generals are not specific enough to constitute a truly evaluative response. They are essentially narratives with an informed commentary, but nonetheless reflect improved operational method.

This battle demonstrated the strengths and weaknesses of 46th Division in late 1918 and mirrored those of the army as a whole. Fresh from an exciting but tough success in crossing the canal, the Division was thrown into another assault at such short notice that many of the batteries could not be in position in time, and the infantry had no opportunity to reconnoitre the ground. Nonetheless, by employing a combined field gun/ heavy machine gun barrage 46th Division was able to reach its main objectives. The deployment of machine guns and light mortars on the flanks of the attacking battalions helped provide the momentum necessary to reach those objectives. However, once the troops sought to move over to the exploitation phase they suffered much higher casualties and were pushed back by German counter attacks. A key reason for the success enjoyed by the Germans was the absence of the close artillery support available in the assault phase. The rolling nature of the countryside probably increased the difficulties of visual observation, but the need to reposition the guns was the critical factor. The opening phase of the operation would appear to confirm Peter Simkins' assertion that by 1918 the British Army could shell any unit into any position. The second phase demonstrates that whilst the British, with their preponderance of material, could dominate set pieces, they were still vulnerable in open warfare.

Whilst it is clearly appropriate for historians to seek answers to the question of how the British Army raised its performance, it is vital to recognise that the arsenal available had increased considerably. Lloyd George's often justified scepticism about British generalship and the calculated mendacity of his memoirs has made him a bete noire of the Terraine School. This has tended to obscure the effect that he had in galvanising industry. Even if the direct benefits of Lloyd George's own tenure of the Ministry of Munitions may be challenged its creation helped to ensure that an abundance of war materiel was available at this critical phase of the war.

Regnicourt

138 Brigade entered Fresnoy-le-Grand on 10 October, a week after it had been the point for German reinforcement to gather before driving the Staffords from Mannequin Hill, illustrating the pressure applied by the British Army in the "100 Days". Reflecting the conditions of open warfare, 1/4 Leicesters "leapfrogged" 1/5 Lincolns and advanced up to the South West corner of the Bois de Riqueval, which was held by the Germans. The Leicesters were then relieved by 1/5 South Staffords. Over the next few days the Staffords battalions relieved each other giving each an opportunity for rest, cleaning and re-organisation. This is an interesting facet of open warfare which is beginning to emerge in the studies of the North West Europe campaign in the Second World War. Whilst it can seem exhilarating to be going forward, and this is heightened by comparison with trench warfare, it is equally draining.

The last major action of 46th Division was to involve 137 Brigade in only a diversionary role. The main role went to 138 Brigade, with 139 Brigade in a supporting role. The situation facing 46th Division was that the Germans held most of the woods between Vaux, Andigny and Regnicourt. Whilst 138 Brigade's advance to the positions now occupied by the Staffords had partially outflanked the woods to the south; the woods provided the Germans with such natural defences that they had not been forced to withdraw. The objective for this battle therefore involved reaching a line Regnicourt-Andigny Les Fermes but this meant beating a path through a triangular area to reach a common base line. The left of 138 Brigade would have to travel almost twice as far as the centre of the Sherwoods line.

To crack this problem, the artillery devised a plan whose technical mastery is stunning. By marking straight lines across the triangle the gunners created a triangular barrage. In effect the barrage meant that individual batteries would have a different number of lifts so that the advancing troops could advance behind a series of standing barrages. The degree to which all the improvements in gunnery during 1917-18 were brought together here is very impressive especially when one considers that, unlike Messines, for example, the front had been fluid for the previous three months.

Equally impressive is the barrage table produced by Major George Wade of 46 Battalion MGC, utilising the skills of the 2nd Life Guards, 6 Battalion MGC and his own 'C' Company. 6th Division was to attack on the left flank of 138 Brigade along a narrow strip, hence the availability of their heavy machine guns. 'C' Company, with four guns, were to open with five minutes of firing at 250 rounds per minute before dropping to 100 rounds per minute until zero plus 123 minutes, i.e. they had to fire steadily for one hour 58 minutes. Since Wade had positioned the guns in different locations they each had their own barrage lines. 2nd Life Guards were all located in the same place and were tasked to imitate the artillery, being assigned ten separate barrage lines but in this case a constant rate of fire of 100 rounds per minute. The Guards role included bounds timed every six minutes during the main part of the advance. An eighteen-minute standing barrage on one line and a twelve-minute standing barrage on the next part of the line were timed to lift together to the next barrage line. This reflected the different distances the troops had to travel. The troops who had the farthest to travel got the least rest, but overall the support available was greater. The 6 Battalion MGC was given five lifts with all guns firing together for the first three and then each half of the company firing on its part of the final protective line. The actual barrage lifts were modified slightly to conform with alterations to the artillery barrage.

For their assault 139 Brigade had two companies each from 1/5 and 1/8 Sherwoods. Each infantry company was allocated one section of the machine gun company in support of their assigned role i.e. advancing, mopping up resistance. Despite the mist and temporary loss of contact, where opposition occurred, the overall plan worked.

The same close co-operation was to apply in 138 Brigade, but the plan was different because this was 46th Division's exposed flank. 137 Brigade was the pivot on the right. Therefore, two sections of the machine gun company were to watch the left flank in case 6th Division's attack failed or the Germans counter-attacked. The remaining eight machine guns, in pairs, were to be established in four posts at pre-determined points as the infantry advanced.[33] Given this careful preparation and deployment of support the success of the operation becomes less surprising. This is 'bite and hold' applied at an operational level.

The infantry found that not everything went smoothly as they endeavoured to occupy the woods. The dummy tanks and figures erected by the Staffords drew considerable German fire,[34] including Green Cross gas, causing the attached machine gunners to continue with their barrage whilst wearing their Small Box Respirators.[35]

138 Brigade had, it believed, applied the new techniques in open warfare well and most of its recent casualties had occurred when it clashed with the Germans on the edge of the Bois de Riqueval.[36]

Despite their assembly area being shelled with gas and high explosive, 1/4 Leicesters on the right and 1/5 Lincolns on the left were ready on time. The units of 6th Division, whom they were to pass through, were withdrawn one hour in advance of the attack set for 5.20 a.m. As indicated above, each battalion had machine gun units attached, whilst the 1/5 Lincolns on the potentially vulnerable left flank also had the support of a section of trench mortars. This desire to protect the flanks with heavy weapons has been noted before and is clearly now an agreed element in the operational method. Given the dense fog prevailing during the assault, the major problems facing 138 Brigade were keeping direction, communication and being able to mop up effectively. By 6.54 a.m. reports were reaching Brigade HQ that the infantry had reached the Regnicourt-Andigny Les Fermes road, but that German units had not been mopped up – this opposition too was suppressed by 11.30 a.m.

As 'C' Company of 1/5 Sherwoods advanced they knew the barrage would lift 100 yards every three minutes with a single round of smoke shell at each lift as a signal.[37] Given the fog and the 'smoke of war' this latter measure may not have been effective. Unfortunately the right of the Sherwoods overtook the barrage and was caught trying to reform by a break in the fog, which exposed them to German machine gunners. Forced to dig in they were rescued by their own 'D' Company whose advance brought them on to the flank of the Germans. Reflecting the more developed approach of the infantry in late 1918 elements of 'A' and 'D' 1/8 Sherwoods worked around to the rear of some well sited German machine guns whilst frontal fire pinned the Germans, the value of close heavy machine gun support proving itself in this action. Being enfiladed, the Germans withdrew though 40 men and 27 machine guns were captured.[38]

33   TNA: WO95/2679, Report on MG Operations, 17 October 1918.
34   TNA: WO95/2684, Report of 137 Brigade.
35   TNA: WO95/2679, 46 Battalion MG Report, 17 October 1918.
36   TNA: WO95/2689, Report by 138 Brigade, 21 October 1918.
37   de Grave, *The War History of the Fifth Battalion The Sherwood Foresters Notts and Derby Regiment*, p.198.
38   Ibid., p.200.

In contrast to the problems faced on 3 October, the Sherwoods were able to obtain heavy and dense fire support at 10.00 a.m. when a German counter attack was seen to be forming in Hennechies Wood. With some supplementary small arms fire, the attack was broken up and all the objectives were secured by 10.15 a.m. Hennechies Wood was itself captured by the French in their attack at 2.00 p.m.

Overall, the plan led to the expenditure of 466,000 rounds of SAA, which is not a lot less than the 537,000 rounds of small arms ammunition issued by the Divisional Ammunition Column for the whole of April 1918. In addition, the company of machine guns operating with 137 Brigade fired 82,000 rounds in barraging the wood. This confirms the importance of abundant war material. This company had also been assigned the task of defending the divisional area in case the Germans countered the manoeuvre by the British.

Given that units of isolated German troops held out and disputed the advance suggests that the British army are not defeating a demoralised German army as Germanophile scholars like to suggest. Such scholars should look to 46th Division and the British Home Front for reasons for Britain's victory rather than continuing to worship at the altar of German militarism. Moltke the Elder was a military genius but the attempt to "bottle" the formula led to ossification and a political system that failed to scrutinise or circumscribe the powers of his successors. However, the sheer weight of metal being deluged on to the Germans, as well as improved morale and technique, all contribute to this and the other victories in the "100 Days". Ludendorff was correct in advising the Kaiser the war could not be won but he balked at admitting the German Army had failed. Hitler was to try to apply the lessons of 1918 by instituting the Four Year Plan to try to ensure Germany would have the resources next time.

The action at Regnicourt-Andigny Les Fermes demonstrates the high level of operational competence that 46th Division and associated units were capable of achieving by late 1918. The integration of all arms, except the now obsolete cavalry, was achieved by careful planning and the benefit of shared experience, in a series of engagements fought just before and over the three weeks following the attack on the Hindenburg Line. The close support provided by sections of heavy weapons specialists certainly foreshadows developments in the Second World War and after. The repeated use of heavy weapons to secure flanks and therefore encourage offensive movement provides clear evidence that 46th Division had devised a clear and successful operational method by the close of hostilities. They had travelled the full length of the learning curve by the time they received news of the Armistice on 11 November 1918.[39]

---

39 The Division was rapidly demobilized in 1919 by the early release of the many miners within its ranks.

10

After the Eleventh Hour

The War Diary of 1/5 Leicesters for 10 November 1918 records that a wireless message was received at 11.15 p.m. regarding an Armistice, but it was too late to tell the men. Since the negotiations in Marshal Foch's railway carriage were still continuing this was presumably a warning message. On the following day the diary recorded that they had received notice of the end of the hostilities.[1] 1/4 Leicesters simply noted on 11 November 1918 that they took over the outpost line. This spirit was reflected in the diary of 1/5 South Staffords, "Everybody took the news very phlegmatically and no outward sign of rejoicing or revelry took place at all". 1/6 North Staffords reacted differently when the Armistice order was made public: "The message was read out to a Battalion muster parade amidst great cheering".[2]

For many of the men it would seem that although the immediate danger was over, the memory of so many who would not return made this moment ambiguous. According to de Grave, it took a day for the 'unbelievable' news to sink in. Apparently, when it did, Company Quarter Master Sergeants were inundated with requests for new items of uniform. Buoyed up by their recent successes and the praise heaped upon them following the breaking of the Hindenburg Line it would seem that at least some of the men were disappointed not to be selected as part of the army of occupation. The War Diary of 1/5 South Staffords recorded "a deep feeling of disappointment and resentment".[3] Interestingly, no such sentiment was expressed in the diary of 1/6 North Staffords who had cheered the news of the Armistice so rapturously. However, 1/5 Leicesters, who like the Staffords had taken the news quietly, were also recording their disappointment.[4]

Superficially, 46th Division had a claim to a place in the Army of Occupation since it had been the first complete Territorial division to arrive in France, in February 1915,

1   LRO: War Diary 1/5 Leicesters, 10-11 November 1918.
2   LRO/SRM: war diaries of battalions cited, 11 November 1918.
3   SRM: War Diary of 1/5 South Staffords,13 November 1918.
4   LRO/SRM: war diaries of units cited, November 1918.

and, but for a very brief interlude, had served continuously on the Western Front. However, the decision on which formations were to go to Germany had already been reached by 9 November 1918. On that date General Sir Henry Rawlinson (GOC Fourth Army) recorded in his diary, that if the Armistice was signed, he and General Sir Herbert Plumer (GOC Second Army) had been told they would lead the armies into Germany to hold the Rhine bridgeheads.[5] Interestingly, Rawlinson said he would be assigned four Corps: IX, IV, V and the Australian Corps. Leaving aside Haig's political savoir-faire in selecting the Australians, he had allocated IX Corps, which included 46th Division to the Army of Occupation. However, Brigadier General J.V. Campbell VC's departure on 10 November 1918 to command 3rd Guards Brigade was a straw in the wind.

For the men, the immediate result of their continuing time in France was that they would become salvage experts. 1/8 Sherwoods spent four hours per morning salvaging equipment from 15-30 November 1918. In the afternoons they were allowed to play sport, presumably as an incentive for tidying up France in the mornings. One match must have provided some satisfaction when the Officers lost their football match with the NCOs on 12 November. Less appealing, perhaps, was the appointment of an education officer; for example, Second Lieutenant Burton in 1/4 Leicesters, to supervise classes for the men designed to help them before demobilisation.[6] In the latter half of November there were battalion, brigade and corps football competitions.[7] However, because of the plethora of fixtures the number recorded is only small though the Adjutant of 1/6 Sherwoods did bother to record their 6:2 victory over the 1/5 battalion.

For some of the men there was only a short wait. Coal miners were needed in England and 46th Division had a disproportionate number. Thirty-three miners left 1/6 Sherwoods on 29 November and 214 more had left by 24 December. Nine quarrymen were also demobilised, but they had to wait for the week between Christmas and New Year. Perhaps this, rather than his low opinion of Territorials, explains why Field Marshal Haig did not select 46th Division for the occupation. During December 1/8 Sherwoods released 230 coal miners to England a considerable proportion of its 768 Other Ranks on Strength on 1 December 1918. As a battalion it was still absorbing new arrivals, since its strength at the end of November was higher than at the beginning, and the reduction in December was less than the number of miners sent home. The perverse effect of this for the remaining men was a surfeit of officers. 1/8 Sherwoods had 34 Officers on 1 November and 745 Other Ranks. By the end of the year the number of Other Ranks was down to 664 but the number of officers had reached 49.

5   CCC: War Journal of General Sir Henry Rawlinson, 9 November 1918.
6   WSF/LRO: war diaries of units cited.
7   WSF: War Diary 1/6 Sherwood Foresters.

1/6 North Staffords released 199 miners from service during December but received 61 reinforcements. 1/4 Leicesters do not detail the departures but by April 1919 the battalion was reduced to a cadre under Major Szaramouicz, Lieutenant-Colonel Edwards having been given command of his old battalion, 1 Bedfordshire. In the case of this battalion it was effectively re-deployed when nine officers and 240 ORs in total were split between three POW companies in early April.[8] By the end of April 1919, 1/8 Sherwoods had only nine officers and 52 men since those not demobilised were sent to POW Companies and similar units. 1/5 Leicesters had been reduced to a Cadre on 25 March when ten officers and 200 ORs under Lieutenant Steele were posted to 11 Leicesters, a Service battalion. It is an interesting comment that it was the Territorials who were posted to a service battalion and not vice versa. Meanwhile, Captain Wollaston MC was to return to England to join 1st Battalion and Lieutenant Colonel Digon DSO was to take command of 3 Connaught Rangers.[9]

Although 46th Division was not destined to occupy Germany its exploits at the Hindenburg Line did occasion a royal visit. On 1 December 1918, King George V accompanied by the Prince of Wales and Prince Henry, came to see the famous Canal and were conducted round by Boyd. Two days later the King passed through the Mormal Forest where 1/6 North Staffords were salvaging and was given an "enthusiastic reception".[10] 46th Division came to an end as its constituent parts were wound down. Perhaps it was unfair that the victors of Bellenglise did not occupy a place in the march across the Rhine but 46th Division only became famous on 29 September 1918 and prior to that date its history, though frequently one of courageous sacrifice, had not brought martial glory.

46th Division had not been initially allocated to Haig's First Army for the planned offensive at Loos. Having nearly been sidelined in Egypt, it is unsurprising that 46th Division was allocated to Third Army, rather than to Fourth Army, for the opening of the Somme Offensive. Nor, under a new commander, had they been selected for Arras, Messines or Passchendaele (the last an unintended blessing). In 1918 Haig had not used 46th Division at Amiens even though they had escaped the worst of the Spring Offensives and when they were eventually used it was to kick in the front door of a fortress. Their perhaps unexpected success was valuable to Haig and key figures like Boyd and Campbell would be rewarded, but for Haig 46th Division was still Montagu-Stuart-Wortley's. As the latter's plaintive post-war correspondence reveals all too clearly for those who had threatened Haig's rise to the top there was no rehabilitation.

8   LRO: War Diary 1/4 Leicesters, 4-6 April 1919.
9   LRO: War Diary 1/5 Leicesters, 20/25/30 March 1919.
10   Ibid., 3 December 1918.

11

Conclusions

This volume started from the premise that the final victory of 1918 owed much to a British Army that had achieved greater operational effectiveness than it had in 1915-1916. Centring the study on 46th Division was designed to test the hypothesis of the "learning curve". As outlined in the Introduction and developed in succeeding chapters, 46th Division parallels the development of the British Army as a whole. As demonstrated at the Hindenburg Line, and in subsequent engagements, 46th Division had reached the point, in the autumn of 1918, where it had a clear operational method equal to that of other leading units of the BEF.

The Learning Curve of 46th Division

In accordance with Bidwell and Graham, it is evident that the 46th Division was only equipped with "home defence" artillery, (obsolete 15 pdrs.) and therefore started behind regular divisions. During its initial spell of trench instruction at least some of the infantry units of the 46th Division failed to impress. This suggests that the 46th Division entered the line in Second Army with a question mark hanging over its effectiveness. In particular, there seems to have been doubt amongst senior commanders regarding the effectiveness of territorial NCOs. Kitchener's decision to raise the "New" armies meant that they rather than territorial divisions were leavened with regular NCOs therefore this deficiency could only be addressed through experience in the field.

During its time with Second Army, in the spring and summer of 1915, the 46th Division learnt the basis of trench holding and there is no substantive evidence that the division was behind other units in this process except the negative form of evidence provided by the absence of references to trench raids. However, this was a learning curve for defence and although the Sherwoods distinguished themselves in responding to the withdrawal of neighbouring units following the flamethrower's emergence on to the Western Front, the 46th Division was no better prepared for offensive operations than the Canadians and it continued to be handicapped by obsolete divisional artillery.

The carnage at the Hohenzollern Redoubt tells us nothing about the capabilities of the division since it was a daylight attack on an enemy alerted by three weeks of fighting, and defending very heavily prepared positions. However, Haig's low opinion of Montagu-Stuart-Wortley nearly removed the 46th Division from the learning curve completely but its transfer to the Middle East was cancelled and it returned to the slow lane of development with Third Army.

During 1916, the 46th Division faced a number of difficulties in progressing along the learning curve. The first problem was that their task at Gommecourt was another one which offered limited prospects for success. The highly visible preparations for the diversionary assault on Gommecourt ensured the Germans were ready. The relative failure of the 46th Division compared to the 56th Division seemed to confirm that it was a less effective assault unit and it was subsequently assigned to a trench holding role. However, it had performed no less well than a number of other divisions on 1 July 1916 and so its position on the learning curve should not be artificially depressed.

The arrival of Major-General Thwaites, in July 1916, seems to have begun a new phase in the learning process. His energetic leadership sees the beginning of active trench raiding and other signs that the division is becoming offensively orientated. However, he and his superiors remain concerned that the NCOs remain a weakness in the operational effectiveness of the division.

The German withdrawal of February/March 1917 offers some evidence that the 46th Division could by then respond effectively to the changing demands posed by semi-open warfare and that Thwaites bears as much responsibility, through regular brigade reliefs, as his NCOs for any slowness in following up on the retreating Germans. Nevertheless, the performance of the 46th Division has improved and they are transferred to General Horne's First Army. Horne deploys them in Lens, and in this urban landscape the 46th Division achieves its first significant success at Hill 65. However, the problems which occur in the assault at Lievin on 1 July 1917 are seen to stem from the 46th Division's lack of push, including some specific criticism of the leadership provided by officers at battalion and company level. Whilst with First Army, 46th Division benefits from the learning curve of I Corps including the Canadians and this is reflected in making steps towards the all-arms company level tactics characteristic of the "100 Days". However, the continuing doubts about its combat effectiveness means that it was not selected for Third Ypres. Therefore the 46th Division maintains its progress along the learning curve through continuous small-scale engagements.

This experience meant that when the division is transferred to Fourth Army in September 1918 it is a much more battle –ready force. The arrival of Major-General Boyd further accelerated learning through the introduction of the latest "blob" formation and a real drive to ensure that all eventualities were planned for. Upon their transfer to the dynamic I Corps in 1917, the 46th Division had "raised its game" and it did so again in Braithwaite's IX Corps. The fog and the superb artillery support on 29 September 1918 were undoubtedly factors in the success of 46th Division but the real improvement in the fighting capability of the division are borne out in the subsequent seizure of the Fonsomme Line and other actions during the last weeks of the war. By November 1918, the 46th Division was using all-arms platoon / company tactics, utilising mortars and heavy machine guns in close support, that show it had travelled as far as any unit down the learning curve of the British Army in the Great War.

The Learning Curve of the British Army

As evidenced by 46th Division, the operational method of the British Army was to carry out a series of "bite and hold" assaults. At the operational level, this methodology involved the provision of artillery support that was sufficient to ensure the infantry could occupy their objectives even when, as at the Hindenburg Line, these included heavily fortified positions. To achieve this effectiveness the artillery, including divisional units, had to operate efficiently and flexibly using gas, high explosives and shrapnel as well smoke (the best use for which was still unclear) to achieve the right balance between destroying defences and counter-battery work.

The increasing sophistication of these artillery operations has been clearly charted by Robin Prior and Trevor Wilson, and others, in relation to major engagements culminating in Amiens on 8 August 1918. This study of 46th Division not only confirms the broad thrust of the received wisdom on artillery development but also provides considerable shading. The integration of mortars and heavy machine guns into barrage tables demonstrates how the British Army applied the enormous materiel available to it by 1918 to best effect. This study also provides considerable evidence that tanks were not the weapon that won the war but that they could be useful in assisting infantry to suppress local opposition from German infantry.

This study therefore confirms the basic hypothesis that the British Army, outside the elite units, followed a learning curve to a successful conclusion by November 1918. Haig had a low opinion of Territorials but by 1918 all divisions had a predominance of conscripts. Perhaps it is possible now to face the fact that in 1918 many more platoons were led by ex-rankers whose knowledge of the job had been gained in the cauldron of war rather than by idealistic youths drawn from a narrow gilded circle of schools. Latin is an excellent medium through which to train minds but the loss of the most promising translator of Horace may have enabled the British Army to replace him with a practical man, better educated than the men under him, but more capable of fulfilling Boyd's more inclusive approach to command and leadership. Territorial battalions were not fashionable in 1914 and it is quite possible that the overall quality rose as subsequent conscripts were distributed evenly.

Major General the Hon. E.J. Montagu-Stuart-Wortley

The "learning curve" of 46th Division was, however, distorted by the circumstances in which it came to France and the relationship between Field Marshal Sir Douglas Haig and their original commander, Major General the Hon. E.J. Montagu-Stuart-Wortley. The conflict between these two men ensured that 46th Division was initially chosen to carry out a pointless assault in broad daylight on the Hohenzollern Redoubt. If Major-General Montagu-Stuart-Wortley had not been so well connected and keen for his command to be blooded then 46th Division might have remained quietly in Second Army improving upon their indifferent initial assessment. Haig had initially been prepared to accept that 46th Division had done their best.

Prime Minister Asquith's decision to pass J.C. Wedgwood's letter on to Haig for comment, just when Haig was successfully ousting Lord French, led to Haig taking up a position in which no blame attached to himself and everything fell upon 46th Division, and especially the shoulders of Montagu-Stuart-Wortley. The evidence, whilst admitting Montagu-Stuart-Wortley's weaknesses, exonerates the Division from the slur cast on them by Haig. The "learning curve" of 46th Division would seem less steep if Haig had not artificially lowered their reputation and if their commander had not been so widely disliked by his peers.

Field Marshal Sir Douglas Haig

Haig was not the "simple soldier" portrayed by his detractors or champions. It is unquestionably time to accept the premise contained in Terraine's title that Haig was a thinking soldier. However, to accept that he is the military paragon beset by devious politicians is to display prejudice in equal manner, albeit diametrically opposite in direction, to those who see him as a "donkey". Like anyone who rises to the top of his profession, Haig was an astute politician. He acted ruthlessly to protect his reputation and to enhance his career.

This study has produced little evidence to link him directly to the Learning Curve. On balance the evidence from Rawlinson's diaries seems to confirm the view that Haig remained wedded to the concept of a breakthrough which would lead to the cavalry returning to their pre-eminence on the field of battle. This took no account of the lessons of four years of total war in which neither side was ever exhausted of resources and therefore flanks could only be turned not broken. Haig continued to see battle like a rugby match in which it would eventually be possible to release the winger to score the decisive try whereas it was actually a match in which both sides had apparently limitless numbers of players to fill gaps.

How the War Was Won

This book has also emphasised the key economic factors that underpinned victory. It is clear from the accounts of front line units that skill and weight of metal overcame German resistance. Therefore, the evidence here contributes to the case that it was the Allies that won the war not the German Army that lost it. However, skilful though the British Army was by the "100 Days" its operational method was based upon the wide availability of diverse weapons with an abundance of quality projectiles. The replacement of the poorer US produced ordnance of 1916 with reliable UK production was an important key to victory. As I have said in various talks, my grandmother who rose to be an inspector and worked on filling new experimental shells showed terrific bravery, fortified by a deep religious faith, as did my grandfather who drove ammunition wagons through "Hell Fire Corner" but my grandmother probably played a bigger role in bringing about victory.

By 1918, the British Army's learning curve had taught it how to win and the British economy had developed the capacity to supply the necessary diversity of material in abundance as 29 September 1918 underlined. To launch the Somme offensive in 1916 Haig had to husband resources so that Rawlinson could mount "the offensive" whereas by 1918 the Hindenburg Line could see a million shells expended, the same amount as the preliminary bombardment in 1916, only six weeks after the offensive at Amiens which included over 500 tanks, a weapon which had only first appeared in September 1916.

The First World War and Memory

I have already alluded to the idea of a lost generation and it is undoubtedly the case that with the decline in the birth rate in late Victorian / Edwardian England a generation of young men from the middle classes were drafted into the grinding machine of the Western Front and their loss was very keenly felt and articulated. This has contributed to the enduring debate about the First World War which has led to the recent spat between the Education Secretary Michael Gove and the History establishment.

Whilst sympathising with some of Mr Gove's frustrations at populist inaccuracies; and being intellectually amused by some of the rejoinders by those who have, in recent years, tended to assert that only the non-academics blame the generals; I feel that Mr Gove needs to recognise that he is only the latest person to try to use History to support an ideology. The best historians will recognise that "our island story" represents a highly selective view of British History but to ignore it altogether would be to leave out a thread in popular perceptions that many historians ignore at their peril.

The Great War shattered the illusion that Britain was the foremost power in the world and, in that sense, marks a major watershed in British History. Britain could have stood aside and played the role the USA eventually played in terms of being an arsenal. Moltke the Younger was not of the calibre of his eponymous elder and therefore a decisive victory in 1914 would probably have eluded him and Britain could then have helped to broker a compromise peace. The Liberal Party which had emerged in the 1850s had always had a strong pacifist / moral approach to foreign policy as the resignations of Burns and Morley confirmed. The decision by Asquith to abandon deeply held core principles rightly condemned the Liberal Party into years of decline which the Labour Party was able to benefit from in addition to the industrial and economic changes in Britain.

In pursuing victory lay the seeds of further decline because the money to finance this economic and military mobilisation had been raised by loans from the United States and therefore a massive increase in the burden imposed by the National Debt. Therefore victory in 1918 served only temporarily to mask a decline in Britain's international power stemming back to the 1870s. Those who pride themselves in the "Special Relationship" need to apprise themselves of the ruthless way in which the USA voted to cut debts to other European powers in the 1920s and re-floated the German economy but held Britain to every Dollar owed until Chamberlain unilaterally cut the payment terms in the Depression. The collapse of the British Empire was due to its economic decline after 1873 and the refusal of a gilded elite to recognise this and then embracing similarly gilded elites in a death struggle which resulted in them falling into a shallow grave into which the USA was happy to bury them and usher in the "American Century".

"Private Baldrick" may now be a figure of political controversy, but it is surely true that no war was ever started by him or fought for him. The men of the 46th Division fought a war in which society required of them an immense sacrifice; their disappointment at retuning to the Western Front in February 1916 and their preparedness to accept their fate tell us an immense amount about them and their society.

As Mayor of Tamworth in 1997 I laid a wreath on behalf of the town at the local war memorial and we went round to the old hospital where the local men killed in the Great War are remembered in the provision of a waiting room and a plaque on the wall bears their names. Like men from so many countries they gave their lives for their country and they deserve to be remembered with honour as do those who returned, wounded and unwounded, from all the battlefronts of World War One.

Not all were lions and many of their leaders were not donkeys but that Britain's governing class could commit so many to such a war of attrition over so long a period means that no subsequent generation has looked upon their country and its leaders in the same way since: the desire to avoid war, if possible, in 1938; the quiet acceptance evident in 1939; the desire for the as yet unfilled promises of WW1 to be fulfilled post-1945; scepticism over Vietnam and the bitter recriminations over the Iraq dossier; through to the popular opposition to involvement in Syria are in a stream flowing from 1914-18 hence its significance as a watershed in British history.

Appendix I

46th (North Midland) Division Infantry & Artillery Orders of Battle

---

September 1915

137th Brigade
    1/5 South Staffordshire
    1/6 South Staffordshire
    1/5 North Staffordshire
    1/6 North Staffordshire

138th Brigade
    1/4 Lincolnshire
    1/5 Lincolnshire
    1/4 Leicestershire
    1/5 Leicestershire

139th Brigade
    1/5 Sherwood Foresters
    1/6 Sherwood Foresters
    1/7 Sherwood Foresters
    1/8 Sherwood Foresters

Artillery Brigades
    I North Midland
    II North Midland
    III North Midland
    IV North Midland

March 1918

137th Brigade
     1/5 South Staffordshire
     1/6 South Staffordshire
     1/6 North Staffordshire

138th Brigade
     1/5 Lincolnshire
     1/4 Leicestershire
     1/5 Leicestershire

139th Brigade
     1/5 Sherwood Foresters
     1/6 Sherwood Foresters
     1/8 Sherwood Foresters

Artillery Brigades
     CCXXX
     CCXXXI

Appendix II

Command roster, 46th (North Midland) Division T.F. 1914-1918

GOC

1 Jun 1914	Major General Hon. E.J. Montagu-Stuart-Wortley
6 Jul 1916	Brigadier General H.M. Campbell (acting)
8 Jul 1916	Major General W. Thwaites
2 Sep 1918	Brigadier General F.G.M. Rowley (acting)
5 Sep 1918	Major General G.F. Boyd

CRA

1 Aug 1914	Brigadier General H.M. Campbell
13 Mar 1918	Lieutenant Colonel Sir S.H. Child Bt. (acting)
22 Mar 1918	Brigadier General Sir S.H. Child Bt. (acting)

GSO1

5 Aug 1914	Lieutenant Colonel W.H.F. Weber
8 Mar 1915	Lieutenant Colonel F. Lyon
14 Jul 1915	Captain L.A.E. Price-Davies VC (acting)
18 Jul 1915	Lieutenant Colonel P.W. Game
19 Mar 1916	Lieutenant Colonel T.H.C. Nunn
3 Apr 1916	Major G. Thorpe (acting)
9 Apr 1916	Lieutenant Colonel A.F. Home
14 Jun 1916	Lieutenant Colonel G. Thorpe
28 May 1917	Major V.N. Johnson (acting)
13 Jun 1917	Lieutenant Colonel G. Thorpe
13 Oct 1917	Lieutenant Colonel F.H. Dorling
23 Jul 1918	Lieutenant Colonel C.F. Jerram

AA&QMG

5 Aug 1914	Colonel J.W. Fearon
27 Oct 1914	Lieutenant Colonel E. Allen
17 Jul 1916	Lieutenant Colonel W.H.M. Freestun
11 Sep 1918	Major H.N. Forbes (acting)
12 Sep 1918	Lieutenant Colonel R. Duckworth

CRE

25 May 1912	Lieutenant Colonel W.E. Harrison
19 Oct 1914	Brigadier General C.V. Wingfield-Stratford
2 May 1918	Lieutenant Colonel E.J. Walthew
22 May 1918	Major W.D. Zeller (acting)
1 Jun 1918	Lieutenant Colonel H.T. Morshead
25 Sep 1918	Captain H.J.C. Marshall (acting)
25 Sep 1918	Captain W.H. Hardman (acting)
27 Sep 1918	Lieutenant Colonel H.T. Morshead (temporary)
28 Sep 1918	Lieutenant Colonel W. Garforth
10 Nov 1918	Lieutenant Colonel H.T. Morshead

137 (Staffordshire) Brigade

10 Oct 1912	Brigadier General W. Bromilow
2 Apr 1916	Brigadier General E. Feetham
18 May 1916	Lieutenant Colonel R.R. Raymer (acting)
5 Jun 1916	Brigadier General H.B. Williams
9 Nov 1916	Lieutenant Colonel W.A. Odling (acting)
17 Nov 1916	Brigadier General J.V. Campbell VC
10 Nov 1918	Brigadier General M.L. Hornby

138 (Lincoln and Leicester) Brigade

9 Aug 1913	Brigadier General A.W. Taylor
22 Feb 1915	Brigadier General W.R. Clifford
15 Aug 1915	Brigadier General G.C. Kemp
29 Apr 1917	Lieutenant Colonel C.A. Evill (acting)
28 May 1917	Lieutenant Colonel G. Thorpe (acting)
13 June 1917	Lieutenant Colonel C.A. Evill (acting)
16 Jun 1917	Brigadier General F.G.M. Rowley

139 (Sherwood Forester) Brigade

9 Sep 1911	Brigadier General C.T. Shipley
27 May 1917	Brigadier General G.G.S. Carey
26 Mar 1918	Brigadier General P.R. Wood
24 Jul 1918	Brigadier General J. Harington

Bibliography

I. Archival Sources

1.1 Churchill College, Cambridge [CCC]
Rawlinson Papers: War Journal of General Sir Henry Rawlinson

1.2 Imperial War Museum [IWM]
Letters and Papers of Lieutenant Colonel P.W. Game
Josiah Wedgwood Papers

1.3 Leicestershire Record Office [LRO]
War Diary 1/ 4 Battalion Leicestershire Regiment, 1914 – 1919
War Diary 1/ 5 Battalion Leicestershire Regiment, 1914 – 1919
Letters of Second Lieutenant A.P. Marsh, 1/5 Leicesters
Poem by Private A.W. Hill, 1/4 Leicesters
Photograph of Private Charles Payne, 1/5 Leicesters
Records of the Leicestershire Territorial Association

1.4 Lincolnshire Record Office/Museum of Lincolnshire Life [MLL]
War Diary 1/ 4 Battalion Lincolnshire Regiment, 1914 – 1918
War Diary 1/ 5 Battalion Lincolnshire Regiment, 1914 – 1919

1.5 Worcestershire & Sherwood Foresters Regimental Museum, Nottingham [WSF]
War Diary 1/ 5 Battalion Nottinghamshire & Derbyshire Regiment, 1914 – 1919
War Diary 1/ 6 Battalion Nottinghamshire & Derbyshire Regiment, 1914 – 1919
War Diary 1/ 7 Battalion Nottinghamshire & Derbyshire Regiment, 1914 – 1918
War Diary 1/ 8 Battalion Nottinghamshire & Derbyshire Regiment, 1914 – 1919

1.6 The National Archives of the United Kingdom [TNA]
Headquarters' Papers, First Army (WO95/158)
Daily Intelligence Summaries (WO95/157)
War Diary 46th Division, General Staff:

February to December 1915 (WO95/2662)

January 1916 to May 1917 (WO95/2663)

June to October 1917 (WO95/2664)

November 1917 to August 1918 (WO95/2665)

September 1918 to March 1919 (WO95/2666)

War Diary QMG and A, 46th Division, 1915 – 1919 (WO95/2666)

War Diary Commander Royal Artillery, 46th Division, February 1915 to June 1916
(WO95/2667)

War Diary 46th Divisional Ammunition Column, 1915 – 1919 (WO95/2675)

War Diary 230 Brigade, Royal Field Artillery (WO95/2673)

War Diary 232 Brigade, Royal Field Artillery (WO95/2674)

War Diary North Midland Divisional Cyclist Company, February 1915 – May 1916
(WO95/2673)

War Diary 'B' Squadron, Prince of Wales Own Yorkshire Hussars (WO95/2673)

War Diary 46 Battalion Machine Gun Corps, March 1918 – May 1919 (WO95/2679)

War Diary 1/1 Battalion of the Monmouthshire Regiment (WO95/2679)

War Diary 46th Divisional Trench Mortar Battery (WO95/2675)

War Diary 137 Infantry Brigade HQ (WO95/2684)

War Diary 3 (Guards) Brigade HQ, August 1915 – December 1916 (WO95 /1221)

War Diary 1 Grenadier Guards, August 1915 – February 1919 (WO95/1223)

War Diary 4 Grenadier Guards, August 1915 – January 1918 (WO95/1223)

War Diary 2 Scots Guards, August 1915 – February 1919 (WO95/1223)

War Diary 1 Welsh Guards, August 1915 – February 1919 (WO95/1224)

The Diaries of Field Marshal Sir Douglas Haig (WO256)

Personal File of Major General Hon. E.J. Montagu-Stuart-Wortley (WO138/29)

1.7 Staffordshire Regimental Museum, Whittington Barracks, Lichfield [SRM]

War Diary 1/ 5 Battalion South Staffordshire Regiment, 1914 – 1919

War Diary 1/ 6 Battalion South Staffordshire Regiment, 1914 – 1919

War Diary 1/ 5 Battalion North Staffordshire Regiment, 1914 – 1918

War Diary 1/ 6 Battalion North Staffordshire Regiment, 1914 – 1919

Lieutenant Campbell Johnston, 'The 46th North Midland Division at Lens in 1917'

'A Sergeant's account of the Hohenzollern Redoubt'

D. Barber, 'Private Percy Fox'

Binns, 'Night Patrol 11/12 June 1915'

'Diaries of a Signaller'

GRW's Account of 29 September 1918

RSM C. Hazelhust DCM, Reminiscences of Highfield Jones Diaries

Papers of Lieutenant-Colonel H. Johnson, 1917-18

Major Magrane, 'Over the Same Ground, 1914-18'

Letters of Sergeant Norton

Rev. Pelling, 'Officers Roll of Honour 1914-18'

Private Roberts, Letter of 27 March 1916

I. Sturland I, 'Terriers-137th Brigade'

II. Published Sources

II.1 Official Publications
Edmonds, J.E., *Military Operations France and Belgium 1915. Vol II. Battle of Aubers Ridge, Festubert and Loos* (London: Macmillan, 1928)
Edmonds, J.E., *Military Operations France and Belgium 1916. Vol. 1 Sir Douglas Haig's Command to 1st July: Battle of the Somme* (London: Macmillan, 1932; reprint Woking: Unwin, 1986)
Edmonds, J.E., *Military Operations: France and Belgium 1918. Vol. 5 26 September-11 November:The Advance to Victory* (London: HMSO, 1947)

II.2 Unit Histories
Anon., *The War History of the Sixth Battalion The South Staffordshire Regiment (T.F.)* (London: Heinemann, 1924)
Anon., *History of The 1st & 2nd Battalions The North Staffordshire Regiment (The Prince of Wales') 1914 – 1923* (Longton: Hughes & Harber, 1932)
Blore, J.E. & Sherratt, J.R., *'Over There' – A Commemorative History of The Old Leek Battery 1908 – 1919* (Leek: The Fairway Press, 1991)
de Grave, L.W., *The War History of the Fifth Battalion The Sherwood Foresters, Notts and Derby Regiment 1914-1918* (Derby & London: Bemrose, 1930)
Meakin, W., *The 5th North Staffords and The North Midland Territorials* (Longton: Hughes & Harber, 1920)
Mills, J.D., *The Fifth Leicestershires* (Loughborough: Echo Press, 1919)
Milne, J.M., *Footprints of the 1/4th Leicestershire Regiment – August 1914 to November 1918* (Leicester: Edgar Backus, 1935)
Montgomery, Sir A., *The Story of the Fourth Army in the Hundred Days, 8 August 1918 – 11 November 1918* (London: Hodder & Stoughton, 1920)
Priestley, R.E., *Breaking the Hindenburg Line – The Story of the 46th (North Midland) Division* (London: Fisher Unwin, 1919)
Weetman, W.C.C., *The 1/8 Battalion Sherwood Foresters in the Great War 1914-1919* (Nottingham: T. Forman & Sons, 1920)
Wylly, H.C., *The Regimental Annual of The Sherwood Foresters, 1920* (London: George Allen & Unwin, 1920)

II.3 Diaries and Memoirs
Ashurst, G.A., *A Lancashire Fusilier at War, 1914 –18* (Marlborough: Crowood Press, 1987)
Bond, B. (ed.), *Staff Officer – The Diaries of Lord Moyne, 1914-1918* (London: Leo Cooper, 1987)
Coppard, G., *With a Machine Gun to Cambrai* (London: Papermac, 1986)
Crutchley, C.E., *Machine Gunner 1914 – 1918* (London: PBS, 1975)

Dunn, J.C., *The War the Infantry Knew, 1914 – 1919* (London: Cardinal, 1987)

Edmonds, C., *A Subaltern's War* (London: Peter Davies, 1930)

Fraser-Tytler, N , *Field Guns in France, 1915 – 1918* (1922; Brighton: Tom Donovan, 1995)

Hesketh-Pritchard, H., *Sniping in France* (London: Leo Cooper, 1994)

Home, A.F., *The Diary of a World War One Cavalry Officer* (Tunbridge Wells: Costello, 1985)

Junger, E., *The Storm of Steel* (London: Constable, 1994)

Nicholson, W.N., *Behind the Lines – An Account of Administrative Staffwork in the British Army, 1914-1918* (Stevenage: Strong Oak/ Tom Donovan, 1989)

Sassoon, S., *Memoirs of an Infantry Officer* (London: Faber & Faber, 1930)

Sheffield, G. & Inglis, G.I.S. (eds.), *From Vimy Ridge to the Rhine – The Great War Letters of Christopher Stone DSO MC* (Marlborough: Crowood Press, 1989)

Sheffield G. & Bourne, J., *Douglas Haig – War Diaries and Letters 1914-1918*, (London, Weidenfeld and Nicolson, 2005)

Sulzbach, H., *With the German Guns – Four Years on the Western Front* (London: Leo Cooper, 1997)

II.4 General Works and Special Studies

Anon., *The Times History of the War, Vols. XX & XXI* (London: The Times, 1919 & 1920)

Ashworth, T., *Trench Warfare 1914-1918; The Live and Let Live System* (London: Pan, 1980)

Bidwell, S. & Graham, D. *Fire-Power – British Army Weapons and Theories of War 1904-1945* (London: Allen & Unwin, 1982)

Barnes, B.S., *This Righteous War* (Huddersfield: Richard Netherwood, 1990)

Bond, B. *et al, 'Look to Your Front': Studies in the First World War by Members of the British Commission for Military History* (Staplehurst: Spellmount, 1999)

Bourne, J.M., *Britain and the Great War, 1914 – 1918* (London: Edward Arnold, 1989)

Bourne, J.M., *Who's Who in the First World War* (London: Routledge, 2001)

Brown, M., *The Imperial War Museum Book of the First World War* (London: Sidgwick & Jackson, 1991)

Brown, M., *The Imperial War Museum Book of 1918 – Year of Victory* (London: Sidgwick & Jackson, 1998)

Chasseaud, P., *Topography of Armageddon – A British Trench Map Atlas of the Western Front 1914 – 1918* (East Sussex: Mapbooks, 1991)

Clark, A., *The Donkeys* (London: Pimlico, 1991)

Conan Doyle, A., *The British Campaign in France and Flanders,* (London: Hodder & Stoughton, 1917)

Coombs, R.E.B., *Before Endeavours Fade* (London: Battle of Britain Prints International, 1983)

Corrigan, G., *Mud, Blood and Poppycock* (London: Cassell, 2003)

DeGroot, G.J., *Blighty – British Society in the Era of the Great War* (London: Longman, 1996)

Ferguson, N., *The Pity of War* (London: Penguin, 1998)

Gilbert, M., *First World War Atlas* (London: Weidenfeld & Nicolson, 1970)

Griffith, P., *Battle Tactics of the Western Front: The British Army's Art of Attack 1916-18* (London: Yale University Press, 1994)

Griffith, P. (ed.), *British Fighting Methods in the Great War* (London: Frank Cass, 1996)

Harris, J.P., *Men, Ideas and Tanks; British Military Thought and Armoured Forces, 1903 – 1939* (Manchester: Manchester University Press, 1995)

Harris, J.P. with Barr, N., *Amiens to the Armistice – The B.E.F. in the Hundred Days' Campaign, 8 August – 11 November 1918* (London: Brassey's, 1998)

Herwig, H.H., *The First World War: Germany and Austria-Hungary, 1914 – 1918* (London: Hodder Headline, 1997)

Laffin, J., *A Western Front Companion, 1914 – 1918* (Stroud: Sutton, 1997)

McCarthy, C., *The Somme – The Day by Day Account* (London: Arms & Armour Press, 1993)

Moorhouse, B., *Forged by Fire; The Battle Tactics and Soldiers of a World War One Battalion – the 7th Somerset Light Infantry*, (Staplehurst: Spellmount, 2003)

Liddle P.H., *The 1916 Battle of the Somme – A Reappraisal* (London: Leo Cooper, 1994)

Macdonald, L., *Somme* (London: Macmillan, 1983)

Macdonald, L., *1915 – Death of Innocence* (London: Headline, 1993)

Middlebrook, M., *The First Day on the Somme – 1 July 1916* (London: Penguin, 1984)

Middlebrook, M., *The Kaiser's Battle* (London: Penguin, 1983)

Mitchinson, K.W., *Pioneer Battalions in the Great War – Organized and Intelligent Labour* (London: Leo Cooper, 1997)

Moore, C., *Trench Fever* (London: Little Brown, 1998)

Neillands, R., *The Great War Generals on the Western Front, 1914 – 18* (London: Robinson, 1999)

Parker, P., *The Old Lie – The Great War and the Public School Ethos* (London: Constable, 1987)

Rawling, B., *Surviving Trench Warfare – Technology and the Canadian Corps, 1914-1918* (Toronto: University of Toronto Press, 1992)

Richter, D., *Chemical Soldiers – British Gas Warfare in World War One* (London: Leo Cooper, 1994)

Scott, P.T., *Home for Christmas – Cards, Messages and Legends of the Great War* (London: Tom Donovan, 1993)

Sheffield, G.D., *The Somme* (London: Cassell, 2003)

Simkins, P., *Kitchener's Army – The Raising of the New Armies, 1914-16* (Manchester: Manchester University Press, 1988)

Simkins, P., *World War 1, 1914 – 1918, The Western Front* (Godalming: Colour Library Books, 1992)

Terraine, J., *To Win a War – 1918, The Year of Victory* (London: Papermac, 1978)

Terraine, J., *White Heat – The New Warfare 1914 – 1918* (London: Leo Cooper, 1982)

Travers, T.H.E., *The Killing Ground – The British Army, The Western Front and The Emergence of Modern Warfare, 1900 – 1918* (London: Unwin/Hyman, 1990)

Travers, T.H.E., *How the War was Won – Command and Technology in the British Army on the Western Front, 1917-1918* (London: Routledge, 1992)

Winter, D., *Death's Men – Soldiers of the Great War* (London: Penguin, 1979)

II.5 Biographical Studies

Bond, B. & Cave, N. (eds.), *Haig. A Reappraisal 70 Years On* (London: Leo Cooper, 1999)

Charteris, J., *Field Marshal Earl Haig* (London: Cassell, 1929)

Cooper, D., *Haig* (London: Faber & Faber, 1935)

Farr D., *The Silent General – Horne of the First Army* (Solihull: Helion, 2007)

Holmes, R., *The Little Field-Marshal – Sir John French* (London: Jonathan Cape, 1981)

Pollock, J., *Kitchener – The Road to Omdurman* (London: Constable, 1998)

Powell, G., *Plumer; The Soldier's General* (London: Leo Cooper, 1990)

Prior, R. &Wilson, T. *Command on the Western Front: The Military Career of Sir Henry Rawlinson* (Oxford: Blackwell, 1992)

Sheffield, G., *The Chief – Douglas Haig and the British Army* (London: Aurum Press, 2011)

Terraine, J., *Douglas Haig – The Educated Soldier* (London: Leo Cooper, 1990)

Winter, D., *Haig's Command: A Reassessment* (London: Viking, 1991)

II.6 Chapters in Books

Beckett, I.F.W., 'King George V and his Generals', in M. Hughes & M. Seligmann (eds.), *Leadership in Conflict* (Barnsley: Leo Cooper, 2000)

Bryson, R., 'The Once and Future Army', in B. Bond (ed.), *'Look to Your Front': Studies in the First World War by Members of the British Commission for Military History* (Staplehurst: Spellmount, 1999)

Simkins, P., 'Co-Stars or Supporting Cast?: British Divisions in the 'Hundred Days', 1918', in Paddy Griffith (ed.), *British Fighting Methods in the Great War* (London: Frank Cass, 1996)

II.7 Journal Articles

Whitmarsh, A., 'The Development of Infantry Tactics in the British 12th (Eastern) Division, 1915-18', *Stand To! The Journal of the Western Front Association*, 48 (1997), pp. 28-32

Index

INDEX OF PEOPLE

INDEX OF PLACES

INDEX OF UNITS & FORMATIONS